A Jewish Arch
from Old Cai

CULTURE AND CIVILISATION
IN THE MIDDLE EAST

Series Editor

Ian R. Netton
University of Leeds

This series studies the Middle East through the twin foci of its diverse cultures and civilisations. Comprising original monographs as well as scholarly surveys, it covers topics in the fields of Middle Eastern literature, archaeology, law, history, thought, science, folklore, art, architecture and language. While there will be a plurality of views, the series presents serious scholarship in a lucid and stimulating fashion.

Qur'an Translation
Discourse, Texture and Exegesis
Hussein Abdul-Raof

The Origins of Islamic Law
The Qur'an, the Muwatta' and Madinan 'Amal
Yasin Dutton

A Jewish Archive from Old Cairo
The History of Cambridge University's Genizah Collection
Stefan C. Reif

A Jewish Archive from Old Cairo

The History of Cambridge University's Genizah Collection

Stefan C. Reif

Professor of Medieval Hebrew Studies
Director of Genizah Research
and Fellow of St John's College
University of Cambridge

CURZON

First Published in 2000
by Curzon Press
Richmond, Surrey

Typeset in Sabon by LaserScript Ltd, Mitcham, Surrey
Printed and bound in Great Britain by
The Bath Press Limited, Bath

British Library Cataloguing in Publication Data
A catalogue record of this book is available from the British Library

Library of Congress Cataloguing in Publication Data
A catalogue record for this book has been requested

ISBN 0–7007–1276–3 (hbk)
ISBN 0–7007–1312–3 (pbk)

For our dearest grandchildren in the Jewish homeland
Gidon, Shoshi, Dani, Nili, Zaki and Ro'i

מנחת שי לצאצאי צאצאינו במולדתנו
גדעון אליה, שושנה מאירה,
דניאלה אסתר, נילי אביגיל,
זכריה פנחס, ורועי דוד פנחס

יהי רצון שזכות אבותינו תגן עליהם
וישגדלו לתורה, לחופה, ולמעשים טובים
וישישבו לבטח בארצנו

CONTENTS

LIST OF ILLUSTRATIONS

INTRODUCTION

Books on learned subjects are written in response to a variety of needs. A scholar may simply be bursting with enthusiasm to share his discoveries with a few fellow experts. The organizers of a seminar or a conference may regard it as their duty to put on permanent record what otherwise might be lost to posterity. Ambitious academics may wish to improve their professional prospects by adding to their list of publications. A series editor may order a particular volume from a known specialist in the field. In none of these cases do the interests of a broader readership figure prominently in the arrangements. What is more, there has long been a tendency on the part of some narrow scholars to judge the academic value of a study in inverse proportion to the number of people who will read and enjoy it. A monograph destined to be directly relevant to the research of no more than a hundred colleagues in the world, to sell two or three times that number, mainly to academic libraries, and to prove dull and uninspiring to anyone else who accidentally dips into its contents has been viewed as superbly successful by those anxious to maintain the exclusiveness of higher learning.

To remain commercially viable, publishers have of course to publish marketable commodities and they have therefore expressed a growing interest in encouraging readable writers to compose saleable treatments of engaging topics. In addition, more and more scholars and academic institutions have come to realize that the results of even the most specialized research can, and indeed should be conveyed to the wider world. The style has to vary in accordance with the target reader, listener or viewer, but the scientific soundness of the presentation need in no way be compromised by the effort to enliven the subject and enthuse those for whom it is uncharted territory. Those who scorn the undoubted educational success and cultural importance of such undertakings are often doing so simply to cover up their own inability to be productive in this connection. The interested public has, for its part, swiftly taken such positive developments to its heart and confidently expressed views on what it needs from scholars. Indeed, its support, and that of its leaders, for advanced research is more likely to be maintained if some broader benefits can be identified and approved. One of most important challenges to higher education is to find ways of providing these benefits without abandoning a commitment to reliable scholarship.

It is now twenty-five years since I was appointed to take over responsibility for the Genizah treasures at Cambridge University Library and it is gratifying to be able to say that many of the aims that I set myself on my arrival have, thanks to the efforts of many colleagues, collaborators and supporters, now been successfully met. One of these aims was not to restrict the activities of the Genizah Research Unit to the kind of technical conservation, manuscript research and bibliographical publication that would be valuable (may I even say invaluable?) to other Genizah researchers in the international scholarly community, but also to convey the excitement of the Genizah texts to those with no more than a modest interest in what was happening a thousand years ago in the Mediterranean area and a limited knowledge of the relevant history and literature. To that end, there have been popular as well as scholarly publications, particularly the Unit's newsletter, *Genizah Fragments*; exhibitions of the Genizah manuscripts in Cambridge as well as elsewhere; an ongoing interchange with the media; and the mounting of information and some experimental manuscript images on the Internet. About 300 lectures on various aspects of the Cambridge Genizah collections have been given, with the result that at least 15,000 people have been introduced to a topic that has left few of them unmoved and uninspired, as they have been presented with details about the lives and loves of people in medieval Cairo streets, and with examples of the languages they spoke and the literature they composed.

That stimulation of emotions has inevitably been accompanied by an arousal of intellectual curiosity. Lectures have almost always been followed by barrages of questions about numerous aspects of what the Genizah archive tells us and how we are to interpret its remarkable evidence. For some, the literary explorers and their discoveries in the nineteenth century, and the unexpected connection then made between Cairo and Cambridge, seem the most fascinating. For others, it is major events and famous people in the Middle Ages who are the stuff of interest, while there are those who warm to the many, mundane matters concerning simple folk that are uncovered in Genizah documents and correspondence. The religiously observant ask questions about continuity and change; the amateur historians enquire about grand developments; and those with a more literary bent request further information about newly discovered works and their authors. What a vast number of them have in common is the expressed desire to read a book that provides them with an instant introduction to all elements of the Genizah story. On being told that no such volume is in existence, their disappointment is palpable and they often make the strong suggestion that one of my responsibilities must surely be to produce one. Interestingly, the same suggestion has also been made by many professional scholars. Some of them are acutely aware that their students feel the need for such a basic reference tool while others have come to the conclusion that they have specialized so much in one aspect of the Genizah that they have lost the thread of what is happening elsewhere in that field. Given all these enthusiastic proponents of a volume that constitutes an intelligent introduction to the Genizah topic, I have finally found the time to meet the request of my potential readership and have prepared the study here being introduced.

In the first chapter, I have gone to the geographical source of the Genizah in the Ben Ezra synagogue in Cairo and tried to explain something of the history and importance of that spiritual centre and the groups of Jews that worshipped there through the centuries. I have also clarified the reasons for the creation of *genizot* in general and for the uniqueness of the Cairo Genizah in particular. It becomes clear from my examination how this marvellous archive came to be amassed, why it is so broad in content, and why some periods are better represented there than others. The various visits to the Ben Ezra synagogue by famous Jews in earlier times are briefly chronicled, as background to the exciting developments in the nineteenth century. Such developments were brought about by a combination of financial greed, manuscript obsession, imperial patronage and scholarly curiosity and led to the receipt and academic exploitation of Genizah fragments in many centres as far apart in various senses as Moscow and Washington.

I have often been asked how Cambridge came to be so interested in Hebrew studies and I have therefore devoted the second chapter to this topic. A most interesting tableau emerges of an ongoing interaction between Jews, Hebrew and Jewish books, and the University of Cambridge over a period of some seven hundred years, and of the personalities who stood at the centre of the picture. The degree of academic interest in Hebrew and Jewish studies varied in accordance with political, social and theological developments but there were undoubtedly times when high levels of learning and of "collection development" were achieved. Jews were often called upon to do the basic teaching but until late in the nineteenth century only Protestant Christians could be appointed to established University positions. At that point, Jews began to be elected to a newly created post in talmudic and rabbinic literature which, though still limited in various ways, turned out to have a major impact on developments.

Those figures who played a central part in the Genizah story of a hundred years ago are closely examined in the third chapter. Details are given of the social, religious and educational backgrounds of Solomon Schechter, Reader in Talmudic and Rabbinic Literature, Francis Jenkinson, University Librarian, and Charles Taylor, Master of St John's College, and it is explained how their characteristics and achievements were of significance for Cambridge's acquisition and early study of the Genizah manuscripts. I have also subjected the twin Scottish women, Mrs Agnes Lewis and Mrs Margaret Gibson, to similar treatment, explaining how their gender and religion excluded them from the University establishment but did not prevent their active role in Semitic manuscript discovery and research. Also introduced here are the contributions made by a Jewish convert to Christianity; a lecturer at Jews' College; a young bookseller who became a Genizah expert; and a young Christian pastor from Germany.

The fourth chapter tells how Genizah fragments were obtained by Cambridge University Library and the Bodleian Library before Schechter's time through Greville Chester and Shelomo Wertheimer and how Mrs Lewis and Mrs Gibson brought two fragments to Schechter in Cambridge in 1896. I argue that the identification of one of these as a Hebrew text of Ben Sira, taken together with his existing controversy with David Margoliouth about the literary history of that book, was the impetus for Schechter's trip to Cairo. The successes of that trip are recounted, including the persuasion of the Chief Rabbi to gift the Genizah to Cambridge scholars, and the efforts of Mrs Lewis and Gibson to clean and dry Genizah fragments in a hotel room! I make use of some personal diaries and correspondence at Cambridge University Library to explain how Schechter and his colleagues worked, usually, but not always, in a friendly atmosphere. Schechter's remarkable scholarly foresight is noted and details are given of how Taylor and Schechter presented the collection to the University and how the Cairo community was thanked.

The Hebrew Bible is the subject of the fifth chapter. It becomes clear from the Genizah evidence that the differences in the consonantal text of various manuscripts a thousand years ago are not significant but that variations of pointing, pronunciation and cantillation among the different Jewish communities was major, inspiring moves towards the development of systematic Hebrew grammar. Overwritten texts are found to conceal beneath them Greek and Syriac texts of the Bible, some of them from as early as the sixth century, and unknown cycles of biblical readings have come to the surface. A wealth of unknown Jewish interpretation of biblical texts, in Hebrew, Aramaic and Arabic, has also been discovered and the Genizah has clarified how the Hebrew Bible was used in everyday life. I have tried to explain why the discovery of the Hebrew Ben Sira and the Damascus Document (later identified among the scrolls from the Judean desert) offer important evidence for the evolution of Jewish religious literature in the pre-medieval period and have given examples of Christian prayers and of Jewish accounts of the life of Jesus as found in the Genizah.

While the talmudic traditions that lie at the heart of rabbinic literature date from at least as early as the first Christian centuries, major developments took place with regard to the nature of that literature in the period before and during the classic Genizah centuries and these are discussed in the sixth chapter. From being a predominantly oral medium, the rabbinic traditions took on an increasingly literary format and I have tried to explain the impact that this made and how the Genizah evidence testifies to associated expansions and innovations. There is much to be learnt from the fragments about the evolution of the talmudic language, text and structure but there are also finds that shed light on the emergence of new forms of rabbinic literature. The prayers became more formalized and the *siddur* was born, giving liturgy a greatly increased literary status. The poetry that once used to embellish the prayers threatened to become even more important than the prayers themselves and assumed all manner of forms. Commentaries on the talmudic texts were composed and transmitted while decisions in Jewish religious law were first recorded in the forms of questions and answers and, later, evolved into treatises devoted to specific topics and codifications. Works have been discovered that reveal how intensely spiritual the lifestyles of some groups had become by the time the Genizah documents were being committed to writing.

The seventh chapter touches on various aspects of the relationships between Jews, Muslims and Christians. Some attention is paid to the role of the Karaites, who opted for biblical and not talmudic Judaism, and to the tales of the Khazars, Arthur Koestler's "thirteenth Jewish tribe." From knowing virtually nothing about the Jews of the land of Israel as they were a thousand years ago, we are now in a position, thanks to the

Genizah, to describe much of their cultural and religious development, and how they compared to those of other centres of Jewry. I have also alluded to the matter of pilgrimage to the Holy Land and to Jewish settlement there in the sixteenth century. The contribution that the Genizah has made to the illumination of the life and work of many a leading Jewish figure is clearly exemplified in the cases of Sa'adya, Judah Ha-Levi and Maimonides. I have pointed out the remarkable degree of novel information now available to us about these outstanding personalities.

There is no doubt that the material that is most widely regarded as fascinating is that pertaining to the daily lives of ordinary folk. In the eighth chapter, I have attempted to summarize the mass of documentation relating to this topic that has been deciphered and made available in many readable publications by Shelomo Dov Goitein and his school of historians. I have cited some of the evidence relating to marriage and explained how arrangements were made and how they were not always successful. What is somewhat surprising is that women were sometimes able to exercise considerable power in the matter of marital arrangements and there is no shortage of examples of women who by no means restricted themselves to domestic activities. Tales are told of travel, commerce and education and include references to an Indian slave who became part of a Jewish family, the ransoming of female captives raped by their non-Jewish captors, complaints about the difficulty of predicting price fluctuations, and children, some of whom anger their teachers by coming late and failing to do their homework, while others antagonize their fellow pupils by being too diligent. Other items here receiving attention are poll tax, synagogue brawls, art and music and I have indicated how medicine, and indeed alternative medicine, played their part in helping people to cope.

The subject of language is tackled in the ninth chapter. I have pointed out that the Genizah texts testify to an explosion of Jewish literacy from the ninth to the twelfth centuries and have argued that it was the Jewish adoption of the codex, or bound volume, that was a major factor in this development. Books, scribal techniques and libraries became a common feature of communal, even personal life and the Jews were undoubtedly worthy of the Muslim description of them as "the people of the book". Hebrew, Arabic and Aramaic are seen to have occupied central roles in Jewish cultural life but the special dialects that the Jews created out of Greek, Arabic, Spanish and German turn out to have been important expressions of their desire to "dance at every wedding." While retaining their loyalty to their religious mother-tongue by writing these languages in Hebrew characters, they were at the same time able to identify with the dominant culture by adopting its vernacular in a variety of contexts. Some details are also provided of how the various levels of education were catered for, among females as well as males, and examples are given of the high esteem in which learning was generally held.

The final chapter transports us from medieval Egypt to modern Cambridge. Now that a hundred years have passed since Solomon Schechter brought back his famous "hoard of Hebrew manuscripts", and the Jewish academic world is busy celebrating this event in many different ways, the time has come to take stock of the achievements of each generation of librarians and scholars. I have therefore divided the century into five fairly self-evident periods and offered an account and an assessment of each. The first, that of Schechter and his contemporaries, was undoubtedly enthusiastic and industrious and the foundations were laid for much subsequent research. There was then a steady move away from institutional interest to individual research and while Cambridge University Library concentrated on other work and on surviving the First World War and the Depression, the centre of Genizah research moved elsewhere, in one case taking over two hundred fragments temporarily with it! In the years just before and just after the Second World War, the oriental staff situation improved and this led to more interest in the Genizah material, culminating in the great expansion of the fifties inspired by Goitein and a few other scholars, particularly from Israel. The final period, that of the past twenty-five years, has seen its own special developments and the chapter is brought to an end with a brief summary of these.

A word of explanation is in order with regard to the style and presentation. I have made a determined effort to reach the reader who is intelligent and interested but in no way a specialist in the field. In order to accomplish this, I have avoided dwelling on the intricacies and technicalities of any one of the many topics here covered. I have also chosen a style of writing that is considerably less formal and academic and tried to avoid taking for granted any advanced knowledge of Genizah matters on the part of the reader. In order to lighten the load on those who find an exclusive concern with text somewhat daunting, I have included a substantial amount of illustrative material. Since my expertise and experience are more closely associated with the Cambridge Genizah material than with similar items found elsewhere, I have concentrated on the collection for which I am responsible. This has not, however, prevented me from providing some details about those other collections and from occasionally referring to specific items included in them. I believe that most of what I have to say about the significance of the Genizah manuscripts for particular subjects in the broader area of Jewish studies is true not only for the Cambridge collections but also for similar material that has chanced to find its way elsewhere.

All that having been said, I hope that I may nevertheless claim, with full justification, that the book remains thoroughly reliable with regard to detail and is based on the Genizah texts themselves or their sound interpretation by Genizah scholars over the years. Aware as I am of the reader's need for verification and further information, I have provided an extensive and annotated guide to reading at the end of each of the ten chapters in which the Genizah fragments themselves and the books and articles devoted to them are cited and discussed. These are in no way less scholarly in content than footnotes but they do not interrupt the flow of the text, may be ignored by those more interested in the general picture, and are couched in a style that is, I hope, more helpful and less dry. In most cases, I have provided additional lists for those who are happy to read studies written in modern Hebrew. In order to ensure that the reader is spared the trouble of cross-referring, and that each chapter may be wholly self-contained, I have occasionally duplicated minor details, in the text and in the reading guides. I am a strong believer in the value of good indexing and am regularly appalled by sloppy editing that opts out of such a provision or does not do its justice. As in so many other volumes, my wife, Shulie, and I have co-operated in the indexing of this volume and very much hope that the result will be found widely useful.

I have of course published many articles on the Cambridge Genizah material over the years and some of the data and findings offered in these have been incorporated in this volume, usually in an expanded and updated form. The three chapters that are most closely based on earlier articles are the second, fifth and tenth, which originally appeared, respectively, as "Hebrew and Hebraists at Cambridge: An Historical Introduction", in my *Hebrew Manuscripts at Cambridge University Library: A Description and Introduction* (Cambridge University Press, Cambridge, 1997), pp. 1–35; "The Cairo Genizah and its Treasures, with Special Reference to Biblical Studies" in *The Aramaic Bible: Targums in their Historical Context,* edited by D. R. G. Beattie and M. J. McNamara (Sheffield Academic Press, Sheffield, 1994), pp. 30–50; and "One Hundred Years of Genizah Research at Cambridge", *Jewish Book Annual* 53 (1995–96), pp. 7–28.

No book is written without the assistance and co-operation of a number of people and it is always a pleasure to be able to put on record one's appreciation of these acts of generosity. I was appointed to a fellowship at the Institute for Advanced Studies of the Hebrew University of Jerusalem for the year 1996–97 and, with the kind permission of the Library Syndicate, the University Librarian and the General Board of the Faculties at the University of Cambridge, was able to take this up. The research and writing done during that year included a number of chapters for this volume and I am deeply grateful to the Institute's Director at that time, Professor David Shulman, and all his splendid staff, for their outstanding helpfulness. My colleagues in the Genizah Research Unit at Cambridge University Library, particularly Dr Avihai Shivtiel and Mr Ellis Weinberger, have responded quickly and productively to my many and varied requests for assistance, as indeed have other colleagues in the Library. Fellow Genizah researchers all over the world have been generous with information whenever approached and many of those listed at the end of the final chapter fall into this category and have earned my warm appreciation. I also owe a deep debt of gratitude to my friend, Mr Joe Dwek CBE, for encouraging, even at times cajoling me into completing this volume and for providing not only moral support but also major financial assistance for that purpose through the Dwek Family Charitable Trust. He was of considerable help when we were first negotiating with Jonathan Price and his colleagues at the Curzon Press, to whom I also owe a debt of gratitude for their commitment to the publication. My wife, Shulie, has, as always, inspired my efforts throughout and has insisted that in the case of this project I never lose sight of the fact that the end-product is aimed at a wide readership. Another source of inspiration, that we both enjoy, is that provided by our delightful grandchildren, whose development, affection and closeness consistently bring us pleasure and satisfaction. May they one day be interested enough in the subject to enjoy reading the volume.

S.C.R.

ONE

A WONDROUS
JEWISH SITE

Over seven hundred years ago, when a few brave souls in England were bearing the torch of learning to damp and distant Cambridge, and almost four centuries before Hebrew was taught at its famous university, a Jewish community known throughout the Islamic empire for its social and political stability, as well as its economic and cultural achievements, had already been flourishing on the Nile for two hundred and fifty years. The community was that of old Cairo and, almost without realizing it, the officials of this significant Jewish settlement were beginning to build up an archive that was destined to achieve scholarly immortality as the Cairo Genizah.

ORIGINS OF OLD CAIRO

Egyptian Jewish centres, such as that of Alexandria, had blossomed during the Hellenistic and early Roman periods and, with their special combination of Greek and Hebrew culture, had made a notable contribution to the development of both Jewish and Christian life and letters. They undoubtedly began to decline in the unhappy conditions that prevailed for them in the early Christian centuries and were given little opportunity of reversing this process under Byzantine rule. It thus seems reasonable to suppose that whatever Jewish population still survived to witness the Islamic conquest of 639–641 c.e. would have greeted the conquerors with at least a modicum of enthusiasm, hopeful of some alleviation of their burdens. Jews from other areas were optimistic about their prospects under the new Muslim régime and a number of them appear to have brought up the train of the invading forces and settled in the newly occupied territory. Among the communities that they established was one at Fustat, the first city to be founded by the Muslims in Egypt, and the initial place of residence of the Arab governors.

1

Positioned on the east bank of the Nile at the head of the delta, dominating access to Lower Egypt, the site chosen by the conquerors had long been acknowledged as one of strategic importance. In pre-Christian times, an important settlement existed there, by the famous river, and was entitled "Babylon", either after a group of Babylonians who once occupied it, or after an Egyptian name corrupted in transmission. A Roman fortress with high walls and impressive towers was built there in the third or fourth century (its remains are still visible) and it was there that the Byzantine Christians surrendered to the invading Arabs on Easter Monday, 641 c.e.

The new Islamic empire followed the lead given by its predecessors and the capital city established at what it called Fustat-Misr in 643 c.e. grew to become the unrivalled centre of Egyptian economic and political life, a position it held for some three hundred years. It did then begin to cede some of its power but had the satisfaction of seeing its role and status inherited by a former suburb some two miles to the north-east, called Cairo (al-Qahira) by the Fatimid dynasty that expanded it as the new administrative capital. The process of Fustat's decline was a gradual one that was not completed until the fifteenth century and in the intervening period the older city remained an important religious and commercial centre. During its earlier heyday, it was one of the wealthiest towns in the Islamic world, with some of its tallest known buildings, a bustling metropolis with affluent minority groups of Christians and Jews.

Paradoxically, detailed information about the Jewish population of Fustat is available only from the beginning of the Fatimid period in 969 c.e., that is, precisely from the time at which the older city's fortunes began to wane. Some scanty references do, however, permit the reconstruction of its earlier history. The community was the most important Jewish settlement in Egypt and took advantage of the communications system of the vast Islamic empire to maintain contact with its co-religionists in North Africa, Babylon and the Holy Land. That the scholarly achievements of the Egyptian Jewish community in general were not insignificant is clear from the fact that it produced one of the most distinguished Jewish sages of all time, Sa'adya Gaon ben Joseph. That scholar, who became head of the leading rabbinical centre in Sura in southern Babylonia, originated from Fayyum, some fifty-five miles to the south-west of Cairo, and there is no reason to assume that the products of that particular community were unique in the Egypt of that period.

Be that as it may, it was Fustat's prosperity rather than its scholarship (which was certainly more distinguished elsewhere) that attracted Jewish

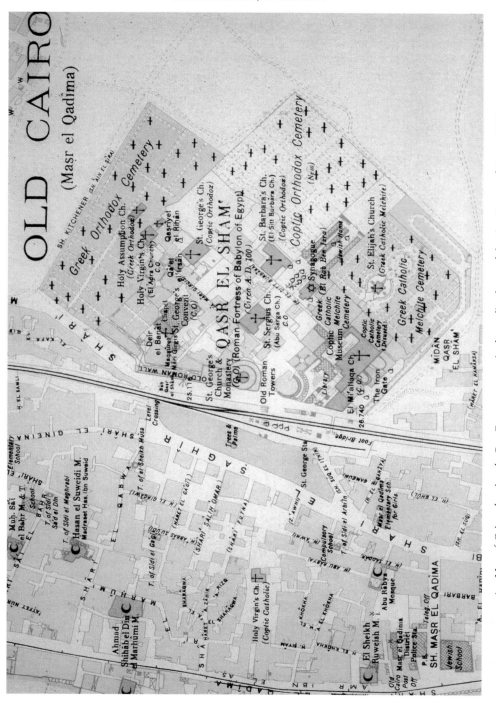

1 – Map of Cairo, showing the Ben Ezra synagogue in the medieval part of the city (Survey of Egypt, 1927)

immigrants from Babylon and Eretz Yisrael and they duly established synagogues in which they could adhere to their own liturgical rites and customs. In addition to these Iraqi and Palestinian congregations that were, as Rabbanites, faithful to the tenets and practice of talmudic Judaism, there was also a large community of Karaites, committed to its own more Bible-based interpretation of the Jewish traditions, and supporting its own synagogue. According to Muslim testimony, one of these places of worship was acquired in 882 c.e. in a rather unusual manner. Faced with a demand by the ruler of Egypt, Ahmad ibn Tulun, for a substantial, financial contribution to the cost of his war effort, the Coptic Patriarch was forced to sell some ecclesiastical property. One of the transactions involved the purchase of St Michael's church by the Jews for conversion into a synagogue. Even if we are persuaded to accept the veracity of this report, it is by no means clear that the synagogue in question is the one in which the Genizah collection was amassed, as claimed by some researchers. The most recent historical and archaeological studies have raised serious doubts about such an identification.

FUSTAT AT ITS ZENITH

It is no coincidence that the Fatimid period (969–1171), which saw Fustat reach the zenith of its commercial power, should also prove the richest in source material for Jewish history. The Jewish community was strengthened by the influx of substantial numbers of immigrants from the Holy Land and from North Africa (especially Tunisia) and numbered a few hundred families. Its members took advantage of the unprecedented degrees of administrative efficiency, economic expansion and religious tolerance that were generally prevalent under the Fatimid dynasty and built the kind of society in which they could expand and consolidate their religious and communal institutions. The distinguished title of *Nagid* was granted to the head of the Egyptian Jewish communities and the appointment, carrying as it did the responsibility of representing the Jews to the authorities, was usually held by one with an influential position at court. During the first century of Fatimid rule, Egyptian Jews looked to the Palestinian religious authorities (*ge'onim*) for guidance but by the twelfth century the situation was reversed and the centre of religious power for the whole Egyptian, Palestinian and Syrian region was to be found in the Fustat/Cairo area. With these and similar developments, the written word, both documentary and literary, naturally acquired a position of growing importance. Through a fortuitous combination of circumstances, a considerable proportion of the vast amount of textual material emanating from the Jewish community, or passing through its hands, was preserved, thus making possible a fascinating reconstruction of medieval Jewish life.

The success story of the Fatimid caliphs in Egypt was also itself somewhat fortuitous. It had more to do with the general political situation in the Mediterranean world of their day than with any inspired leadership or novel policies on their part. The collapse of the former centre of Mediterranean trade in Tunisia and the gradual replacement of Byzantium by the Italian republics as the controllers of commerce on the northern shores of the Mediterranean gave Egypt the opportunity of dominating eastern Mediterranean trade. Its merchants forged strong commercial links with India and East Asia and produced what was effectively a contemporary economic miracle. On the military side, Fatimid Egypt did not dominate the area but neither was there any other power strong enough to overthrow her. Something of a balance was maintained between the emergent Seljuk Turks, the inconsistent Crusader forces, and the Fatimids themselves, and this amounted to a satisfactory situation for the Egyptian centre. On the domestic front, Fatimid achievements had their roots not so much in how the rulers directed their subjects but rather in the degree to which they permitted them to exercise their own initiatives. The energy, administrative ability and economic enterprise of Tunisians, Christians and Jews were given their head and major advantage thereby accrued to the state. At the same time, by their relatively liberal approach to the people and their skilful use of propaganda, the administration ensured that it remained internally tolerable and that no pretexts were given for outbursts of popular dissatisfaction.

No matter how tolerant the atmosphere, the Jews could, however, never be more than second-class citizens in the Islamic environment, and were always liable to active persecution when religious fanaticism took hold of those with the power to indulge in its cruder manifestations. Even during the halcyon days of the Fatimid hegemony, storms could sometimes break out and there is evidence to suggest that members of the Shi'ite Isma'ili sect, to which the Fatimid rulers belonged, were among those with a tendency to disturb the calm. The worst instances of religious intolerance occurred in the latter part of the reign of the caliph, al-Hakim (996–1021). Not psychologically the soundest of the Fatimid dynasty, he ordered the Christians and the Jews to wear marks of identification and denied them the right to ride horses or purchase slaves. He followed this up in about 1012 by ordering their forcible conversion and the destruction of their churches and synagogues. What was a rather extraordinary event under the Fatimids became a more run-of-the-mill occurrence under later dynasties when the whole situation deteriorated for both the city of Fustat and its Jewish community.

THE CITY'S DECLINE

The earliest manifestations of this decline may already be detected during the Fatimid period itself. As early as the middle of the eleventh century, during the latter and somewhat blighted part of al-Mustansir's reign, Fustat suffered years of severe famine, aggravated by the outbreak of epidemics. The city seems to have recovered from this setback, just as it did more than half a century later when the problem was the collapse of buildings that had not been maintained in a satisfactory state of repair. Although efforts to rebuild and to reconstruct were sufficiently successful to ensure that recovery and further development remained possible in most of the Fatimid period, the situation changed as the dynasty moved into its final years. In a measure designed to foil the advance of the Crusader army, which was approaching its environs in 1168, the city was evacuated and burnt down. Though later rebuilt, it was hardly in a position to withstand the additional catastrophes of famine and plague visited upon it a few decades later. Indeed, it was during the Ayyubid dynasty (1171–1250), founded by Saladin, famous scourge of the Crusaders, who had seized power at the convenient deaths of both his overlord Nur-al-Din and the deposed Fatimid caliph, that fatal blows were struck at Fustat's centrality. As Egyptian sea power waned and its rulers became more introspective, the once great commercial centre of Fustat finally had to acknowledge the pre-eminence of Cairo, its sometime suburb. While the grandson of Moses Maimonides still followed the example of his father and grandfather and resided in Fustat, subsequent generations of the family, still occupying the position of *Nagid*, moved north, to join the majority of the population in Cairo. By the end of the fourteenth century, there were four synagogues in the newer settlement as against three Jewish places of worship in the older centre.

The Mamluk period (13th–16th centuries) may justifiably be designated as one of the darkest ages in Egyptian Jewish history. The administration was reorganized and placed in the exclusive hands of Muslims who adhered strictly to Islamic law. The large-scale persecution of religious minorities was the order of the day and, not content with imposing discriminatory legislation on the Jews, the Muslim rulers resorted to grave physical violence, at one stage even insisting on the total closure of synagogues. Under such conditions, it is hardly surprising that the Jewish community suffered economic decline and a reduction in population. On the cultural side, the relative paucity of local Jewish sources dating from the Mamluk period is a further reflection of the wretched plight in which the community then found itself. Things finally took a turn for the better in the early sixteenth century, when power passed into the hands of the Ottoman Turks, and the arrival of sizeable numbers of refugees, as a result of the Spanish Expulsion, breathed fresh life into the ailing Jewish body. The structure of the community had already undergone considerable change in earlier centuries with the gradual integration of both the Palestinian and Babylonian immigrants into the dominant Tunisian element, and their ultimate disappearance as independent entities. The Spanish influx took this process a stage further and effected a tripartite division of the Rabbanite community into *Musta'rabīn*, the native Arabic-speaking faction; *Maghribyīn*, that is, those who had their origin further west in North Africa; and *Sefaradim*, the refugees from the persecutions in Spain and Portugal.

SEFARADIM AND OTTOMANS

In the subsequent jockeying for power and influence within the community at large, it was the last-mentioned, the newest arrivals, who, by dint of their cultural heritage, self-confidence and clear-cut identity, emerged victorious. The religious and lay leadership became predominantly Sefaradi and communal customs were gradually altered to accommodate them to the rites familiar to the Spanish emigrés. The newly reconstituted community took full advantage of the economic opportunities afforded by the Ottomans during the early part of their rule and shouldered heavy responsibilities relating to the financial administration of the country. It also came to enjoy considerable improvements in its status and conditions, as well as in its standards of Jewish learning. The halt called by the Ottomans to the intellectual, political and economic decline of Egypt proved, however, to be no more than temporary. Financial extortion, court intrigue, political corruption and arbitrary execution came to typify the régime and the position of the Jews once again bordered on the intolerable. The office of *Nagid* was abolished by the government in the second half of the sixteenth century and Jewish officials in the state treasury took over the function of representing their fellows to the authorities, often at the ultimate personal cost. A large proportion of the Jewish community suffered

2 – Synagogue officials depositing worn-out texts in the Genizah
(diorama at the Nahum Goldmann Museum of the Jewish Diaspora, Tel Aviv)

extremes of poverty and ignorance. Jewish learning stagnated and Jews were not spared the crudest physical attacks. It was during this early Ottoman period that the Jews of Cairo, fearful of being attacked on their way to the Basatin cemetery some distance outside the town, were forced to hire Muslim guards, to arrange clandestine funerals, and to abandon some of their burial customs.

This depressing state of affairs remained substantially unaltered until the nineteenth century. Then, in the wake of Napoleon Bonaparte's eastern expedition, the violent emergence of Egypt as a kingdom independent of Turkey, and the reforms of Mohammed Ali, the country suddenly found itself the subject of close attention on the part of the contemporary colonial powers. European influence began to make itself felt and culminated in the construction of the Suez Canal in 1869. The steps taken by Britain and France to protect their financial investment in the country, and the ultimate occupation by a British military force in

1882, brought the nineteenth century into Egypt and Egypt into the nineteenth century. With the attendant economic expansion, Cairo emerged as an important modern capital and its population, which became considerably more cosmopolitan, almost tripled in the course of the century. The number of Jewish inhabitants, which had stood at about 4,000, made a similar, proportional increase over the period, although by that time no more than a handful of Jewish families were resident in Old Cairo, or Misr al-'Atiqa (or al-Qadima), as it had come to be called. With the exception of the occasional outburst of anti-Semitism – even the recurrence of the pernicious but historically persistent blood-libel – the situation greatly improved for the Jews, who were able to look to the colonial powers for a degree of protection and assistance. It was the leadership of a vibrant and confident community that was able to welcome Solomon Schechter when he arrived in search of literary treasures at the end of 1896 and to crown his efforts with astonishing success.

BEN EZRA SYNAGOGUE

The successful amassing of these treasures took place in the Ben Ezra synagogue of Old Cairo and the history of that institution makes remarkable reading. Local Jewish tradition has it that it was on that site

9

that Moses appealed to God to bring the plague of hail to an end and there are those who will confidently point out to visitors precisely where the infant Moses was placed in the bullrushes. It was there, it is claimed, that the prophet Jeremiah recited his laments over the destruction of Jerusalem and its first temple, and the synagogue is credited by some as housing the tomb of one of the biblical prophets. Ezra the scribe is said to have persuaded a sceptical generation of Egyptian Jews of his religious credentials by transcribing a Torah scroll with magical powers and depositing it among that community's archives. His name is traditionally associated with various parts of the synagogue and this association is possibly the reason why it came to be called the Ben Ezra synagogue at the beginning of this century. In the Genizah documents of a thousand years ago, it is referred to as *Kanīsat al-Yerūshalmiyīn* or *Kanīsat al-Shāmiyīn*, after the Palestinian Jews who founded it or were among its early occupants, while from the fifteenth century onwards it was known as *Kanīsat Eliyahu,* after the prophet Elijah. In its precincts are to be found a memorial stone and a well, both reputedly with the capacity to heal the sick, and, according to one tradition, Elijah himself once made an appearance in the area. It has even been claimed that a snake once protected the entrance to its manuscript treasures.

If its legends have captured the hearts of the pious, its documented chronology has been no less captivating for anyone with an interest in history. Contrary to an oft-cited opinion, it seems not originally to have been a church but to have been purpose built in the middle of the tenth century for a growing Jewish community. There is a tradition among the Karaites that it originally served their community rather than that of the Rabbanites and they point to the Karaite material found in its Genizah by way of evidence. In view, however, of the close relations that existed between the two communities at the time of the synagogue's foundation, that factor is not decisive. What is beyond doubt is that a synagogue has occupied this same site for a thousand years, a historical feat surely achieved by no other Jewish house of worship. Having been founded in a period of relative tolerance and prosperity, and having flourished alongside synagogues of Iraqi (=Babylonian) and Karaite Jews, it was demolished on the orders of the fanatical Shiʻite Caliph al-Hakim early in the eleventh century. Following its careful and impressive reconstruction in about 1040, it still had an imposing appearance and role. This can indeed be verified by those parts of its ornate wooden doors that are still to be found in various museums around the world. Many old customs brought by Jews from the Holy Land (including the reading of the Torah in three years rather than one) survived there. The communal

3 – Searching for Genizah treasures in the Basatin Cemetery near Cairo, 1979
(Cambridge University Library)

leadership continued to be centred on the site, even after most of the population had moved to the more modern city of Cairo. It had an extensive library and beautiful furnishings, full details of which have been reconstructed from the reports to be found in some of the Genizah manuscripts. Its greatest claim to fame comes from the Genizah collection that preserved such manuscripts and some explanation is due of how that priceless medieval collection came to be in the Ben Ezra synagogue, awaiting popular curiosity and scholarly examination in the modern period.

AMASSING THE GENIZAH

The earliest occurrences in Hebrew literature of the root *gnz*, from which the word *genizah* is derived, are in late sections of the Hebrew Bible, where it refers to the storage of valuable items. Given that these examples have Persian linguistic elements and that aspects of these texts may reflect a Persian imperial environment, it is probable that the entry into Hebrew was through Persian. Nevertheless, the root is attested not only in Hebrew and Aramaic but also in Arabic, Ethiopic and Late Babylonian with the meanings of "hide", "cover" and "bury" and it is

11

not impossible that it had authentic Semitic origins. In the rabbinic literature of the first few Christian centuries, it carries similar senses and is used to describe special treasures stored away by God, such as the Torah and the souls of the righteous. In that part of such literature dealing with religious law, however, it takes on a technical sense, describing the removal from circulation of some item that is or has at some stage been regarded as sacred, whether legitimately or illicitly, and is now ruled inappropriate for ritual use. Such items may include religious texts controversially claiming to be authoritative, materials once used in worship, capricious transcriptions of the four-letter Hebrew name of God (tetragrammaton), or artifacts about whose sacred status there is unresolvable doubt.

As Jewish law developed and synagogal ritual became more institutionalized, it became customary for communities to set aside a *bet genizah*, or simply *genizah*, into which could be consigned texts of the Hebrew Bible that were damaged or worn, as well as other Hebrew texts, including works regarded as heretical, that contained biblical verses or references to God. The rationale for such behaviour lay in an interpretation of the third commandment that proscribed the obliteration of the name of God but the principle appears to have been extended by many Jewish communities to the protection of a variety of Hebrew and Jewish literature, all of which might lay some claim to a degree of sacredness. If it is true, as I have claimed, that the adoption of the codex by the Jews in about the eighth century led to an explosion of Jewish literary activity, the problem of the disposal of obsolete items must soon have become a pressing one, and the use of a *genizah* a more frequent and standard occurrence.

Assuming that such an extensive application of the law was in fact a feature of oriental Jewish communities of the post-talmudic and early medieval periods, it is only to be expected that *genizot*, or what would in today's world constitute precious archival collections, were amassed in many areas of Jewish settlement. There is indeed evidence that while some communities made "assurance double sure" by burying the unwanted texts in the ground to await the natural process of disintegration, there were others that removed them to caves or tombs, sometimes storing them first in suitable vessels. It is not implausible that the Qumran Scrolls represent just such a *genizah,* although there is clearly room for dispute about the immediate reason for the removal. Sadly, however, the survival rate of such *genizot* has not proved impressive, the ravages of time and climate on the one hand and the vicissitudes of Jewish history on the other either ensuring a return to dust, or denying later generations adequate knowledge of where a search might even be commenced. Fortunately, however, in the case to hand, the first stage of consignment into the synagogue *genizah* appears not to have been followed by removal to a cave or burial place and scientific study of Jewish literature has consequently been greatly enriched.

The long survival of the Jewish community on the same site in Fustat; the dry climate of Egypt; the central importance of the city to Muslim and Jewish history for a number of centuries; and the reluctance of the Jewish communal leaders to take any action in the matter of its *genizah*, other than to expand its contents with all forms of the written word – all these factors contributed to the survival there of a collection of

fragmentary Jewish texts that is at least as significant as the Qumran Scrolls and may arguably outstrip the latter in overall historical significance. Generation after generation appear to have arranged the collection from homes and institutions in and around Cairo of texts that were no longer to be circulated, and thousands of them were consigned to the *genizah* of the Ben Ezra synagogue. To the great advantage of the historian, the custom was liberally interpreted by its synagogal authorities there and the deposits were not confined to sacred literature.

In a move that was to make its collection unique in terms of world culture and history, the community of Fustat chose to preserve much of the written word that passed through its hands, regardless of its religious status. There thus came to be amassed all manner of ephemera that had more to do with the daily activities of ordinary folk than with the ideology of rabbis and scholars. In an age that certainly predated the concern for the preservation of archives, the explanation for their behaviour may be that they saw Hebrew letters, or even any texts written by or about Jews, as either intrinsically sacred, or bearing a degree of holiness because of the frequent occurrence there of references to God, the Hebrew Bible or other religious subjects. The peak of this archival activity, if it may anachronistically be described as such, was during the Fatimid period, precisely when the community reached the zenith of its social, economic and cultural achievements.

VISITORS AND COLLECTORS

Whatever its exciting classical origins and its major medieval achievements, the Ben Ezra synagogue from the fifteenth to the nineteenth century was more noteworthy for pilgrimage and tourism than for vibrant communal life and seemed destined to slip into insignificance. Accusations by the Muslim authorities in 1442 that the Jews had committed some affront against Islam in the synagogue led to the demolition of its *bimah* (raised platform), the torture and conversion of some of its members, and the imposition of a swingeing fine. The resulting lack of communal funds lead to a neglect of the building's fabric, a situation exacerbated in 1473 by a fire, which also affected the nearby Babylonian synagogue. The merchant traveller, Meshullam of Voltera, made specific mention of the "synagogue of the Prophet Elijah" in 1481, noting that the general area of old Cairo was "a total ruin, and few people live there". Conscious as they were of the traditional importance of the site and the special place it occupied in the affections of Cairene Jewry, the leaders of the community were apparently successful in petitioning the Muslim authorities for permission to rebuild and managed to find the funds necessary to undertake this task. This is clear from the report of his visit written by the distinguished scholar, Obadiah of Bertinoro, in 1488. As well as commenting on the Ezra scroll, he was able to remark on the beauty and antiquity of the synagogue and he reported that it was called after Elijah the prophet who "is said to have appeared there to the pious in the south east corner, where they keep a continuous lamp burning." He also related that its columns were so attractive that the caliph had to be bribed not to remove them for his own use. He does, however, point out that by that time the building was used for prayer only on the sabbath. Some fifty years later, the more affluent Cairo community not only arranged for some of its members to spend the sabbath there but also maintained ten poor people (*baṭlanim*) in the area to ensure the required quorum (*minyan*) for prayer.

By the eighteenth century, Jewish and non-Jewish visitors from Egypt, Morocco, Italy and England were still fascinated by the building, the Ezra scroll reputed to be housed there, and the old inscriptions around the synagogue. At the same time, they had to acknowledge that it was used mainly for accommodating visitors and that the Jews of Cairo came there only on *Rosh Ḥodesh* (New Moon) to worship. The German-Jewish adventurer (and great-uncle of Heinrich Heine), Simon van Geldern, was, however, something of a trailblazer for later manuscript research, recalling that in 1752–53 he had searched for "Hebrew books and writings which had become unusable". It is conceivable that the tales of the Ezra scroll had led him to Fustat as a possible source of rare hebraica. Perhaps a need to fund his penchant for gambling encouraged such an interest in book bargains and he may have been the first to emerge from Fustat's Palestinian synagogue with some literary spoils.

It was the scholarly visitors of the second half of the nineteenth century who ensured the immortality of the synagogue. Between 1859 and 1872, during which time further reconstruction and renovation took place, they appear to have alerted the synagogue officials to the financial gain that could accrue to them if they were willing to part with some of the many thousands of Hebrew documents that had been amassed in the synagogue's *genizah* over the centuries. The Ashkenazi talmudist and traveller from Jerusalem, Jacob Saphir, described the state of the synagogue and the community as he saw it during visits he made in 1859 and 1864. On the earlier occasion he succeeded in catching sight of the ancient Torah scroll attributed to Ezra and came to some sceptical conclusions about its authenticity. During his second visit, he persuaded the two of those in authority to allow him access to the *genizah*, despite warnings about the snake that allegedly protected the entrance, and later reported the results:

> After I had laboured for two days and was covered with dust and earth, I removed a few folios of some old books and manuscripts that I had chosen, but did not find any valuable information in them. Who knows what else there is below? I was tired of searching, but I certainly came across no snake or similar reptile and, thank God, no harm came to me.

The Polish Karaite leader, Abraham Firkovich, who was an enthusiastic collector of manuscripts, appeared on the scene in 1864–65 and a substantial proportion of his extensive collection, now in St Petersburg, undoubtedly came from the Karaite synagogue in Cairo. Firkovich was neither explicit about the provenances of his finds nor averse to doctoring what he found to support an early date for the emergence of Karaism. It therefore remains unclear, even after much recent investigation of the matter, whether or not some of his haul, including many choice historical items, came from the Ben Ezra synagogue. What is clear is that he knew of the importance of its *genizah* and that, if his financial situation had permitted it, he might have persevered longer in Cairo and pre-empted Schechter's discoveries of more than thirty years later.

The Russian Orthodox Church built up an extensive centre of activity in Jerusalem in the second half of the nineteenth century, the remnants of which are still to be found today in the centre of the modern city. The archimandrite, Antonin (Andrei Ivanovich) Kapustin, was resident there from 1865 until his death in 1894 and on one of his trips to Cairo he too acquired Genizah fragments, over a thousand in number, which were, like the Firkovich acquisitions, subsequently taken to St Petersburg.

It was the ancient Christian churches of old Cairo that first attracted the English clergyman, Greville Chester, and were fully described by him in a publication of 1872. He also provided details of the Ben Ezra synagogue, noting the tradition that it had once been a Coptic place of worship and expressing the hope that it "could be rescued from its present state of profanation and restored to Christian worship." Evidently, Chester was again on hand when the old building was demolished in 1889 and was able to obtain some precious fragments that he brought back with him to Oxford and Cambridge.

Over the next twenty years or so, particularly during the reconstruction of the synagogue between 1889 and 1892, exciting fragments of medieval Jewish literature found their way to various centres of learning, and particularly important roles were played in this process of manuscript relocation by Elkan Nathan Adler, brother of British Chief Rabbi Hermann Adler, and the Jerusalem rabbi and bibliophile, Solomon Aaron Wertheimer. Indeed, both these scholars were able to publish little-known Jewish texts and to establish considerable reputations as a result of their forays among the fragments from Fustat. Wertheimer's fragments were sold to various institutions, especially to the Bodleian Library in Oxford (which also acquired some Genizah items from the assyriologist and traveller, Archibald Henry Sayce), as well as to Cambridge University Library. Adler's manuscripts were purchased from him in 1922 by the Jewish Theological Seminary of America in New York. The American Jewish orientalist, Cyrus Adler, later to be President of Dropsie College in Philadelphia and of the Jewish Theological Seminary in New York, purchased some fifty fragments from an antiquities dealer in Cairo early in 1891 and showed them to Neubauer in Oxford and Schechter in Cambridge not many months later. His collection was ultimately deposited in the library of Dropsie College in Philadelphia (now the Center for Judaic Studies at the University of Pennsylvania).

4 – Elkan Nathan Adler, Anglo-Jewish lawyer and bibliophile, 1861–1946
(by Lafayette, in *Jewish Historical Society of England Miscellanies* V, 1948)

The greatest haul of literary treasures was, however, made by the Reader in Talmudic and Rabbinic Literature at the University of Cambridge, Solomon Schechter, who followed a lead given by his Presbyterian friends, the pious and learned Scotswomen, Agnes Lewis and Margaret Gibson and, with the assistance and guidance of the Master of St John's College, Charles Taylor, succeeded in bringing 140,000 Genizah fragments to Cambridge University Library. Thus was inaugurated an era of learning that has brightly illuminated numerous aspects of medieval Jewish life in the Mediterranean area. Schechter made his literary expedition at the end of 1896, brought his discoveries back to Cambridge in 1897, and, with Charles Taylor, presented the collection to the University of Cambridge in 1898.

MORE RECENT TIMES

Contrary to what is sometimes claimed, Schechter did not empty Cairo and its environs of all its Genizah material. American, Hungarian and

French scholars also claimed their shares of the spoils and, in addition to fragments that made their way to other institutions in England, such as the British Museum (now British Library) and the John Rylands Library (now the John Rylands University Library of Manchester), both via the private library of Moses Gaster, and to the Selly Oak Colleges in Birmingham, substantial collections were acquired by Charles Freer of Detroit in 1908 (now at the Smithsonian Institution in Washington) and by Jack Mosseri, of the Cairo Jewish family, as announced by him in 1913. The Mosseri Collection, still in the hands of his family but now in Paris, is the only major set of Genizah manuscripts remaining in private hands. There are also fragments in the library of the Alliance Israélite Universelle in Paris, as well as in Strasbourg, Budapest and Vienna. The trade in such items was not yet over by the beginning of the century and individuals were still able to purchase medieval Jewish fragments from dealers for a number of decades.

Between the Ben Ezra synagogue's reconstruction in 1892 and the Second World War there was a distinct flourishing of the Cairene Jewish community. Wealthy Jewish families such as the Cattawis, Mosseris and Romanos restored much of the Ben Ezra's fabric, constructed communal housing for the needy, and welcomed many visitors from around the world, especially those serving the European powers. The Cambridge Jewish scholar, Herbert Loewe, wrote a lively report of crowded and enthusiastic communal festivities at the synagogue during his visit of 1906 and published it in the *Jewish Chronicle* of 20 July, 1906. He described it as "a perfect storehouse of fable and fancy" and chaffingly pronounced it "quite wonderful how many miracles they have managed to crowd into that small building". During both World Wars, Jews on active service enjoyed the hospitality of Jewish families in Egypt and the total Jewish population was as high as 75,000. In 1930, Ralph Green was appointed administrator of the Ben Ezra and was responsible for many initiatives in the fields of construction and welfare. But the establishment of the State of Israel and the Arab-Israeli wars reduced the Egyptian Jewish community from that number to a few hundred and, by the 1970s, the synagogue was again dilapidated, damaged and damp with no prospect but that of ignominious neglect and abuse. Tourists acquainted with the exciting Genizah story made special efforts to find the synagogue, only to have their enthusiasm severely dampened when they arrived at the sorry scene.

Thanks to the generosity of Edgar Bronfman, the Canadian philanthropist and president of the World Jewish Congress, and the devoted efforts of his sister, the distinguished architect and preserva-

5 – Ben Ezra synagogue before restoration, 1990 (*Fortifications and the Synagogue*, ed. P. Lambert, Weidenfeld & Nicolson, London, 1994, page 32)

6 – Ben Ezra synagogue after restoration, 1991 (*Fortifications and the Synagogue*, ed. P. Lambert, Weidenfeld & Nicolson, London, 1994, page 33)

tionist, Phyllis Lambert, founder and director of the Canadian Centre for Architecture in Montreal, the synagogue's story – at least as far as its building is concerned – has a happy ending. With the active (but not easily achieved) co-operation of politicians and communal leaders, architects and archaeologists, conservators, historians and photographers, the building was superbly restored. After a few fits and starts, a programme that first got under way in 1981 was successfully concluded after about ten years and a splendid volume entitled *Fortifications and the Synagogue: The Fortress of Babylon and the Ben Ezra Synagogue, Cairo* was edited by Lambert and published in London in 1994. Every aspect of the Ben Ezra's communal and physical history is covered in its ten chapters and the seven informative essays are accompanied by a sumptuous variety of plates and diagrams. A particularly interesting appendix offers the reader the opportunity of browsing through the lively comments of nineteenth- and twentieth-century visitors to the synagogue and provides excellent background information for those interested in the remarkable Genizah story.

Guide to reading

Lambert's volume provides a wealth of detail concerning the histories of old Cairo in general and of the Ben Ezra synagogue in particular. The more ancient archaeological aspect is covered by Peter Sheehan while Charles Le Quesne deals with the later archaeological evidence, as well as providing information about legends, modern history and Genizah scholarship. Menahem Ben-Sasson's article surveys the tenth to the fourteenth centuries and cites many Genizah texts, and his Hebrew University colleague, Joseph Hacker, makes use of his expertise in the Ottoman period to deal with the subsequent four hundred years. If that volume is more concerned with the Jewish side of Cairo's history, it may be balanced by the treatments of two related subjects in the new edition of *The Encyclopaedia of Islam*. J. Jomier's entries on "Al-Kahira" (IV, Leiden, 1978, pp. 424–44) and "Al-Fustat" (II, Leiden and London, 1965, pp. 957–59) are highly informative and explain the political, social and economic background to developments. That same reference work contains a short but useful contribution by S. D. Goitein on the general topic of the "Geniza" (II, Leiden and London, 1965, pp. 987–89).

Paul Kahle was among the small group of non-Jews devoted to Genizah research and the first chapter of his volume *The Cairo Geniza* (2nd edition, Oxford, 1959) discusses the history, discovery and contents of the Genizah. It then goes on to explain its relevance to the Dead Sea Scrolls, Karaism, the Khazars and Jewish liturgical poetry. Kahle's volume was the standard reference work in English for a number of years but must now be used with care since much of the information and many of the theories have recently been superseded. If, for instance, data is now required about the location, history and nature of the various Genizah collectors and the collections they left around the world, Benjamin Richler's *Guide to Hebrew Manuscript Collections* (Jerusalem, 1994) is the first place to look. He directs the Institute of Microfilmed Hebrew Manuscripts at the Jewish National and University Library in Jerusalem and is *au fait* with all the latest developments in the field of Hebrew manuscript research. His volume consists of an alphabetical guide to all the individuals and institutions involved, and many appendices detailing the whereabouts of specific collections. S. D. Goitein's classic set of volumes *A Mediterranean Society* (5 volumes, plus index volume, prepared by Paula Sanders, Berkeley, Los Angeles, London, 1967–93) will be cited many times through this volume. Goitein's general introduction to the Genizah is to be found in the first volume, pp. 1–74. Other brief introductions to the Genizah are Norman Golb's essays "Sixty Years of Genizah Research" in *Judaism* 6 (1957), pp. 3–16 and "The Contents of the Genizah" in *Perspectives in Jewish Learning*, ed. M. Harris (Chicago, 1965); the entry in the *Encyclopaedia Judaica* 16 (Jerusalem, 1972), cols. 1333–42, which is a vast improvement on the thin treatment in the body of the work (7, pp. 404–7); S. C. Reif's A *Guide to the Taylor-Schechter Genizah Collection* (2nd edition, Cambridge, 1979); Simon Hopkins's "The Discovery of the Cairo Geniza", inspired by his period as a research assistant in the Genizah Research Unit at Cambridge University Library (1975–78), and published in a little known South African serial *Bibliophilia Africana* 4 (1981), pp. 137–78; and J. Sadan's comparative study "Genizah and Genizah-like Practices in Islamic and Jewish Traditions", *Bibliotheca Orientalis* 43 (1986), pp. 36–58. Genizah research in America, beginning with Cyrus Adler in 1891, is neatly summarized in Menahem Schmelzer's pamphlet *One Hundred Years of Genizah Discovery and Research: The American Share* (National Foundation for Jewish Culture Lecture Series, no. 2, New York, 1998). Victor (Lebedev) Bochman's article "Hidden Treasures: 100 Years since the Discovery of the Cairo Genizah", *Ariel* 106 (1998), pp. 7–14 has useful information concerning the Arabic and Karaite material but suffers from a number of inaccuracies.

For further information about more specific developments in the history of the Jewish communities of Egypt through the various periods, one should in the first instance consult three volumes produced by students of Goitein. The first volume of Moshe Gil's three heavily documented Hebrew volumes on the history of Palestinian Jewry in the early centuries of Islamic rule (Tel Aviv, 1983) has been revised and translated into English as *A History of Palestine 634–1099* (Cambridge, 1992). It cites Islamic and Christian sources, as well as Jewish texts, especially from the Genizah, and, in view of the close relationship that often existed between the Holy Land and Egypt, it provides rich information about both centres. That relationship was sometimes dominated by Egypt and sometimes by Palestine and Mark Cohen explains how a crucial change took place in the eleventh century. In his *Jewish Self-Government in Medieval Egypt* (Princeton, 1980), he traces the development of the Jewish community and how it took over the leadership of regional Jewry. A broad picture of precisely how Jews related to Arabs in the Middle Ages is clearly painted by Norman Stillman in *The Jews of Arab Lands* (Philadelphia, 1979). The coverage ranges from the beginning of Islam to modern times and historical survey is accompanied by translated sources, with the Genizah texts and the Egyptian centre well represented. The nature of that centre as it attracted colonial attention in the modern period is dealt with in the fourth volume that should be cited in this context. Jacob Landau's *Jews in Nineteenth-Century Egypt* (New York, 1969) was translated from the Hebrew original published in Jerusalem two years earlier. Academically sound without being difficult to read, Landau's study introduces the reader to the people, places and trends of the period immediately leading up to the discovery and scholarly exploitation of the Genizah source.

In addition to reading the original editions of Gil and Landau that have just been cited, those at home in Hebrew can also benefit from a number of other books and articles. There is the somewhat idiosyncratic article by N. Allony, "Genizah and Hebrew Manuscripts in Cambridge Libraries", that appeared in *Areshet* 3 (1961), pp. 395–425 and the same writer's "Genizah Practices among the Jews" in *Sinai* 79 (1976), pp. 193–201. There is very little in the field of Hebrew bibliography that did not attract the attention of A. M. Habermann who dealt with the Genizah in his booklet *The Cairo Genizah and other Genizoth* (Jerusalem, 1971), while the halakhic aspects are covered by the relevant entry in the *Encyclopaedia Talmudica* 6 (Jerusalem, 1954), cols. 232–39. A survey of the synagogue was reported by M. Ben-Dov in his article "The Ezra Synagogue in Cairo", *Qadmoniot* 15 (1982), pp. 33–39 and Mark Cohen offered a detailed reconstruction of the building activities that led up to the scattering of the collection in the 1890s in his paper "The Cairo Genizah and the Custom of Genizah among Oriental Jewry", *Pe'amim* 24 (1985), pp. 3–35. The origins of the Firkovich collection and its relationship to Genizah collections in general are analysed by Menahem Ben-Sasson in an article entitled "Firkovich's Second Collection: Remarks on Historical and Halakhic Material" in *Jewish Studies* 31 (1991), pp. 47–67, with an update in a lecture prepared by himself and Ze'ev Elkin for the Ben Zvi Institute in February, 1997 and entitled "Abraham Firkovich and the Cairo Genizah: New Evidence". The text of this lecture is expected to be published shortly in *Pe'amim*. The introduction to Neil Danzig's important volume *A Catalogue of Fragments of Halakhah and Midrash from the Cairo Genizah in the Elkan Nathan Adler Collection of the Library of the Jewish Theological Seminary of America* (New York and Jerusalem, 1997) also contains useful information about the Cairo Genizah in general and the Elkan Nathan Adler fragments in particular.

TWO

THE CAMBRIDGE CONNECTION

Remarkable as it may seem, the Cambridge connection with Hebrew goes back in time almost as far as the commitment of the Cairo Jewish community to preserving its Genizah archive. Although Hebrew was not included in the basic courses of study pursued by Christians at the University of Cambridge until the sixteenth century, the middle-sized Norman Jewish community in the city, residing between the Round Church and today's Market Square, produced its own Benjamin the Grammarian as early as the twelfth century, presumably with a local collection of Hebrew books on which to base his studies. Such interest in hebraica among the Jews undoubtedly had its parallel among their Christian neighbours. Across the English Channel in France, Hugh of St. Victor, the Augustinian abbey in Paris, was at that time championing an approach that stressed not only the importance of Hebrew Scripture but also of its traditional Jewish interpretation.

Those interested in converting the Jews also felt the need to match the Hebrew linguistic talents of their theological competitors and such orders as the Dominicans and the Franciscans were particularly successful in doing so. The Church leadership also made its contribution by encouraging the study of eastern languages and in 1312 its General Council ordered the establishment of teaching posts in Hebrew, Arabic, Aramaic and Greek at five European universities. By the time that a "common library of the scholars" had emerged at the University of Cambridge in the early fifteenth century and found itself a place on the Old Schools site, between St Mary's Church and Clare College, Hebrew was no longer such an alien tongue in English academic circles. Some important hebraica and Latin books closely relating to Jews and Judaism were acquired by the various Cambridge libraries, and a recently published list of such pre-Elizabethan Cambridge holdings puts the total number at over fifty. Nine of those were once in the University Library, but only four still remain there.

23

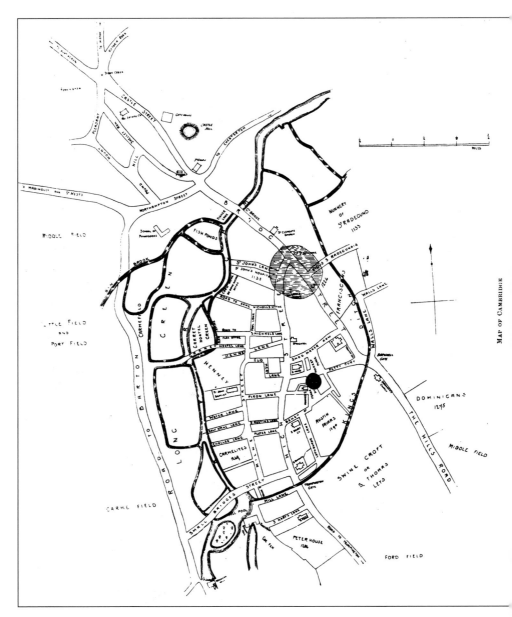

7 – Medieval Cambridge with the Jewish areas marked (H. P. Stokes, *Studies in Anglo-Jewish History*, published for the Jewish Historical Society of England, Edinburgh, 1913)

EFFECTS OF REFORMATION

Revolutionary developments in the sixteenth century provided Hebrew with a more permanent place in the university curriculum. New modes of Christian thought, culminating in the Protestant Reformation, challenged the Catholic Church's traditional interpretation of the Bible. Religious thinkers laid new stress on the literal meaning of the Hebrew text and on the need to study the various Semitic languages. The newly available printing-presses were utilized by leading Christian hebraists to introduce their religious brethren to the Jewish Bible commentators and grammarians who had excelled in such learning. In Cambridge, as early as 1516, John Fisher, Bishop of Rochester and Chancellor of the University, who was still trying to steer a middle course between the new humanism and the old scholasticism, included a requirement in the first statutes that he drew up for St. John's to the effect that some students should devote themselves to the study of Hebrew literature. The later statutes of 1524 and 1530, which the same benefactor drew up for that college, go even further, suggesting the study of Hebrew for suitable students, and listing Hebrew among the five classical languages in which formal conversations in the dining hall and disputations were exclusively to be conducted. Provision was also made for a lecturer in Hebrew, at a salary of £4–5 per annum, to tutor the senior students each day.

Whatever their theological and political differences, Thomas Cromwell, Fisher's successor as Chancellor, was certainly happy to follow his predecessor's lead in this matter, and his Royal Commission of 1535 instructed the University to maintain a university lecturer in either Greek or Hebrew at its own expense. The financial burden proved something of an obstacle to the success of the project and in 1535 and 1537 the lectureship in mathematics had to be suspended to provide the salaries of the Greek and Hebrew lecturers. Welcome relief and a sounder basis for the post came with the foundation of the Regius (that is, royal) chairs by Henry VIII in 1540, at stipends of £40 per annum, at first charged upon the plundered revenues of the Cathedral Church of Westminster but from about 1547 payable by Trinity College. This office of "our Hebrew reader in Cambridge", granted its own coat of arms featuring the Hebrew letter *tav* in 1590, was early occupied by a number of distinguished hebraists. Paul Fagius, a gentile pupil of the German Jewish grammarian Elijah Levita who taught in Italy, did much to popularize his teacher's work. John Immanuel Tremellius, an Italian Jewish convert to Protestantism, lectured while the ideologically suspect Thomas Wakefield retained the official title. Edward Lively was chosen by James I as one of the translators of the new English version of the Bible decided upon at the Hampton Court Conference of 1604, to whom other translators were to refer any problems concerning obscurities in the Hebrew and mistakes in earlier English translations.

Not surpisingly, given its theological rationale, the scope of the teaching was limited by an injunction of 1549 to the Hebrew scriptures and the grammar of the language, and the professors apparently had little success in engendering enthusiasm for the subject among the student body. Nevertheless, the presence in the two English universities of itinerant Jewish scholars, giving private Hebrew lessons and consulting library collections, the establishment of some college lectureships in Hebrew, as at Gonville and Caius in 1585, and the requirement at Caius that "all bachelors should attend the Hebrew lectures" are further indications that Hebrew studies were well founded in England by the end of the sixteenth century. Indeed, Emmanuel and Sidney Sussex expected their fellows to be proficient in Hebrew and a proportion of the Cambridge theologians were competent hebraists. Meanwhile, the Reformation had brought similar developments in the Scottish centres of higher education. Three universities were established in Scotland in the fifteenth century – St. Andrews (1412), Glasgow (1451) and Aberdeen (1495) – and were followed by Edinburgh in 1583. Hebrew and related languages were certainly being taught there in the sixteenth century.

It was during the last quarter of the same century that Cambridge University Library took its first faltering steps into the modern world. Having commenced the century with over 600 books, its holdings had, by 1557, been eroded through neglect, unscrupulous borrowing and the ravages of the Reformation, to less than 200. The dedicated efforts of Andrew Perne, Master of Peterhouse, did, however, succeed in restoring the library to usefulness. A University Librarian was appointed, the first surviving regulations were drawn up for the administration of the Library, and leading scholars and clerics of the day were persuaded to become its benefactors. Through their generosity, as well as that of Perne himself, the number of books at the library increased to almost a thousand by the end of the century. Although a few have yet to be traced, most of the works with Hebrew and Jewish connections included among these benefactions are happily still to be found in the Library. They include a Bomberg Hebrew Bible (1517–18); a first edition of David Qimḥi's Hebrew lexicon, *Shorashim* (Rome, before 1480?); and Qimḥi's commentary on Psalms 1–10 in the Latin version of Fagius (Constantinople, 1544), once owned by Thomas Cranmer, famous cleric and statesman under Henry VIII.

ROUNDHEADS AND CAVALIERS

The King James (or, Authorised) Version, among the translators of which were two holders of the Cambridge Hebrew chair, was published in 1611 and the subsequent period of fifty years represents something of a golden age for Hebrew scholarship in England. Hebrew texts and translated rabbinic works made their appearance, the numbers of hebraica at the Bodleian Library in Oxford and at Cambridge University Library were substantially increased, and some native scholars, holding distinguished college and university posts, numbered Hebrew and other Semitic languages among their various accomplishments. Among such men at Cambridge, the best known are probably Robert Sheringham, senior fellow at Caius, John Lightfoot, Master of St. Catharine's, and Ralph Cudworth, Master of Clare and then of Christ's and Regius Professor of Hebrew. Only the latter two escaped serious disruption of their academic lives during the political upheavals that marked the period of the Civil War and the Puritan Commonwealth, others suffering the indignity of ejection from their college appointments, and worse. Until his reinstatement at the Restoration, Sheringham taught Hebrew and Arabic in Rotterdam where he was nicknamed "the Rabbi", while Lightfoot, who "by constant reading of the rabbis became almost a rabbi himself", collaborated with Brian Walton on the compilation of his *Polyglot*. Cudworth, leader of the "Cambridge Platonists", contributed a Hebrew piece to the volume with which Cambridge congratulated Charles I on his return from Scotland in 1641, composed an enthusiastic Hebrew poem for the publication with which Cambridge greeted the "accession" of Richard Cromwell in 1658, and penned more Hebrew verse, no less enthusiastic, for the volume of congratulations dedicated by the same university to Charles II.

The academic self-indulgence that led scholars to praise their political leaders in a language that the latter could not read was also to be found among preachers desirous of impressing their congregations with the sheer incomprehensibility of their sermons. The Westminster Assembly of 1644 attempted to strike a blow for more democratic religious education by prohibiting the use of Hebrew in the pulpit but there is evidence to suggest that churchgoers felt cheated if homilies were delivered in a language wholly within their intellectual grasp. Further evidence of the importance attached to the study of Hebrew in the seventeenth century, in the colonies as well as at home, is contained in the first scheme of study for Harvard College, in the North American Cambridge, which prescribed Hebrew, Aramaic and Syriac as subjects of weekly instruction for all students.

Such interest in Hebrew and Jewish sources also developed a political dimension when the scholarly interests of distinguished orientalists such as the jurist John Selden matured into philosemitic convictions and provided important support for Oliver Cromwell's proposal to permit the Jews to resettle in England. The issue was a contentious one, as indicated by the strong feelings expressed in a number of pamphlets about the Jews published at the time. Those opposed to the proposal did their best to whip up support among the general population, who were in any case ill-disposed towards the Jews, by spreading malicious rumours about their intentions. Among these were the libels that the Jews were negotiating the purchase of the Bodleian Library, Cambridge University Library and/or St. Paul's Cathedral for conversion into a synagogue. Estimates of the precise financial reward that Cromwell would personally receive for his part in arranging such transactions provided a useful double-duty calumny for those without sympathies for either the Lord Protector or the potential immigrants.

Among the delegates invited to attend the Whitehall Conference of 1655 and to decide whether there was any legal impediment to Jewish admission and, if not, on what terms they might be invited to return, were a number of leading theologians, among them Professor Cudworth of Cambridge. Although there is no surviving record of any formal decision having been reached at this Conference, the next ten years saw the establishment of a small Jewish community in London, approved by the Council of State, and the confirmation of its rights by the restored monarch. It was to be some time before Jews were permitted, or indeed inclined, to play any major part in the development of Hebrew studies in the United Kingdom but their presence alone was bound to have at least some effect on the situation.

MAJOR ACQUISITIONS

This keen interest in Hebrew and related subjects also made itself felt at Cambridge University Library in the second quarter of the seventeenth century. The Library was fortunate to have at its head Abraham Whelock who, though a trifle neurotic, brought to the position a devotion, energy and scholarly standing which did much to transform its administration, holdings and reputation from the mediocre to the outstanding. From the beginning, Whelock, whose academic accomplishments led to his appointment in 1632 as the first holder of the Arabic lectureship endowed by Sir Thomas Adams, set himself the task

28

of expanding the Library's collection in the oriental field in an economical fashion. Enjoying as he did the friendship and respect of many of the leading orientalists of the day, he was able to ensure that when they gave thought to the matter of presenting or bequeathing their literary treasures, his own institution was not forgotten. Among important manuscripts gifted during his tenure of office were a part of Moses Naḥmanides' pentateuchal commentary, with a Latin translation; Robert Sheringham's edition of the mishnaic tractate *Yoma* with his impressive Latin translation and commentary; and the first volume of Christopher Cartwright's learned and informative discussion, in Latin, of the running comments on the text of Genesis made by a wide range of Jewish exegetes. These accessions, however, pale into insignificance when compared with two illustrious collections of orientalia which Whelock saw safely on to the University Library shelves in exciting circumstances.

In May 1625, six months after the death of the distinguished Dutch orientalist, Thomas van Erpe, or Erpenius, negotiations were entered into between his widow and the authorities of the University of Leiden, at which he had occupied a chair, for the purchase of his library of printed books and manuscripts. By November, no agreement had yet been reached and George Villiers, Duke of Buckingham (cultured philanderer and favourite of James I), taking advantage of the breakdown in negotiations, made a swift purchase of the manuscripts for £500. The Duke's ownership of these manuscripts, and the hope that he would build a new library for Cambridge University in which they would be housed, apparently played no small part in his successful nomination for election as Chancellor in 1626, but in 1628, before the University could benefit from his bounty, an assassin's knife put an end to his life and, as it then seemed, to the University's schemes. Yet Whelock took up the matter of the manuscripts and succeeded in persuading the Duke's widow, the dowager duchess Catherine, to present them to Cambridge University Library. Of the eighty-six manuscripts that duly arrived in June 1632, thirteen were in Hebrew and one in Judaeo-Arabic, and they clearly demonstrate in which specific area of Jewish literature the interests of Erpenius lay. Biblical and rabbinic texts, and one translated medical treatise, account for six, while the remaining eight, dated in the fifteenth and sixteenth centuries, constitute a miscellany of tracts, translations and commentaries, touching on the work of famous Greek, Christian, Islamic and Jewish philosophers.

The renowned jurist, John Selden, known for his scholarship and a sympathetic approach to Judaism, also earned the gratitude of

Cambridge for his role in persuading Parliament to divert two other exceptional collections of books to its University Library. The fate of the first of these, the 10,000 volumes of the Lambeth Palace Library, became the subject of parliamentary debate after Laud's impeachment and unhappy end and the abolition of episcopacy, and were delivered to Cambridge in the academical year, 1648–49. The Library's holdings were thus enriched by the presence of an extra twenty-nine printed volumes of *Biblia Hebraica*, and seventeen "Rabbinnici", consisting of a variety of post-biblical works, in manuscript and print, ranging from part of the censored edition of the Talmud printed by Froben (Basle, 1578–81) to Constantijn L'Empereur van Oppijck's edition of the mishnaic tractate *Middot*, with his Latin translation and commentary (Leiden, 1630), and the Hebrew version of Calvin's Geneva Catechism produced by Tremellius in 1554. The privilege of holding these volumes was however withdrawn when Anglicanism was restored and Lambeth felt uninclined to write off its loss. Of more central significance is another collection of orientalia that Selden was also instrumental in bringing to Cambridge since this complemented the Erpenius manuscripts and was destined to become one of the University Library's permanent attractions for hebraists.

This collection was originally brought together, much of it apparently in 1643, by one Isaac Faragi (traditionally but wrongly pronounced Pragi at Cambridge University Library for many years), an otherwise unknown Italian Jew who functioned as rabbi and/or bookseller. Faragi sold his books to the London dealer famous for his collection of Civil War and Commonwealth pamphlets, George Thomason, for about a quarter of the £500 which Parliament eventually paid for them, but Thomason apparently did much to earn his handsome profit. He sensed the contemporary interest in orientalia and took steps to cater for it. In 1647 he published a catalogue of books bought in Italy, devoting ten pages to a detailed description of the Faragi books and drawing attention to the unique character of this rabbinical and oriental material. Thomason shrewdly recognized Selden as a potential customer and sent him a copy of those ten pages.

His expectations were not disappointed. Spurred on by Selden "the Lords and Commons, in Parliament assembled" ordered the payment of £500 to the bookseller and the presentation of the collection to the "Public Library of the University of Cambridge", and entrusted Selden and John Lightfoot with the safe consignment of the books. The arrival of eleven manuscripts, ten Hebrew and one Persian, in the Faragi collection meant a significant increase in the Library's holdings of such

8 – The building that housed the University Library 100 years ago and is now used for
administrative offices (Cambridge University Library)

material. The manuscripts included a fourteenth-century Ashkenazi
text of the halakhic decisions of Isaiah of Trani; a north French
commentary on Job by Berekhiah from the same century; and a
lavishly illuminated medical text-book emanating from fifteenth-
century north Italy. It was, however, in the quantity of its printed
hebraica that the acquisitions brought a most profound improvement.
The Library could now boast the new ownership of approximately 400
printed Hebrew items, including six volumes from before 1501. The
later items, emanating mainly from Italy but also from Polish and
Turkish presses, were bound together in about a third as many volumes
and constituted a representative sample of the hebraica being published
at the time. Not only is the biblical, talmudic-midrashic and halakhic
literature covered but there are also numerous works on kabbalah,
philosophy and medicine. To his intense satisfaction, Whelock was
surrounded by hundreds of Hebrew volumes to match the thousands of
general volumes he had seen on to the shelves and the University
Library's collections of hebraica dwarfed what was available at
individual colleges.

SLOWER PROGRESS

The progress made in Hebrew studies at Cambridge in the latter part of the seventeenth century hardly compares with the dynamic developments of the decades immediately preceding. The most distinguished Cambridge hebraist of the period was in fact a Jew, and a loyal one at that. Isaac Abendana was informally engaged, as was the baptised Jew Paul Colend (formerly, Moshe) Scialitti, as a Hebrew tutor at Trinity, and probably also gave private lessons in the subject. His claim to fame, however, lies in literary rather than pedagogical achievements. The need for a Latin translation of the Mishnah was being keenly felt by Cambridge theologians and the University, taking advantage of Abendana's presence between 1663 and 1675, engaged him on the task. He was paid £89.2s.6d for his translation as well as some indexing and binding, and the rate of payment was one pound per tractate. Although Abendana's translation was, in the words of Israel Abrahams, a "monument to his own erudition", various factors combined to ensure that it was never published. Abendana, whose brother Jacob became Haham of the Spanish and Portuguese Congregation in London in 1681, eventually made his way to Oxford and published popular guides to Jewish rites and customs, for which he found a readier and more profitable market.

At Cambridge University Library too the promise of the earlier years was not maintained. The return of the Lambeth books, the death of Whelock and the University's failure to expand the staff to cope with the more extensive responsibilities of an enlarged library depressed the institution while the high standards set by Whelock gradually gave way to more perfunctory levels of organization. Thomas Fuller's criticism of its staff contained in his reference in 1655 to "library-*losers* (for library-*keepers* I cannot call them)" gradually came to have more and not less justification. In spite of this general situation, however, some important acquisitions were made in the hebraic and oriental areas. The library of Richard Holdsworth, Master of Emmanuel, contained over a hundred "libri hebraei" and "bibliae hebraicae"; the bequest of Henry Lucas, who had represented the University in Parliament, included a handful of books of Jewish interest; and Edmund Castell, Professor of Arabic, willed thirty-eight oriental manuscripts, nineteen of them apparently in Hebrew. In addition to other Hebrew gifts from various individuals, including forty-six printed books purchased by the Vice-Chancellor, John Howorth, from the London Jewish merchant, Solomon Gabay, a substantial benefaction, (to prove invaluable when Hebrew manuscripts were purchased in number in the nineteenth century), came from Tobias Rustat who had been in service with the second Duke of Buckingham and then, for the best part of both their lives, with Charles II.

The scholars of eighteenth-century Cambridge enjoy no great reputation for intellectual industry or sober pursuits. Little enthusiasm was displayed for either giving lectures or undertaking research and, in the inevitable deterioration of standards, Hebrew fared no better than most subjects. Complaints that members of the University were dealing with Jewish peddlars indicate that Cambridge interest in Jewish sources was at that time just as likely to be commercial as literary. The long-established lectureships at Caius and St. John's were often reduced to sinecures while those who occupied the Regius chair distinguished themselves, if at all, in subjects other than Hebrew, and in a fondness for the pulpit. Their sole contribution to Hebrew scholarship, if contribution it be, is to be found in the Hebrew poems they and other clerics provided for official volumes composed by members of the University on auspicious public occasions. The University's *Historical Register* records that one was a "miserly refuge", that another was "a notorious gourmand", and that a third hanged himself in his college rooms. In the absence of keen interest, highly qualified candidates, and significant financial inducement (the stipend remaining at £40 a year), Trinity College which was responsible for the election, remuneration and the provision of fellow's rights, had problems in filling the post. The kind of difficulty that the electors had to face is amply illustrated by the record of one particular candidature in 1771. On being asked several times by the electors whether he was ready to be examined, the candidate, Thomas Churchil of Clare College, would give no direct answer and, on being pressed, declared he would give the electors no further trouble and withdrew!

This dearth of enthusiastic and competent hebraists posed something of a problem for Caius College which was still interested in imparting a knowledge of Hebrew to some of its students. Once again, the services of a Jew were called upon and one Israel Lyons, a silversmith by profession, was, for a number of years, paid £5 a year by that college to give Hebrew instruction to its junior members. Lyons styled himself "Teacher of the Hebrew Tongue in the University of Cambridge" in two of his publications. Indeed, the University archives record that he was paid a total of £80 between 1741 and 1769 for giving Hebrew tuition, as well as £6.5s.6d for an edition of the Hebrew Bible published in Amsterdam in 1724–28. In addition, he contributed to the University's official volume of condolence on the death of Queen Caroline in which he is described as *L(inguae) S(acrae) Informator.* He thus seems to have enjoyed a close though obviously not quite formal relationship with the University and other Jews appear to have performed similar functions.

The lull in the University Library's acquisition of hebraica that had characterized the end of the seventeenth century was not replaced by any dynamic developments in the eighteenth. Although the Copyright Act of 1709 gave the University Library the right to a copy of each book published in the country, only an estimated sixth of the books published in the second half of the century were deposited there. Since the number of oriental books produced in England at the time was not in any case substantial, there must have been few Hebrew volumes among them. Approximately 150 printed books and a handful of manuscripts from the King's or Royal Library, purchased and presented by George I in 1715, were in Hebrew but, considering that the total number of the former was in excess of 30,000 and of the latter possibly about 1,790, the haul was hardly impressive. Among the manuscripts definitely to be traced to that collection, originally amassed by John Moore, Bishop of Ely, are a fourteenth-century Hebrew Bible from Spain, fifteenth-century copies of the second part of Jacob ben Asher's code and David Ha-Nagid's Judaeo-Arabic midrash on Numbers, and a minute sixteenth-century Sefaradi prayer-book. In addition, the Rev. George Lewis presented some Persian manuscripts and "oriental curiosities which proved a great attraction to tourists" and a generous benefaction made by William Worts in 1709 was destined to play a part in expanding the Hebrew collection a century later.

VICTORIAN EFFICIENCY

In the universities of nineteenth-century Britain, the new drive for propriety, industry and efficiency stood in stark contrast to the tendencies of the previous century and led to higher standards of scholarship and administration. Hebrew studies were particularly fortunate in benefitting from this trend as well as from a number of other developments. The Empire's expansion encouraged orientalists to widen their intellectual horizons and to press for educational recognition of their scholarly interests. With the gradual removal of their religious disabilities (Cambridge was among those places that ensured that it was gradual), Jews became eligible to study and teach at universities without abrogating loyalty to their faith and thus to contribute more directly to general scholarly achievements. Not that the Jews flocked to take degrees in Hebrew; as immigrants and first generation citizens they were concerned with the more mundane aspects of settling into their new environment. Their presence, however, together with that of some scholars who had fled the persecutions of eastern Europe for the more liberal countries to the west, and of others who had been influenced by the new scientific approach to Jewish learning in the rabbinical seminaries of central Europe, fostered a further interest in Hebrew and a revival of the seventeenth-century fascination with post-biblical Hebrew literature. When University College, London, opened its doors, a chair of Hebrew was advertised and a Polish-born Jew, Hyman Hurwitz, was appointed to the post in 1827.

Although the sixteenth-century statutes relating to the Regius chair of Hebrew at Cambridge had regulated the method of appointment, the frequency of lectures and the total extent of salary and benefit, the decline in the value of the stipend in the seventeenth century, and in the application of regulations in the eighteenth, had brought about a situation which required the attention of the nineteenth-century Commissioners. The new statutes for the Regius professorships, confirmed by order of Queen Victoria in May 1860, cleared up the confusion by restoring what was best in the original foundation and merging it with the contemporary requirements, and the financial problems of the Hebrew chair were eased by an 1840 Act of Parliament that provided for the attachment of a Canonry of Ely from the date of the next appointment. The situation had already begun to improve from as early as 1831 with the appointment of Samuel Lee as Professor of Hebrew.

With merit playing a greater part in appointments than hitherto, Trinity's monopoly was broken and while it is true that Lee and his two successors, W. H. Mill, first holder of the attached Ely Canonry, and Thomas Jarrett, are better known as polyglot orientalists than accomplished hebraists, they did re-establish the tradition for high standards of scholarship. Jarrett was Hebrew lecturer at St. Catharine's from 1828 to 1832 and it was the reversion of such college appointees as Jarrett, and John Crowfoot at Caius, to competent and active roles in the teaching of the language that assured its revival. As the "senior" oriental subject, Hebrew also benefitted from the establishment of a Board of Oriental Studies in 1861 and Jarrett was its first presiding officer. A further encouragement to the study of the language was provided by Robert Tyrwhitt who in 1817 bequeathed a generous sum, the income from which was to be used for Hebrew scholarships and the general promotion of Hebrew learning. The fund was augmented by the University in 1862 and many a distinguished hebraist won his first academic recognition as a Cambridge Tyrwhitt scholar.

Jews, who formally established a local congregation in 1847 and met for worship in a house behind the Round Church, continued to play a part in the development of Hebrew. Solomon Lyon (1754–1820) is said to have established a Jewish boarding-school at Cambridge, the first of its type in the country, and to have taught Hebrew to some junior members of the University destined to become such distinguished personages as the Duke of Sussex, the Bishop of Gloucester, and the musician and composer, Isaac Nathan. Rabbi Joseph Crool, an eccentric personality best known for his opposition to the activities of the London Society for Promoting Christianity among the Jews, and his view that Jewish emancipation should be avoided since it would lead only to assimilation, continued Lyon's work and was himself succeeded as *Praeceptor Linguae Sacrae* by Herman Hedwig Bernard whose conversion to Christianity seems not to have dampened his enthusiasm for either Hebrew or Rabbinics. Works from the pens of Lyon, Crool and Bernard contributed to the flowering of Hebrew and Jewish letters in the period leading up to Jewish political emancipation.

The Library too made physical, administrative and bibliographical progress in the first half of the nineteenth century and the Rustat and Worts benefactions were arranged in such a way as to provide some income to assist with the purchase of books. The first significant accession of oriental books for about a century took place in the first decade of the century. The missionary, Claudius Buchanan, Professor and Vice-Provost of the College of Fort William in Bengal between 1800 and 1807, presented not only the relatively unimportant missionary tracts that his college was producing in the local dialects but also some valuable Hebrew and Syriac works. Among the manuscripts donated were twenty-five in Syriac, including the famous "Buchanan Bible", twenty-one in Hebrew for one of which Rabbi Crool provided an English translation, and one each in Ethiopic and Persian, while the printed material included twenty-nine Hebrew and eleven Syriac volumes.

The subject matter of the Hebrew books from Buchanan ranged over a wide area and some of the printed editions were already over two centuries old. As far as the Hebrew manuscripts are concerned, particularly worthy of mention are items relating to the history of the Black and White Jews of Cochin; halakhic and kabbalistic works transcribed in the century or two before Buchanan acquired them; a sixteenth- or seventeenth-century pentateuchal scroll and a sixteenth-century Ashkenazi copy of Judah b. Beṣalel Löw's super-commentary on Rashi. In one of his own publications, Buchanan gives an account of the Jewish community of Cochin, which he had encountered during a visit to the Malabar coast in 1806–7, and of how he had, not without some unpleasant clashes, obtained many of these manuscripts from them.

As thoughts turned to the provision of general catalogues, so consideration was also given to the need for a catalogue of the oriental manuscripts and on 11 May 1825 Dr Daniel Guildford Wait was authorized by the Senate to compile such a reference work. The catalogue was to be modelled on those produced for the Bodleian in Oxford and for the Escurial in Spain, and was to contain brief manuscript descriptions, each headed by a Roman numeral and including some quotations from the original, the whole printed in two columns on folio sheets. However well defined the intention, the plan seems to have come to nought and it certainly did nothing to solve the financial problems of the unfortunate Dr Wait who was later imprisoned for debt.

Despite its general progress, the Library still lacked dynamic and efficient leadership and a modern system of administration. Criticisms of its deficiencies were especially made by the outspoken Johnian, J. E. B. Mayor, and Joseph Power eventually resigned the Librarianship in 1864, to be succeeded by the Library's chief critic. This appointment, no less than that of Henry Bradshaw as a young assistant in 1856, and subsequently as the superintendent of manuscripts and early printed books in 1859, was destined to be of profound significance for the institution's future development.

9 – Henry Bradshaw, Cambridge University Librarian,
1867–1886 (Cambridge University Library)

FLOWERING OF HEBREW STUDIES

The latter half of the nineteenth century saw a flowering of Hebrew learning at Cambridge that matched the finest achievements of the past and set standards difficult for subsequent generations to surpass. Writing in 1882, Charles Taylor, Master of St. John's, cited the following assessment of the situation that he had read, with obvious approval, in a current periodical: "Possibly at no time since the seventeenth century, when some of the greatest modern hebraists were Cambridge men, has Hebrew learning been more actively and accurately pursued in Cambridge than now." For the undergraduate, this pursuit of Hebrew learning first took place at the college level, where a succession of sometime Tyrwhitt scholars initiated their protégés in the language of the "Old Testament". Seven colleges taught Hebrew and among the lecturers were future professors of Arabic and Divinity, a prospective college master, and three members-to-be of the Old Testament Revision Committee. Perhaps the most successful, and certainly the most popular and enthusiastic of such lecturers, was the conservative Anglican, Peter Mason, at St. John's. As well as training and inspiring generations of hebraists, Mason also wrote two text-books, one of them jointly with

38

Bernard in the field of rabbinics, and when, in spite of the support of thirty-one former pupils, his candidature for the vacant Regius chair in 1882 was unsuccessful, his supporters compensated him for the indignity by subscribing funds for the establishment of a Mason Prize for Biblical Hebrew. Further inducements to the study of Hebrew during this period were an earlier University Prize established by subscription in 1865 and a later scholarship created under the terms of the will of John Stewart of Rannoch, to which the first election was made in 1894.

Christ's College, under the masterships of James Cartmell, C. A. Swainson and John Peile, championed a liberal attitude to nonconformists and strongly promoted Hebrew studies. It was also particularly generous, perhaps at the urging of W. H. Lowe and his circle, in providing college affiliations for distinguished hebraists and semiticists such as Schiller-Szinessy, Robertson Smith, Schechter and Abrahams, whose earlier studies had not been conducted at Cambridge. The achievements of such men more than justified that college's faith in them.

The renewed interest in Hebrew and related subjects also made itself felt in University teaching and examining. An undergraduate examination ("Tripos") was introduced for Semitic languages, apparently without controversy, in 1872, but those responsible for drawing up the equivalent syllabus for Theology were faced with a problem that was to become almost endemic to their Faculty business in the years to follow, namely, the place of Hebrew in their programme of studies. Following protests in 1871 by distinguished hebraists that Hebrew scholarship had been "omitted from the proposed scheme", the syndicate responsible agreed to include Hebrew passages for pointing and proses for translation into classical Hebrew in the new syllabus. Consideration was continually given to the possibility of widening the scope of the Semitic languages and literatures taught at the University, a recommendation was made for the appointment of a number of University lecturers in Hebrew, and post-biblical Hebrew and Jewish studies were formally included in the Semitics examination syllabus. It became the norm for the most distinguished scholars of their day, men such as William Wright, William Robertson Smith and R. L. Bensly to be appointed to Semitics chairs and long lists of outstanding candidates, nine in the case of the Regius chair of Hebrew to which A. F. Kirkpatrick was appointed in 1882, found themselves competing for election to such posts.

Developments at the University Library were no less encouraging. After the halting progress of previous decades, J. E. B. Mayor, in the

10 – W. H. Lowe of Christ's College, non-Jewish scholar of rabbinic
literature and lecturer in Hebrew at Christ's 1875–1891, with details
of his weight in the rowing club (Cambridge University
Boat Club, photograph album for 1870)

short period of three years in which he held the office of Librarian,
applied his vast learning, innovative mind and direct manner to that
institution's problems and succeeded in demonstrating how they were to
be solved in the modern world. For him, part of the solution lay in
ascertaining how similar difficulties were dealt with at other famous
scholarly libraries, and adapting the best of their methods for Cambridge
use. For all his administrative prowess, he ever remained the dedicated
scholar and it was in this guise that Solomon and Mathilde Schechter
later came to know him. Reminiscing about her years in Cambridge,
Mathilde wrote of him that he was "one of the great men of learning, a
type which has almost disappeared to make way in the University for the
modern up-to-date professors. It is the men of affairs who are now the
leaders in the University, the men of science in particular."

Henry Bradshaw, the young man without whose help Mayor would,
on his own admission, have "thrown up his position in disgust"

succeeded to the Librarianship in 1867 when his predecessor returned to full-time scholarship. With his wide knowledge of languages, his fascination with all manner of manuscripts and incunables, and his devotion to well-ordered procedures, he attracted donations of a variety of valuable manuscripts and printed books and, perhaps more importantly, ensured that the Library budget was large enough, and special funds such as the Rustat and Worts benefactions available enough, to enable him to purchase rare material when it came on to the market. The far-sighted Board of Oriental Studies appreciated that as the Library's oriental holdings grew, so would the need increase for a larger budget and for additional specialist librarians to deal with them. Its members suggested that the oriental department should be "placed under the separate management of a person especially chosen for his proficiency in Oriental learning" and concluded: "Experience has shown that not a few of the most eminent orientalists have owed their distinction to a familiarity with their special branches of study acquired in the discharge of their duties as librarians. The proposed office of Curator of the Oriental Department might be tenable in conjunction with a Readership in any branch of Oriental Literature".

The curatorship, in a somewhat restricted form, was established in 1899 and held by Solomon Schechter in 1900–02. Indeed, when Henry Bradshaw was succeeded by Robertson Smith, the Library came under the control of an orientalist but, despite hard work and long hours, the latter's term of office (1886–89) was too brief to make any great impression and he soon returned to his Semitic studies. By that time, a spectacular five-fold increase had been recorded in the Library's holdings of Hebrew manuscripts. During Bradshaw's librarianship, over six hundred Hebrew manuscripts were added to the collection and a goodly proportion of these catalogued. This was due to Bradshaw's co-operation with a remarkable figure who exercised a formative influence on Hebrew studies in nineteenth-century Cambridge, Solomon Marcus Schiller-Szinessy.

A REVOLUTIONARY HUNGARIAN RABBI

Perhaps the most striking aspect of Schiller-Szinessy's life is the novel nature of so much of what he did. Born in Altofen (now Budapest) in 1820, he was one of the earliest in a long line of distinguished Hungarian scholars who combined the advantage of a western education with the best of traditional talmudic learning, and the first Jew to be appointed to the faculty of the Lutheran Eperies Evangelical College. There can have been few rabbinic luminaries in his day who could match his active involvement in front-line operations in 1849 on behalf of the Hungarian revolutionaries and he followed this up in 1856 by becoming the minister of the newly formed, or perhaps more accurately "Reformed", Manchester Congregation of British Jews, where he set about introducing innovations in the synagogue services. He enjoyed an unexpected romance with a Unitarian Christian in Manchester and, on her acceptance as a convert to Judaism by the Grand Rabbin of Paris, married her in 1863. In that same year, Schiller-Szinessy came to Cambridge to earn his living, as many of his earlier correligionists had done, by freelance teaching. In 1866, the University of Cambridge, at the prompting of some of its more liberal graduates and after very carefully examining its conscience, formally appointed the Rabbi as Praeceptor in Rabbinic and Talmudic Literature. The appointment was not made without serious opposition, the proposal finally being carried on 17 May by 76 votes to 64. The Test Act of 1871 gave the University the opportunity of granting him further recognition and, having been appointed Reader in Talmudic and Rabbinic literature in 1875, he was, in the following year, probably the first Jew to proceed to the M.A. degree on conventional lines.

Schiller-Szinessy's controversialist bent led him into all manner of difficulties with both the Orthodox and Reform communities, to resignations from posts, and to public disagreements with his fellow Anglo-Jewish academics, Adolf Neubauer and Solomon Schechter, in which vituperative accusations were hurled in both directions. Nevertheless, in his twenty-seven years at Cambridge, he established rabbinic scholarship as an integral part of Oriental Studies and created a school of hebraists who were to win distinction in the academic and ecclesiastical worlds, among them Charles Taylor, Master of St. John's; W. H. Lowe, editor of the Cambridge Manuscript of the Mishnah; J. J. S. Perowne, Bishop of Worcester; W. Aldis Wright, Secretary of the Old Testament Revision Committee; and numerous professors of Oriental Studies. As he himself said, he was "the disciple of great teachers and the teacher of great disciples".

As far as Schiller-Szinessy's palaeographical skills are concerned, his presence in Cambridge was noted in 1865 by Bradshaw, then in charge of the University Library's manuscripts under Mayor. He privately engaged him to compile "a minute and elaborate catalogue" of the Library's Hebrew manuscripts, relying on Schiller-Szinessy's specialist knowledge and himself providing the bibliographical expertise required. The first fruits of this endeavour appeared in 1876 and covered seventy-two manuscripts, and a second volume, with descriptions of an

11 – S. M. Schiller-Szinessy, Reader in Talmudic and Rabbinic Literature
in the University of Cambridge, 1866–1890 (by Fischer, *Transactions
of the Jewish Historical Society of England* 21, 1968)

additional twenty-five manuscripts, was printed but never formally
published. Before his death in 1890 Schiller-Szinessy had completed
descriptions of about two-thirds of what had become a collection of
about eight hundred manuscript works, and these, in the form of a
handwritten catalogue of six bound volumes, remained, for many years,
the most comprehensive guide to the collection. It was no doubt through
his prompting that Bradshaw purchased so many valuable Hebrew
manuscripts, especially from the leading nineteenth century Jewish
bookseller in Austria, Samuel Schönblum of Lemberg, and from Hirsch
Lipschütz of Cracow, as well as from Fischl Hirsch (= J. Fischl), W. H.
Black, N. Coronel, B. Quaritch, J. Saphir and M. Scharfmesser.

Although Schiller-Szinessy benefitted from the University's progress in acknowledging the rights of minorities to equal treatment, he was made aware in at least one area that acknowledgement was not yet complete. The possibility of a religious test remained part of the statutes for the Regius chair of Hebrew until 1927 and undoubtedly continued to influence developments in later years. When he presented himself as a candidate for that post in 1882, the electors admitted him provisionally and permitted him to lecture before them like all the other candidates but "by a majority of votes expressed the opinion" that he was "not qualified to hold the Professorship". There is no doubt about the mention of a religious test in the fourteenth statute and it therefore seems that at least one of the electors was sufficiently liberal to suggest that the Vice-Chancellor was not *obliged* to impose such a test and that he might therefore decline on this occasion to exercise this right. How he would have dealt with the matter of the attached Ely Canonry is not apparent. The University's support for post-biblical Jewish studies was not yet wholehearted since Schiller-Szinessy's salary was not raised to a reasonable level until 1879, nor his position established as permanent until 1885. Even at that date, part of his salary had to be met by a personal subscription of Charles Taylor whose generosity, well motivated though it was, set an unfortunate precedent for later years.

As far as the University Library's acquisition of Hebrew manuscripts is concerned, the closing decade of the nineteenth century and its initial equivalent in the twentieth saw the further indulgence of such an interest but one that was destined to become the final expression of serious activity in a long history of important collection. That it proved to be final, and indeed a glorious finale to previous efforts, may jointly be credited to Schiller-Szinessy's successor as the University's talmudic specialist, Solomon Schechter; to the newly appointed University Librarian, Francis Jenkinson who followed Robertson Smith in chronological terms but Bradshaw in professional ones; and to Charles Taylor, Master of St John's College, devoted hebraist and liberal polymath.

Guide to reading

A fuller and carefully annotated version of the above chapter, entitled "Hebrew and Hebraists at Cambridge: An Historical Introduction", appears in S. C. Reif's *Hebrew Manuscripts at Cambridge University Library: A Description and Introduction* (Cambridge, 1997), pp. 1–35. Those interested in locating the precise sources of the information used and cited would do well to consult that version and to make use of the index that is included on pp. 551–55 of the same volume. Details of the broader history of the Jews in England, as well as specific aspects of that history in Cambridge, for the period covered by this chapter, rather than the more modern era, may be found in the classic studies of H. P. Stokes, *Studies in Anglo-Jewish History* (Edinburgh, 1913), as updated by the important researches of R. B. Dobson in "The Jews of Medieval Cambridge", *Transactions of the Jewish Historical Society of England* 32 (1993), pp. 1–24; J. Picciotto, *Sketches of Anglo-Jewish History*, an 1875 publication revised and annotated by Israel Finestein (London, 1955); and Cecil Roth, *A History of the Jews in England* (third edition, Oxford, 1964). A more recent volume that has dealt with these subjects is that of David S. Katz, *The Jews in the History of England* (Oxford, 1994), which has especially valuable information on nineteenth-century Cambridge on pp. 374–82.

On the historical development of the University of Cambridge from its earliest origins until the late nineteenth century, a series of four volumes, entitled *A History of the University of Cambridge*, is currently being published by Cambridge University Press under the general editorship of C. N. L. Brooke, to replace J. B. Mullinger's dated but still useful two volumes on *The University of Cambridge* (Cambridge, 1873 and 1884). The first volume, *The University to 1546*, by Damian Riehl Leader, appeared in 1988; the third, *1750–1870* by Peter Searby, in 1987; and the fourth, *1870–1990* by Brooke himself, in 1993. The second volume, *1546–1750* by Victor Morgan, is still awaited. A briefer but more readable account is given by Elisabeth Leedham-Green in *A Concise History of the University of Cambridge* (Cambridge, 1996) but, unsurprisingly, neither her volume, nor any of the more lengthy volumes pays much attention to Jews or to hebraists, since they were generally no more than marginal to the University's overall interests. The acquisition of hebraica was perhaps a little more significant at times and the histories of the University Library consequently touch on this topic, at least tangentially. Useful information is contained in Charles Sayle's *Annals of Cambridge University Library* (Cambridge, 1916) and there is a small but helpful booklet by J. C. T. Oates, *Cambridge University Library: A Historical Sketch* (Cambridge, 1975; a revised version of the entry in the fourth volume of the *Encyclopaedia of Library and Information Science*). The subject has, however, been thoroughly dealt with more recently in Oates's *Cambridge University Library: A History. From the Beginnings to the Copyright Act of Queen Anne* (Cambridge, 1986) and in David McKitterick's complementary volume *Cambridge University Library: A History. The Eighteenth and Nineteenth Centuries* (Cambridge, 1986).

More details relating to the influence of the Reformation on the universities in general and on Hebrew studies in particular may be found in H. Rashdall, *The Universities of Europe in the Middle Ages* (Oxford, 1936) and in J. E. B. Mayor, *Early Statutes of the College of St. John the Evangelist in the University of Cambridge* (Cambridge, 1859). Some recent books dealing with Christian hebraists and of importance for the topics discussed in this chapter are G. Lloyd Jones, *The Discovery of Hebrew in Tudor England* (Manchester, 1983); William McKane, *Selected Christian Hebraists* (Cambridge, 1989); and Stephen G. Burnett, *From Christian Hebraism to Jewish Studies: Johannes Buxtorf (1564–1629) and Hebrew Learning in the Seventeenth Century* (Leiden, New York, Köln, 1996). On the subject of the particular manuscripts and manuscript collections that existed in Cambridge at various times, there is intriguing data in Raphael Loewe, "Hebrew Books and Judaica in Mediaeval Oxford and Cambridge" in *Remember the Days: Essays on Anglo-Jewish History presented to Cecil Roth*, ed. J. M. Shaftesley (London, 1966), pp. 23–48; M. Beit-Arié, *The Only Dated Medieval Hebrew Manuscript Written in England* (London, 1985); and A. Dalby, "A Dictionary of Oriental Collections in Cambridge University Library", *Transactions of the Cambridge Bibliographical Society* 9 (1988), pp. 248–80.

Indispensable reference works for the personalities and events of nineteenth-century Cambridge are J. Venn and J. A. Venn, *Alumni Cantabrigienses* (Cambridge, 1922–54); *The Dictionary of National Biography* (London, 1908–09); and the two volumes by D. A. Winstanley, *Early Victorian Cambridge* (Cambridge, 1940) and *Later Victorian Cambridge* (Cambridge, 1947). For further information on Schiller-Szinessy and Robertson Smith, see R. Loewe, "Solomon Marcus Schiller-Szinessy, 1820–1890. First Reader in Talmudic and Rabbinic Literature at Cambridge", *Transactions of the Jewish Historical Society of England* 21 (1968), pp. 148–89, and *William Robertson Smith: Essays in Reassessment*, ed. William Johnstone (Sheffield, 1995), especially S. C. Reif, "William Robertson Smith in Relation to Hebraists and Jews at Christ's College, Cambridge", pp. 210–23. Another paper by S. C. Reif relating to Schiller-Szinessy's appointment at Cambridge in 1866, "A Usurper among Christian Hebraists", is scheduled to appear in a volume entitled *Hebrew Study from Ezra to Ben-Yehuda*, edited by William Horbury, and being published by T & T Clark in Edinburgh.

THREE

DETAILS OF THE CAST

Given the long history of Hebrew studies at Cambridge, the broadening interest in Jewish learning, and the recent arrival of many precious Hebrew manuscripts, the stage was set at the end of the nineteenth century for exciting new developments. Henry Bradshaw and R. H. Bensly had ensured a major increase in Hebraica at the University Library; W. H. Lowe had brought Jews into the Senior Common Room at Christ's College; and Schiller-Szinessy had persuaded an initially sceptical group of dons that a Jew could teach rabbinic literature without offending the religious susceptibilities of young Christian gentlemen. When the Hungarian rabbi died fairly suddenly in March 1890, efforts were quickly made to fill the post in a similar fashion and by October of the same year Solomon Schechter was already living and teaching in Cambridge. His appointment had been greatly eased by an array of outstanding references provided on his behalf by Jewish and non-Jewish scholars from many institutions at home and abroad. No matter how well the stage was set, progress in the plot was dependent on the parts to be played by a number of leading figures. The literary riches of the Cairo Genizah had begun to be diverted hither and thither and a number of visitors had sensed that historical documents were there for removal and investigation. That the trickle of texts turned into a flood and that the close study of their contents became a pilgrimage is due to the enthusiastic interests and industrious activities of a few Cambridge personalities in the last decade of the Victorian period.

SCHECHTER IN CONTINENTAL EUROPE

Solomon Schechter was born in the middle of the nineteenth century in a Rumanian village somewhat distant from where his parents and grand-parents had once flourished. The Hebrew name that they gave to the son born to them in either 1847 or 1849, namely, Shneur Zalman, is a clear

47

indication of the background of Schechter's parents, Isaac and Ḥaya. The name was that of the founder of the ḥasidic sect of Lubavitch or Ḥabad and testifies to the fact that the *shoḥet* (ritual slaughterer), Isaac Schechter, belonged to that particular group of Orthodox eastern European Jews that had originated in Belorussia. Stressing the potential of the ordinary worshipper for the achievement of mystical communion with God and the everyday ways in which this could be achieved, Shneur Zalman's brand of ḥasidism also demonstrated a strongly developed interest in study. The Schechter parents had doubtless moved to Focsani (Fokschan) in Moldavia to escape the worst excesses of Russian anti-Semitism but emancipation and civil rights proved just as illusory there as elsewhere.

Young Shneur Zalman (or Solomon, as he styled himself when he moved westwards) was physically and intellectually powerful and later claimed that he had inherited passion and energy from his mother while attributing any religious and scholarly tendencies that he might have to the influence of his father, who had been his first teacher. The other influences were naturally those of the eastern European *shtetl* (small town Jewry), the ḥasidic *shtiebel* (small and informal place of worship) and the *yeshivah* (academy for rabbinic studies). In addition, he obtained access, apparently through a local *maskil* infected with the germ of enlightened thought, to books and articles that broadened his mind, at least within the sphere of Jewish scholarship, and led him to seek further education elsewhere. As a teenager he moved on to Lwow (Lemberg), the capital city of Eastern Galicia, still then an outlying province of the Austro-Hungarian Empire, and studied with the expert halakhist, Rabbi Joseph Saul Nathanson. Nathanson was not only an outstanding interpreter of Jewish religious law but also had other intellectual tendencies that may have left their mark on the young Rumanian ḥasid. He was critical of ḥasidism, opposed "progressive" Judaism but without encouraging communal separatism, and made lenient rulings when circumstances demanded them. Schechter may have been going through something of a crisis in his religious and educational outlook at this time since he returned to his native town for a while, continued his studies, and even contracted an unhappy marriage.

The combination of a commitment to Judaism, a passion for broader learning, and an undoubtedly radical streak, led him to seek further education in the the more historically based institutions of Jewish learning in central Europe. Having earlier divorced his wife after only a year of marriage, he abandoned the Rumanian *shtetl* forever (physically, if never altogether spiritually) and entered the Vienna Rabbinical Seminary. Its founder, Adolf (Aaron) Jellinek, saw it as his mission to

48

spread scientific Jewish learning, a moderately liberal interpretation of Judaism, and a love of Jewish community and culture. As well as coming under the general influence of Jellinek, Schechter acquired a historical approach to the study of talmudic and halakhic literature from I. H. Weiss and the ability to subject midrash to text criticism and modern exegesis from Meir Friedmann (Ish-Shalom), both teachers more sympathetic to Jewish tradition and the continuity of the Hebrew language than Jellinek himself. It was indeed perhaps because of their similar background, restlessness and religious outlook that Friedmann was so dear to Schechter in his Vienna years. While in that city, Schechter took the opportunity of improving his general education with courses at the university, made a living as a Hebrew teacher, and obtained a rabbinical ordination.

By 1879 he was again looking for new pastures and ready to travel further along the road of westernization, this time via the Hochschule für die Wissenschaft des Judentums that had been founded in Berlin in 1872. Indeed, at this stage of his intellectual and religious development, the young eastern European ḥasid was less enchanted with his background than he would later lead us to believe and the only publications to have come from him by that time had been two satires on ḥasidism. Though officially not attached to any specific form of Judaism, the Hochschule was certainly associated more with progressive than with orthodox trends and this perhaps gave Schechter the opportunity of indulging in what many of his family would certainly have regarded as religious heresy. Although there were personally orthodox teachers, such as the critical talmudist Israel Lewy, at the Hochschule, and more clinical and sceptical scholars, such as the renowned bibliographer Moritz Stein-schneider, also available in Berlin to inspire him with their lectures, Schechter chose to be closest to Pinkus Fritz Frankl. This more centrist rabbi and scholar whom he had known in Vienna, was now Geiger's successor in Berlin and a teacher at the Hochschule, and it was in his home that Schechter found lodgings. Perhaps under Frankl's influence, he deepened his love of scientific Jewish studies, retained an attachment to traditional observance if not to orthodoxy, and nurtured a growing animosity to the kind of German intellectual anti-Semitism that he encountered in the lectures that he attended at the university. He had, however, still not found his ideal milieu and his students in Berlin, Claude Montefiore from England and Richard Gottheil from the U.S.A., both of them religiously liberal, beckoned to him to exchange the Germany that he was finding politically and socially uncomfortable for the Anglo-Saxon environment in which he might feel more at home.

12 – Solomon Schechter in London, 1887 (Norman Bentwich,
Solomon Schechter: A Biography, Philadelphia, 1938,
Library of the Jewish Theological Seminary of America)

SCHECHTER IN ENGLAND

Thus it was that he arrived in England in 1882 as Montefiore's tutor, destined to spend twenty years there, but always subsidized by the generosity of his English student. Though he did not find in the Anglo-Jewish community the appreciation of Jewish culture that he was anxiously seeking, Schechter taught and inspired a group of leading Jewish intellectuals in London called "the Wanderers", read widely and began to write English, and never felt threatened by the kind of relaxed and inclusive orthodoxy championed by Chief Rabbi Nathan Marcus Adler and his son and successor, Hermann. Schechter never took to the centralized bureaucratic system that the Chief Rabbinate and the United Synagogue orchestrated, nor to the Anglo-Jewish cleric, whom he regarded as a mere flunkey or religious functionary with little or no scholarly achievement, but he did enjoy the liberal environment of

50

England, and the Anglo-Jewish establishment always gave him full rein to express his biting criticisms while still accepting him as one of its own. The close company in which he was best able to express his strong views, "the Wanderers", was dominated by the writer Israel Zangwill, the literary critic and editor Joseph Jacobs, and Schechter himself. Other participants were the editor of the *Jewish Chronicle*, Asher Myers, the Tutor at Jews' College who later became a leading exponent of Liberal Judaism, Israel Abrahams, and Lucien Wolf, publicist, historian and first president of the Jewish Historical Society of England in 1893.

While in England, he established his scholarly credentials, much as Montefiore hoped he would, by the critical and historical study of Hebrew manuscripts in the rich collections of that country, as well as in other parts of Europe, by his publication of first scientific editions of such works as *Avot de Rabbi Nathan* and of more general articles in the newly founded *Jewish Quarterly Review*, by teaching at Jews' College, and by contributing items on Jewish learning to the *Jewish Chronicle*. Almost inevitably, given his character and opinions, he became involved in controversies with other scholars but his marriage to Mathilde Roth of Breslau in 1887 brought him the kind of personal and domestic security, affection and support that certainly smoothed some of the rougher edges of his personality and toned down at least the religious side of his radicalism. It also brought him a daughter, Ruth, and a son, Frank, both born in London, and a second daughter, Amy, born in Cambridge. But Schechter had still not found what he was seeking in the professional world and his next venture, lasting from 1890 to 1902, was to be in the rarefied academic atmosphere of Cambridge where he could be sure (or so he thought) that learning would count above all other considerations in the assessment of his standing among his peers.

If an intensely scholastic environment in which to continue his textual studies was all that he was seeking, Schechter might well have remained in Cambridge for the rest of his life since it was there that he made his most important contributions to Jewish learning. He continued his work on Hebrew manuscripts in general, and began to prepare descriptions of those codices that his predecessor, Schiller-Szinessy, had not included in his catalogue of the Hebraica at Cambridge University Library. Editions of *Aggadat Shir Ha-Shirim* and *Midrash Ha-Gadol* were published in Cambridge and he also undertook the kind of Jewish theological summaries that Montefiore desperately wanted to see him produce and that were ultimately included in his volumes of collected essays. His greatest and most original coup was, however, his expedition to Cairo in 1896–97 in search of the source of the medieval Hebrew fragments that had come westwards in previous years and his return to Cambridge with what turned out to be 140,000 items of inestimable significance for the rewriting of Jewish social, literary and religious history in the Middle Ages, especially in the Mediterranean area. It was as a result of his imagination and enthusiasm, as well as of his erudition, that the recovery of the "hoard of Hebrew manuscripts" from the Genizah of the Ben Ezra synagogue in medieval Cairo became a reality. His energy and single-mindedness ensured that the major areas represented in that collection began to be carefully investigated before he left Cambridge in 1902. Not only did a number of original studies result from his Genizah discoveries; the example he set served as a trail-blazer for the hundreds of books and thousands of articles that have followed in the century since he set out for Cairo.

SCHECHTER IN AND OUT OF CAMBRIDGE

But to imagine that Schechter ever felt, or was made to feel, fully at home in the courts, cloisters and combination rooms of the colleges on the Cam is to underestimate the gap that still existed between such an exotic personality and the conventional surroundings in which he worked. It is true that William Robertson Smith, University Librarian when Schechter arrived and subsequently Sir Thomas Adams's Professor of Arabic, had been instrumental in having him appointed as university lecturer and accepted as a member of Christ's College. In addition, many leading members of the university, such as Charles Taylor, Master of St John's College, and Francis Jenkinson, Robertson Smith's successor as University Librarian, enjoyed and valued his remarkable mind and prodigious learning. Nevertheless, his main friendships were with those who stood outside the established academic society. The rights of ethnic and religious minorities always concerned him and he and Mathilde were friendly with those then battling for women to be permitted equal entry into the University. The Scottish Presbyterian sisters, Margaret Gibson and Agnes Lewis, and the literary and poetic raconteur and librarian, Erik Magnusson, developed fairly close relations with him. His warmest friendship was undoudtedly the one he enjoyed with the famous and pioneering anthropologist, James Frazer, a fellow of Trinity for most of his professional life who never obtained a tenured teaching appointment at the University of Cambridge.

Given that Schechter was always dependent on Claude Montefiore for part of his salary, that he was not appointed to a chair, and that no college saw fit to offer him a fellowship, it may fairly be argued that what Lilly Frazer said about her spouse James might equally well have been echoed by Mathilde about her husband Solomon, had she been but half as outspoken as her counterpart: "...you have touched a real sore in saying that Cambridge has shown strange neglect in not providing for him. This is the greatest grievance that we feel... Dons are people who run in grooves and have no imagination... I always tell my husband that such as he is, he is – and that suffices..." On their many afternoon walks together, Frazer and Schechter no doubt exchanged complaints about the Cambridge establishment and its concern to protect its conventions but it would not be accurate to lay the entire blame on the University for the further failure of Schechter to settle down fully. Having gradually abandoned intensely religious institutions for enthusiastically academic ones, he had lost the close Jewish connection somewhere along the way and felt the need to return to a milieu that could combine the best of both traditions. In such a milieu he might be able to train a future generation of intellectual rabbis and the by-product of such a return might be to the Jewish religious advantage of his three children. They were having to be brought up in a tiny Jewish community where services were held only during term-time, where sabbath could be a lonely affair unless visitors came from London (as they often did), where observing the Jewish dietary laws was not easy, and where apostate Jews were more common than observant ones.

So it was that Schechter's final move was to America, to the Jewish community that had for a number of years already signalled to him that it required his religious ideas, his industry and his fire. There he re-established the Jewish Theological Seminary as a scholarly institution with a commitment to traditional Judaism, provided an intellectual power-house that propelled the Conservative movement and its United Synagogue of America for about three-quarters of a century, and disseminated popular presentations of Jewish learning that were, by the time of his death on 20 November 1915, having an impact on a broad spectrum of the community. Whether by doing so, he finally found his fulfilment is another matter since it cannot have been easy for such a maverick personality to become a figure of authority and to weigh himself down with administrative burdens. He resented the failure of the Seminary's supporters to create an adequate financial endowment and regretted what he saw as a lack of appreciation of scientific Jewish scholarship. His relations with his educational colleagues, inside and outside the Seminary, were at times strained and, although he had wished it otherwise, he eventually had to acknowledge the need to create not an umbrella Judaism to cover left and right but another

13 – Francis Jenkinson, Cambridge University Librarian, 1889–1924
(Cambridge University Library, by Sargent)

denomination that was neither Orthodox nor Reform but Conservative. It was not uncommon for Schechter in his American years to express frustration and a sense of failure; as Mel Scult has recently put it, "the Seminary succeeded, but unfortunately Schechter did not know it."

JENKINSON'S EDUCATION

Mathilde Schechter's characterization of Francis Jenkinson as "cultured and aristocratic", though brief, may be used as an accurate description of the environment in which he was born and reared. On his father's side he derived from West Country nobility and his maternal line was of equally distinguished status in the Northern Scottish county of Elginshire (now Grampian). Both families, as well as being physically impressive, had demonstrated interests in art, natural history, music and literature. The estate of his maternal grandfather, Sir William Gordon-Cumming, was Altyre, 2–3 miles south of Forres and it is likely that his birth, on 20 August 1853, took place in the mansion house of the estate. Though born in Scotland, it was in the counties of Berkshire, Oxfordshire and Wiltshire, to the west of London, that Francis was to spend his boyhood and schooldays. Those early years were marred by the tragic and accidental death of his mother in December 1859, following which his father entered the church in Reading, where the family, including his sister Nelly, lived until 1872. Young Francis briefly attended school at Woodcote, between Reading and Wallingford, but it was at the public school of Marlborough that he received his education throughout his teenage years, from 1865 until 1872.

Marlborough had been founded in 1843 to provide the usual public school education but, more unusually, to do so at a subsidized rate of fees for the sons of clergymen. It was therefore particularly appropriate for Jenkinson Junior and it was not difficult for him to reach the school from Reading since the Great Western Railway had opened a branch line to Marlborough a year before he enroled. Contemporaries testify to his high level of intelligence, his broad interests in the acquisition of information, and his independence of mind, while at the same time making no mention of that industrious obsession with detailed study that is often the hallmark of the pure academic. Such an obsession on his part was reserved for other pursuits. From an early age until the end of his life the study and collection of flies, moths and butterflies was his passion and he was fascinated by various aspects of the natural world, especially ornithology. Robust health was denied him and he suffered from chronic headaches, so that sport did not represent an attractive proposition to him. If, however, he was more of an individual than a team man, he was always known for his kind heart and helpful nature.

The major educational influence on him during his days at Marlborough came from the remarkable pedagogue who presided over the fortunes of the school from 1850 to 1870, Dr George Granville Bradley. It was Bradley who removed the uglier excesses of the traditional public school from the young institution entrusted to him and who stimulated his charges to detailed enquiry, accuracy of information, and a dissatisfaction with vagueness and imperfection. It is reported that Alfred Lord Tennyson, when asked why he sent his son, Hallam, to Marlborough, replied that he had not sent him to Marlborough but to Bradley. While the younger pupils stood in awe of his intellect and demanding standards, those in the upper forms were able to develop an intimacy with him that allowed them to enjoy at first hand the intensity and enthusiasm of a dedicated teacher and to be personally inspired by such characteristics. Bradley brought with him from Rugby, where he had been both pupil and master, the educational philosophy of Thomas Arnold, and Francis Jenkinson was one of those who enjoyed the benefit of an exposure to its practical application. In spite of never having driven himself to his intellectual limits, he was able to win recognition as one of the school's brightest boys and to enter Trinity College, Cambridge, to read classics, as scholar and exhibitioner, in October 1872.

At university, as at school, Jenkinson equipped himself well and came close to carrying off a number of prizes but he remained devoted to broader learning, to his insect research and to music. He cultivated a number of friendships, remained among the more serious of his circle, and achieved first class honours in classics in 1876. Following two further years of somewhat relaxed study and teaching, he was elected to a Trinity fellowship, followed by a lectureship in 1881 and a tutorship in 1882. He continued to teach (including "Newnham young ladies... which is... great fun") until 1889 and his sensitive personality and genteel manner no doubt impressed his students, as they had done his teachers and companions. This activity did not, however, turn out to be his natural métier. He voluntarily served as curator of various antiquarian and zoological collections, in which capacity he could demonstrate his growing commitment to the acquisition of interesting objects, their careful presentation and exhibition, and the provision of guidance to those willing to examine and analyse them. Such a commitment, married to a love of books and their detailed examination, and to general learning, represented the ideal makings of an academic librarian and it required only the personal inspiration of an eminently qualified mentor to turn the potential into the real. Henry Bradshaw, Cambridge University Librarian from 1867 until 1886, was the man who provided it. Bradshaw used his wide knowledge of languages, his devotion to well-ordered procedures, and his fascination with manuscripts and early printed volumes to advance the process of modernizing the Library. Although his own special interests were in typographical history, liturgical editions and Irish books, he presided over a considerable expansion of numerous other areas, including that of orientalia in general and hebraica in particular.

JENKINSON AT THE UNIVERSITY LIBRARY

In the 1880s Jenkinson came under the influence of the second "Brad" in his life and found himself considerably attracted to the bibliophilia, methodology and acquisitive tendencies that characterized the University Librarian's term of office. He assisted Bradshaw with his Library work, became something of an amanuensis to him, and developed a fine style of handwriting, clear as well as attractive, that was in no small measure modeled on that of the University Librarian. Having also been a member of the Library Syndicate, he had every reason to expect that on Bradshaw's sudden death in 1886 he would be appointed to succeed him. When he heard, however, that William Robertson Smith, the erudite and controversial semiticist and historian of the Bible, at that time The Lord Almoner's Professor of Arabic, had been proposed, Jenkinson, who had never been, nor would ever become ambitious and vigorous in the advancement of his own career, gave the proposal his full support. Robertson Smith's presence in the Library, in Christ's College, and in the University as a whole, very much contributed to the promotion of oriental studies but his specialized talents were not long suppressed by his administrative duties and he left the way open for the appointment of Jenkinson as University Librarian when he returned to his Arabic studies as Sir Thomas Adams's Professor in 1889.

The new Librarian now entered an office that he was to hold until his death thirty-four years later. Sadly, for fourteen of these years he lived alone at 10 Brookside, since his marriage to Marian Sydney Wetton on 6 July 1887 was tragically ended with her premature death, following a brief illness, six months later on 5 January 1888. Though admitting of no particular religious belief, Jenkinson had the inner strength and goodness of a fine individual that enabled him to overcome such personal adversity and remain the quiet, reliable and helpful man of learning who eased the way for so many explorers of the Library's uncharted

bibliographical territories. Though he did publish a number of items relating to numismatics and classics, as well as to books and libraries, and contributed regularly to the *Entomologist's Monthly Magazine*, publication was no more his forté than was teaching. His strength lay in the quiet order that he brought to the affairs of the Library and to the traditions of accurate description and generous guidance that have survived for over a century since he championed them. His love of books, the close and important contacts he cultivated, and his fastidiousness about the preservation of items that some might have dismissed as ephemera, ensured that the University Library not only remained a major storehouse of scholarly publications but also the recipient of such remarkable and indeed unique treasures as the Taylor-Schechter Genizah Collection, the Acton Collection (rich in foreign historical works), the War Collection (mainly propaganda and other ephemeral literature relating to the 1914–18 hostilities), and various other benefactions. He himself was well aware that responsibility for such a library demanded an impressive array of talents and exercises and he once drew up a list for the Library Syndicate that enumerated fourteen areas of required activity.

It should not be supposed that Jenkinson enjoyed administration as such or that he was a born organizer or innovator; far from it. He simply took pride in providing, himself and through a devoted and knowledgeable staff, a sound and scholarly service to his readers and in maintaining his institution's academic status and meeting any challenges to its privileges or threats to its rich collections. He was popular with his staff but never shirked from exercising authority when necessary. Though he responded to the needs of his day when he had to, the overall theme of his stewardship was one of consolidation rather than innovation. He did support the Library Syndicate's decision in 1921 to undertake the building of an expanded library on a new site but it is significant that the successful outcome of the project did not occur until more than a decade after his death. That he overcame bouts of ill-health and reached the biblically allotted age was in no small degree due to the care and happiness provided for him by his marriage to Margaret Stewart ("Daisy") in 1902. On his own evidence, she brightened his existence by her music, her sympathy and her companionship and, though never themselves parents, they developed close relations with the children of relatives. Keen and accomplished letter-writer that he was, Jenkinson did not hesitate to include youngsters among his correspondents and his ability to communicate meaningfully with them is another indication of his sensitivity and humanity. When Jenkinson, who had held his fellowship at Trinity since 1878, died in a Hampstead clinic on 21 September 1923, there were many tributes and marks of respect to a man who was, as reported by a senior staff member and historian of the University Library of a subsequent generation, regarded by many as a saint.

Despite very different backgrounds, Jenkinson and Schechter had a number of common characteristics. They both loved genuine learning and respected religious traditions but retained a suspicion of the organized bureaucracy that sometimes dominated them. Loyalty and friendship meant a good deal to them and they were devoted, in their own ways, to promoting the University Library's welfare and maintaining the excellence of its collections. Temperamentally, however, Jenkinson was a cultured Cambridge gentleman, reserved and tolerant, while Schechter was an unkempt, cosmopolitan intellectual, absent-minded and volatile. One could not but be impressed by Schechter's creativity and enthusiasm; one had to accept that Jenkinson was a staid consolidator of earlier initiatives. The remarkable fact is that while the University Librarian found the correct channels for the talmudist's scholarly brilliance, the latter reciprocated by bringing into the Library priceless orientalia, productive research and outstanding scholarly visitors. Jenkinson maintained the catholic interest in manuscripts nurtured by Bradshaw and, though a classicist himself, was responsive to the discovery, presentation and offer of oriental items. He encouraged Schechter's study of Hebrew manuscripts, even when that meant travel abroad for his Jewish colleague, and Schechter took responsibility for continuing his predecessor's work on describing the Hebrew manu-scripts at Cambridge University Library. Schechter's contacts with many Jewish centres abroad, as well as in London, ensured a steady stream of hebraic offers and his high degree of expertise in the rabbinic field enabled him to make wise choices and suggest sensible prices. Many letters from Schechter to Jenkinson, as well as numerous notes in Jenkinson's diaries, make this clear. They also demonstrate more generally the major results of their relationship and interaction and the manner in which their joint endeavours inspired and promoted the new subject of Genizah research.

TAYLOR'S LIFE AND WORK

Another scholarly partnership entered into by Schechter was the one that he enjoyed with Charles Taylor. Taylor had been born in 1840 into an affluent Bedfordshire family that had settled in London and acquired considerable property in the capital city. His early days were spent in the central and prosperous environment of Regent Street but his father had died when he was five years old and his mother had moved with her three young sons to Hampstead. Having excelled in a wide variety of subjects at St. Marylebone Grammar School and at King's College School, he came up to Cambridge in 1858 as a student at St. John's College, where he was destined to spend the remaining fifty years of his

14 – Charles Taylor, Master of St John's College Cambridge, 1881–1908
(Master and Fellows of St John's College, Cambridge)

life. He won a College Scholarship and came ninth among all those in the University examined in mathematics and also performed adequately as a student of Classics. In 1863 he obtained a first class degree in Theology, with distinction in Hebrew, and a year later was elected to the University's Tyrwhitt's Hebrew scholarship, to a Naden Divinity Studentship at St. John's, and to a College Fellowship. He was ordained as a Deacon of the Church of England in 1866 and as a Priest a year later.

Taylor was kind, quiet and industrious. His love of learning was not motivated by ambition but by an intense desire for accuracy and comprehensiveness. Though hospitable, courteous and loyal to his friends, he was shy in company and preferred to converse with only one or two companions, at times doing so with wit and humour. Institutions with which he was closely associated enjoyed the benefit of his great generosity and he preferred to donate money rather than to seek ways of adding to his family's considerable wealth. He was open to suggestions for change but only when the relevant facts and arguments were thoroughly researched and presented. This made him a cautious but fair administrator and ensured that his views were welcomed and respected. He was sincerely committed to traditional Anglican beliefs and practices while remaining moderate and tolerant enough to understand and respect other religions. However devoted to detailed scholarship, he was no cloistered academic, enjoying walking, rowing and mountaineering, not only for the physical exercise they provided but also for the contribution they made to character building. When he married Margaret Dillon in October 1907 he seemed, in the words of Israel Abrahams, "to grow younger and to throw off some of his reserve" but their happiness was brought to an abrupt end after only a few months by the fatal heart attack that he suffered in Nürnberg in August, 1908.

The half-century spent by Taylor at Cambridge was full of achievement, honours and service. He was appointed a College Lecturer in Theology in 1873, elected to an honorary fellowship of King's College, London, in 1876, and played an important part in effecting the changes that resulted from the work of the Cambridge University Commission that began in 1877. He was elected Master of St. John's College in 1881, received an honorary LL.D. from Harvard in 1886, and served as Vice-Chancellor of the University of Cambridge from 1887 to 1889. He also represented the University in local government. Remarkably, he continued to make important contributions to the various fields of learning that he had mastered as a young student, publishing important books and articles in mathematics, theology, biblical studies and rabbinics and demonstrating a mastery of the Semitic languages no less than the Classical ones.

TAYLOR AND HEBREW STUDIES

Taylor was fortunate enough to be the student of the devoted hebraist, Peter Mason, at St. John's College and to have acquired from him a devotion to the study of the Hebrew Bible. Although Mason, as a conservative Anglican churchman, was among those who did their best in 1866 to prevent the appointment of Rabbi Schiller-Szinessy as Lecturer in Rabbinic and Talmudic Literature, he was by no means opposed to the teaching of the subject, merely to its being taught by a Jew rather than an Anglican. He himself was at home in the broader Hebrew field and transmitted to his students an enthusiasm for finding their way around it. Unencumbered by traditional ecclesiastical reservations, Taylor made a point of learning as much as he could from Schiller-Szinessy (perhaps even when the rabbi was still teaching only privately) and came to be counted among an impressive group of young Cambridge hebraists who, under the influence of these two undoubtedly different but equally inspiring teachers, attempted, sometimes successfully, to promote Hebrew studies in a more liberal fashion than some of their colleagues could bring themselves to tolerate. Taylor returned to a seventeenth-century English tradition, neglected for some two centuries, that stressed the importance of early rabbinic Judaism for the better understanding of the rise of Christianity. At the same time, he never allowed his personal theological commitments to dictate a negative approach to the Talmud and its adherents but consistently dealt with the subject in a manner that was at once intelligent, scientific and sympathetic.

In noting the recognition that he enjoyed as one of the Christian masters of rabbinic learning in England, Europe and America, a younger contemporary of his at St. John's College with similar education and interests, John Henry Hart, praised Taylor for what he had done to vindicate the relevance of "this difficult department of knowledge" to the "study of the primitive Christian literature". He was also impressed by that fact that "he was one of the few who did not affront their Jewish rivals by a tone of tolerant superiority." Having specialized in the field for about ten years, Taylor produced his *Sayings of the Jewish Fathers* in 1877. This edition of the (second-century?) collection of the theological wisdom of the rabbis constituting the tractate *Avot* provided the Hebrew text with a translation, commentary and detailed notes and brought together a remarkable blend of Jewish exegesis, Christians parallels and Classical learning. The first edition owed much to the inspiration of Schiller-Szinessy who described it as "the most important contribution to these studies made by any Christian scholar since the time of Buxtorf" (in Basle three centuries earlier). But Taylor did not call a halt at that point. He continued to research the subject and, with the help of Solomon Schechter, was able to produce an expanded version in 1897 that remains worthy of close consultation one hundred years later. Although in the course of a lifetime of rabbinic studies, Taylor must have come across statements and ideas that were not to his theological taste, Israel Abrahams, when writing his obituary for the *Jewish*

Chronicle, could not recall a single instance when he had "uttered a depreciatory word about Pharisaism."

The financial assistance, advice and encouragement that Taylor provided for Schechter when he set out on his Cairo trip in 1896 was neither the first nor the last of such generous acts on the part of the Christian hebraist. During Schiller-Szinessy's tenure of the talmudic and rabbinic post, Taylor had done much to ease the rabbi's way in an environment that was not universally friendly. When the salary was held by the University at a lower rate than equivalent teaching positions, Taylor had personally provided a subvention that made it possible to raise it. He had also provided his Jewish colleague with an additional source of income by purchasing from him books and transcriptions of manuscripts, had responded sympathetically to Schiller-Szinessy's notes about others' plans for Semitics that were not to the rabbi's liking, and had exchanged scholarly information with him. When the Reader in Talmudic had put his name forward as a candidate for the Regius Chair of Hebrew that fell vacant in 1882, Taylor had been one of those who entertained some doubts about rejecting the application out of hand. It was true that a Christian religious test could be applied and that a canonry at Ely Cathedral awaited the successful candidate, but Taylor nevertheless argued for allowing the candidature and for softening the blow when a majority of the electors declared it invalid.

During Schechter's twelve years in Cambridge, Taylor continued to be helpful in similar ways. He donated funds that enabled Schechter to travel abroad to consult Hebrew manuscripts, helped to arrange an additional source of income for him in the University, and published, sometimes together with Schechter, the results of Genizah research. Like Jenkinson, he spoke up for Schechter in University circles and was a moderating influence on the Rumanian scholar's intensities. Later, he not only contributed to the cost of Salomon Buber's 1905 edition of the *Sefer Ha-'Orah* as a memorial to Rashi (d. 1105) but also sent to Lemberg his personal copy of a precious thirteenth-century Hebrew manuscript of *Siddur Rashi*, so that Buber could make use of it for his scientific edition. He built up an outstanding collection of Hebrew manuscripts which he made available to his Jewish scholarly colleagues and he ensured the continuity of this availability by bequeathing all of them to Cambridge University Library. To return to Hart's assessment of Taylor, by way of summary, "he had insight into the minds of the Jews in particular, and insight generally."

15 – Mrs Margaret Gibson, on a camel in the Near East, 1893
(Westminster College, Cambridge)

THE "GIBLEW" TWINS

Mrs Agnes Smith Lewis and Mrs Margaret Dunlop Gibson were born as twins in 1843 in the little town of Irvine on the Ayrshire coast of Scotland, some 25 miles south-west of Glasgow. They were unfortunately bereft of their mother after only three weeks but somehow, through the devotion of their father, the lawyer, John Smith, the interest of the local Presbyterian minister, William Robertson, and their boarding school at Birkenhead, Agnes and Margaret received a sound education in religion, literature and languages. Such an education, combined with a huge fortune fortuitously and unexpectedly inherited by their father from an American cousin and bequeathed to them by him in 1866, provided the inspiration and the means for the private study of the Classical and Semitic languages and for trips to the Near East that resulted in the acquisition of many exciting manuscripts. The remarkable partnership of these two formidable women and their exclusive devotion to each other were only briefly interrupted by the marriage of Margaret to the ailing clergyman, James Young Gibson, in 1883, and of Agnes to the obsessive academic, Samuel Savage Lewis, in 1888, neither husband surviving more than about two years in the happy state. On settling in Cambridge, Mrs Lewis and Mrs

64

Gibson, though disadvantaged and marginalized by their gender and their religious non-conformism in central University circles, became pillars of the Presbyterian community and close friends of many of the less conventional and more liberal dons in the city.

Given the difficulties facing women scholars at that time, and indeed for many decades afterwards, the achievements of Agnes and Maggie were truly remarkable. For almost half a century, until the end of the First World War, they travelled, researched and published extensively, contributing significantly to the fields of Classical and Semitic studies, as well as writing more popular books.

During their intrepid journeys in the Eastern Mediterranean, they discovered and purchased rare Syriac, Arabic and Hebrew items that had a major impact on scholarship and themselves edited texts of considerable importance to the early history of Christian literature. At St. Catherine's Convent in Sinai they retrieved a precious manuscript that was being recycled as a butter-dish and they were among the first to write about female spirituality. In 1897, they financed and supervised the transfer of the English Presbyterian Theological College to Cambridge where, as Westminster College, it enjoyed the benefit of their patronage for many years. Although the Cambridge establishment could never bring itself to regard them as anything but eccentric amateurs attempting to impose themselves on a predominantly male academic environment, they received honours and recognition from many other institutions. By the time of their deaths in 1920 (Maggie) and 1926 (Agnes), they had played a major role in ensuring that women would soon have to be fully recognized in even the most conservative of educational environments.

On expressing an interest in mastering Syriac before their 1892 travels to the Middle East, Mrs Lewis and Mrs Gibson had been given private lessons (female attendance at his University lectures was at that time out of the question!) by one of the local experts, R. H. Kennett of Queens' College, and had been referred to a young and promising scholar, Francis Burkitt, for guidance and practice in writing the language. Soon to become University Lecturer in Palaeography and later Norrisian Professor of Divinity, Burkitt not only taught and inspired the twins but also, together with his wife, and with the Benslys, accompanied them on one of their later trips to Sinai. He became one of the leading figures in the study and publication of difficult Greek and Semitic texts and was close to both Taylor and Schechter.

16 – Mrs Agnes Lewis, disembarking from a boat in Egypt, 1893
(Westminster College, Cambridge)

OTHER WORTHY PLAYERS

Indeed, neither research nor the production of critical editions is possible without the initial industry of those who tackle the basic problems of decipherment, identification and description. In this connection, Herman Leonard Pass and Hartwig Hirschfeld played worthy roles. Pass was a student of Jews' College, the Orthodox London seminary, who continued his studies at Cambridge and, having there converted to Christianity, was ordained as an Anglican priest in 1916. He was on hand and ready to tackle the biblical items among the Genizah finds. Jews' College's contribution to the Genizah scholarship of the day is further represented by the work done by Hartwig Hirschfeld, its lecturer in Arabic and Syriac, who also taught at University College, London. It was Hirschfeld who was invited to examine and briefly describe the Arabic and Judaeo-Arabic parts of the Taylor-Schechter Collection.

While Pass and Hirschfeld were employed at the University Library only on a temporary basis, Ernest James Worman worked there from 1895 until his death in 1909. At that time, it became customary for youngsters untrained in research and librarianship to be employed in the University Library, given language training in the University, and ultimately engaged on specialist work. So it was that Worman, a bookshop salesman of twenty-four, was chosen from no fewer than 116 applicants. He soon proved himself quietly industrious, admirably thorough, and linguistically talented. After the departure of Hirschfeld in 1902, he became the Library's expert in the classification of the Judaeo-Arabic material, an achievement recognized by his appointment in 1908 as Curator in Oriental Literature.

The final character to be introduced here is the German scholar of theology and Semitics, Paul Kahle. Having complemented his Arabic and Hebrew studies in Germany with lengthy periods in the Middle East, he directed the Institute for Oriental Studies at the University of Bonn for some fifteen years. Following a clash with the Nazi authorities, he fled to Oxford where he spent the remainder of a long and fruitful career. Unlike those who occupied the Regius chair of Hebrew at Cambridge during the years of early Genizah research and were more devoted to the literary and theological study of the "Old Testament", Kahle took a great interest in rabbinic sources, mastered the reading of Hebrew manuscripts and worked closely with Jewish scholars.

Guide to reading

It is somewhat surprising that there are no up-to-date and balanced biographies of Schechter, Jenkinson or Taylor. Norman Bentwich's *Solomon Schechter. A Biography* (Philadelphia, 1938) is a detailed account of his life and achievements but remains respectful and cautious as far as his personality and character are concerned. Bentwich was a close friend of the family who was anxious to stress the conventional rather than the radical elements in his hero's make-up. Cyrus Adler's obituary "Solomon Schechter. A Biographical Sketch" in the *American Jewish Year Book* of 1917 does have some important data and insights but is of a similar ilk. A few articles have recently attempted to correct the bias. Mel Scult has made important contributions by writing about Mathilde Schechter in his "The Baale Boste Reconsidered. The Life of Mathilde Roth Schechter (M.R.S.)" in *Modern Judaism* 7 (1987), pp. 1–27, and by chronicling and analysing Schechter's years in New York in "Schechter's Seminary", his contribution (pp. 43–102) to the first volume, entitled *The Making of an Institution of Jewish Higher Learning*, of the two-volume study *Tradition Renewed: A History of the Jewish Theological Seminary* (New York, 1997), edited by Jack Wertheimer. A closer and more critical account of the Cambridge years has been attempted by S. C. Reif in his article "Jenkinson and Schechter at Cambridge: An Expanded and Updated Assessment", *Transactions of the Jewish Historical Society of England* 32 (1993), pp. 279–316, and the importance of Schechter as a rabbinic scholar has been assessed by Jacob Sussmann in a lecture given at the World Congress of Jewish Studies in Jerusalem, 1997, and scheduled for publication in its proceedings. An extensive and well annotated list of Schechter's publications is provided by A. S. Oko in his *Solomon Schechter M.A. Litt.D.: A Bibliography* (Cambridge, 1938) and Schechter's attitude to biblical criticism has been discussed by David J. Fine in "Solomon Schechter and the Ambivalence of Jewish *Wissenschaft*", *Judaism* 46 (1997), no. 181, pp. 3–24. It may be added that the forthcoming biography of Schechter's daughter, Ruth, promised by Baruch Hirson, may finally overturn any notion of his having been in any way an establishment figure, even on the Jewish side.

Some three years after the death of Jenkinson, his brother-in-law, also a Cambridge "don", H. F. Stewart, wrote an appreciation of him in the volume *Francis Jenkinson. Fellow of Trinity College Cambridge and University Librarian. A Memoir* (Cambridge, 1926). Once again, the writer is too close to the subject to be dispassionate and he is certainly little interested in Jenkinson's role as a collector and conservator of hebraica and judaica. Although it is a much shorter treatment of the University Librarian, the entry compiled by S. Gaselee for the *Dictionary of National Biography 1922–1930* (London, 1937), pp. 453–54, is more academically sound and the relationship with Schechter is assessed in Reif's article just noted. Charles Taylor, sometime Vice-Chancellor of the University of Cambridge and long time Master of St. John's College, does not even merit a biographical volume that is biased and personal. Given his eminence in so many areas, it is strange that all that we have to rely on are the appreciative obituaries that were published in the St. John's College magazine, *The Eagle*, 30 (1908–9), pp. 64–85 and 197–204; *Dictionary of National Biography. Supplement 1901–11* (London, 1912), pp. 480–82; and *Who Was Who 1897–1915* (Sixth edition, London, 1986), p. 513.

On Cambridge as Schechter found it at the end of the nineteenth century, there are important insights in R. Ackerman's *J. G. Frazer. His Life and Work* (Cambridge, 1987), as well as in the volume edited by William Johnstone, *William Robertson Smith: Essays in Reassessment*, (Sheffield, 1995), and in the chapter entitled "Hebrew and Hebraists at Cambridge: An Historical Introduction", in S. C. Reif's *Hebrew Manuscripts at Cambridge University Library: A Description and Introduction* (Cambridge, 1997), pp. 1–35. Mrs Lewis and Mrs Gibson are a great attraction for historians, hebraists and feminists, and there is a delightful biography by A. Whigham Price, *The Ladies of Castlebrae* (Gloucester, 1985), that provides details, evaluation and photographs.

A few further details about Pass and Hirschfeld may be found in J. A. Venn, *Alumni Cantabrigienses* II/V (Cambridge, 1953), p. 42, and in the *Jews' College Jubilee Volume*, ed. I. Harris London, 1906), pp. cxii–cxvi. Worman's origins before he was appointed to a post in the University Library are intriguingly obscure but his social, religious and academic contributions to Cambridge life in the second half of his life are well summarized in a booklet published in his memory shortly after his death. It was entitled *Ernest James Worman 1871–1909* (Cambridge, 1910) and contained brief essays by a number of friends and colleagues, including Francis Jenkinson and Israel Abrahams. Paul Kahle's life and work were appreciatively assessed by Matthew Black in his obituary "Paul Ernst Kahle 1875–1965", *Proceedings of the British Academy* 51 (1965), pp. 485–95 and his Jewish student, the distinguished scholar of liturgical poetry who later settled and taught in Jerusalem, Menahem Zulay, offered some interesting insights in an article published in the Hebrew periodical *Molad* 4 (1950), pp. 355–57.

FOUR

TEXTS IN
TRANSIT

Given that those with a keen interest in literary antiquities were already making off with some of the contents of the *genizot* in Cairo before Schechter arrived in Cambridge in 1890, it is a little strange to find no significant mention of such fragmentary manuscripts at Cambridge University Library until 1891. There is one deed of sale dating from the rabbinical court of Abraham, son of Maimonides, in Fustat in 1233 that looks remarkably like many other Genizah fragments and may have arrived at the Library as early as the 1880s. There are also a few other such items that may have been acquired at any time during the 1880s and 1890s. Unfortunately, the records are vague with regard to their original provenance and the manner of their acquisition. What is clear, however, is that between 1891 and 1896, about a hundred Genizah fragments were acquired by the Library and that within those five years it gradually dawned on Schechter that there must be a rich source of such items awaiting discovery, removal and systematic study.

PRE-SCHECHTER GENIZAH

The earliest of such acquisitions were the result of generous gifts made by the Reverend Greville Chester, an Anglican Egyptologist and author. A graduate of Balliol College, Oxford, Chester was a well-known traveller and collector of orientalia, who presented various Genizah items to Oxford and Cambridge and whose works included his *Catalogue of the Egyptian Antiquities in the Ashmolean Museum, Oxford*, published in 1881. He was clearly well advised and intelligently supplied by his source since his gifts to Cambridge included a fifteenth- or sixteenth-century Italian Hebrew prayer-book, a Karaite tract from about the twelfth century dealing with the calendar and with the dates of the Jewish festivals, and some thirty-three important liturgical pieces, all of them from the Genizah. Most of them date from the tenth to the twelfth centuries and are of considerable assistance in the reconstruction of the prayer-books of Babylon and Palestine in general and of Saʿadya Gaon in particular. Central prayers for daily, sabbath and festival use, rather than liturgical poetry for occasional recitation, predominate and there seems have been a consistency in the choice of the texts and an interest in one particular field.

The fragments that came to the Library from Rabbi Solomon Aaron Wertheimer were altogether broader in content but in no way of lesser importance. Wertheimer, a rabbinic scholar and bookseller of Jerusalem, was born near Pressburg, Slovakia, in 1866 and died in Jerusalem in 1935. He located and identified many important manuscripts, including some of the earliest known Genizah fragments, and sold them only because of his family's need for subsistence. Between 1893 and 1896, he corresponded with the University Library in Cambridge, regularly offering detailed lists of the fragments at no more than a few shillings per item. What is remarkable is not that such precious thousand-year old texts were offered at such giveaway prices but that, after discussions between Jenkinson and Schechter, a fair proportion of them were rejected!

What was retained amounted to more than sixty pieces and extended over a number of subjects. The fields of Bible, midrashic literature and

17 – Rabbi Solomon Wertheimer of Jerusalem, Genizah editor and dealer, 1866–1935 (Ktav Yad Ve-Sefer Institute, Jerusalem, 1990)

71

rabbinic law are represented but the emphasis is very much on liturgical poetry, legal documents and personal letters. The content is novel and the dates generally range from the eleventh to the thirteenth centuries, giving the distinct impression that either Wertheimer or Schechter, or perhaps both of them and Jenkinson, had a special interest in those items that would lead to the rewriting of Jewish social and literary history in the early medieval period. It did, however, take Schechter a year or two to appreciate fully the extraordinary potential of these damaged and worn folios and the need to acquire more of them and to devote himself to the difficult task of their decipherment. He was perhaps too busy with his careful historical analysis of rabbinic tracts to apply himself to the fragments until, that is, he found that two of them were of special importance for such study.

These two fragments were actually in the Bodleian Library in Oxford, and not at Cambridge University Library, and had arrived there in the previous few years as part of Oxford's share of the literary spoils of Egyptian synagogues. They were both from the twelfth century, the first from the tractate *Keritot* in the Babylonian Talmud and the second from the tractate *Berakhot* in the Jerusalem Talmud. Schechter was excited not only by the fact that these manuscripts provided texts that predated and challenged the standard editions but also by the older linguistic characteristics preserved in them. The grammar, spelling and dialect demonstrated clearly that the fragments represented the earliest known, and therefore the relatively unspoilt versions of such texts. With the assistance of the Anglo-Jewish cleric, Simeon Singer, and the generous participation of Cambridge University Press, Schechter prepared editions of the fragments in 1895 that were dedicated to Isaac Hirsch Weiss on his eightieth birthday and made their appearance in 1896. In their introduction, the editors make direct reference to the acquisitions recently made by the Bodleian Library and demonstrate their awareness of the promise that they hold for scientific Jewish studies in the future: "These consist mostly of fragments, but they date from so early a period and present so many unique examples that it is by no means an exaggeration to say that their publication will open entirely new fields of research to the student of Jewish Literature."

THE BEN SIRA CONTROVERSY

Another subject that contributed to Schechter's growing interest in the importance of such fragments was the controversy about the original Hebrew of the apocryphal book of Ben Sira (Ecclesiasticus). This collection of proverbs and popular wisdom had been written in the second pre-Christian century and had survived into the late medieval and early modern worlds primarily in Greek and Syriac versions used by the Christian Church. The question being faced by historians of Jewish literature was whether to use any of the rabbinic sources for the reconstruction of the original Hebrew or to rely exclusively on retranslations from the Greek and the Syriac. In this connection, rigid positions had been taken up early in the decade by David Samuel Margoliouth and, partly by way of response, by Schechter himself.

Margoliouth, for his part, originated from a Jewish family whose route from eastern to western European culture was somewhat different from that of Schechter. His father, Ezekiel, and another relative, Moses, were converted to Anglican Christianity and became active missionaries among the Jews, with a considerable reputation among those anxious to bring the Church's message to the chosen people. David won a scholarship to the English public school, Winchester College, and carried off an assortment of university prizes as a student of classics at New College, Oxford, before turning his attention to oriental studies and winning election to the Laudian Chair of Arabic in 1889. With a deep voice, an "exotic and vivid appearance" and an outstanding linguistic ability, Margoliouth was one of the great Oxford characters of his day. In matters academic, he delighted in adopting sceptical positions, such as when he denied the authenticity of the Elephantine Papyri and of pre-Islamic Arabic poetry, but in the ecclesiastical context he remained thoroughly conservative. It would appear that not until his late years did he feel any special sympathy for the people from whom his family had stemmed.

The inaugural lecture of the newly appointed Laudian Professor of Arabic in the University of Oxford was published in 1890 and dealt with none other than Ben Sira. Since the holder of the chair was required to lecture on the Semitic languages ("Arabic, Chaldee and Syriac"), Margoliouth thought it singularly apt to continue the work he had begun in his Kennicott Prize Dissertation of 1887 and to tackle the matter of the original Hebrew of Ben Sira. Having examined all the versions, he concluded that the most reliable evidence was to be found in the Greek and Syriac versions and proceeded to reconstruct a specimen Hebrew text based on their renderings. He was obviously of the view that the rabbinic testimony was of little consequence and indeed took the opportunity of a sideways swipe at the "whole Rabbinic farrago" and of including a theologically tendentious statement about the "grave of the Old-Hebrew and the old-Israel".

18 – Professor D. S. Margoliouth, 1858–1940, Laudian Professor of Arabic
in the University of Oxford (Warden and Fellows of New College, Oxford)

Given his interest in dating rabbinic language and literature and in establishing its chronological relationship to the latest books of the Hebrew Bible, it is not surprising to find that one of Schechter's first publications after his appointment at Cambridge, and indeed an early contribution to the newly published *Jewish Quarterly Review*, was an article on Ben Sira. Since talmudic and midrashic texts cite Hebrew verses from that work, it was obviously important to him to list, analyse and annotate these so that they could better be assessed in the context of "solving the great Sirach difficulties". Encouraged and assisted by Claude Montefiore, Schechter also provided translations of the relevant texts, as well as demonstrating impressive erudition in his detailed end-notes. Clearly he had at the back of his mind the notion that he might at some later stage be able to argue for, if not prove, an authentic Jewish transmission of the Hebrew text of Ben Sira, and he saw in the rabbinic texts a stage in that possible transmission.

There can be little doubt that Margoliouth's theories constituted the immediate inspiration for Schechter's study. Hebraists were not generally impressed with Margoliouth's reconstruction and a controversy got under way between him and the leading semiticists, T. K. Cheyne, S. R. Driver and A. Neubauer, as recorded in the columns of the

74

19 – Solomon Schechter's letter of 13 May 1896, identifying the Ben Sira fragment
(Cambridge University Library)

Expositor during the 1890s. For Schechter the matter appears to have called not only for a discussion concerning Semitic languages but also for a scholarly crusade (if that term may be used in this context!) in defence of Jewish literary traditions. It was insufficient for him to claim that the Greek and Syriac versions were unlikely candidates for the role of authentic transmitters; more than that, they were no less than "defaced caricatures of the real work of Sirach".

CHERCHEZ LES FEMMES

The battle lines had been drawn and the skirmishes continued for five years. Only then was a new weapon discovered that had the potential to settle the matter once and for all and, paradox of all paradoxes, it was a woman who brought it to England and thus contributed to the debate about the kind of language in which a great literary misogynist had written Ecclesiasticus. Indeed, the credit must go not to one woman but to two, Agnes Lewis and Margaret Gibson, whose scholarly reputations became interdependent for a short but important period with that of Schechter. Having in the spring of 1896 brought home a haul of manuscripts from Jerusalem, the plain of Sharon and Cairo, they were able to call on the services of the Reader in Talmudic to help them identify items that were written in a form of Hebrew unfamiliar to them from their Old Testament studies. On 13 May, Schechter examined the fragments in their dining-room and quickly identified one as a vellum leaf of the Palestinian (=Jerusalem) Talmud, itself a significant find, given the paucity of manuscript sources for that work, and his earlier fascination with a similar fragment housed at the Bodleian. It was, however, another "scrap of paper" that attracted his closer attention and that he immediately wished to take with him for further study and for possible publication. Within a matter of hours he had communicated the result of his research to his women friends by way of telegram and letter, the text of the latter conveying the intensity of his excitement:

> Dear Mrs Lewis, I think we have reason to congratulate ourselves. For the fragment I took with me represents a piece of the original Hebrew of Ecclesiasticus. It is the first time that such a thing was discovered. Please do not speak yet about the matter till tomorrow. I will come to you tomorrow about 11 p.m. [*sic!*] and talk over the matter with you how to make the matter known. In haste and great excitement, Yours sincerely, S. Schechter.

Although he expressly requested them to keep the matter confidential, he himself could not control his enthusiasm and spread the word among colleagues at the University Library. Mrs Lewis immediately wrote with the news to the *Athenaeum* and the *Academy* and Schechter published the text in the July issue of the *Expositor*. What he had identified was a Hebrew text of parts of Ecclesiasticus 39–40 and he was convinced that it represented a reliable witness to the original language of the book. Now surely, he must have thought, the scholarly controversy had been settled in his favour. Little did he realize then that Margoliouth would not be convinced even when seriously challenged by Nöldeke and that the opposing view would not finally be refuted until discoveries by Yigael Yadin at Masada in 1964.

Adolf Neubauer, expert in Jewish studies who had long been aware of the importance of *genizah* collections in the Near East for Mediterranean scholarship, and Arthur Cowley, erudite semiticist, had, within five weeks of Mrs Lewis's letter appearing in the *Athenaeum*, located another nine leaves of the same manuscript of Ecclesiasticus at the Bodleian Library in Oxford. It is possible that they were already working on such a project but more probable that Mrs Lewis was right when she later

20 – The 10th-century fragment of Ben Sira purchased by Mrs Lewis and identified by Dr Schechter (Or.1102) (Cambridge University Library)

made use of best British understatement and wrote that it was "natural to think" that it was her letter of 13 May, published on 16 May, that had been "of some assistance in guiding Messrs Neubauer and Cowley to this important result".

Schechter himself has little to say about which precise scholarly quest inspired him to undertake a trip to Cairo in the winter of 1896–97 in search of manuscripts. The undertaking was clearly important enough for him to cancel a previous intention of participating in Herbert Bentwich's Zionist pilgrimage to the land of Israel with the Maccabeans. Undoubtedly, the kind of medieval Hebrew, Aramaic and Arabic fragments that had appeared in Oxford and Cambridge in the previous

77

few years and that had been purchased by Cyrus Adler in 1891, and the fact that some of them had been written in Cairo, had made him think about the possibilities of further discoveries. It is equally likely that the success of the Anglo-Jewish lawyer, Elkan Nathan Adler, in bringing home a sack of palaeographical treasures from the Egyptian capital a year before, during his second visit there, had not gone unnoticed. Surely, however, Schechter's excitement about the Ben Sira fragment brought to him by Mrs Lewis and the feverish activities of Neubauer and Cowley, and his determination to find more manuscripts of the Hebrew text, were major factors in his decision to travel East in pursuit of the source of such a precious item and in the expectation of discovering many more like it.

THE TRIP TO CAIRO

By December, 1896, Schechter was ready to set out for Cairo. He had taken advantage of the kind offer of his hebraist colleague, Charles Taylor, to defray all his expenses and had not therefore required to approach the University authorities for a travel grant and the unwelcome publicity and competition that this might have brought for his plans. With the warm support of leading Cambridge dons such as the moral philosopher and campaigner for women's rights, Henry Sidgwick (brother-in-law of Arthur James Balfour), and the Scots medical scientist at St. John's College, Donald Macalister, and a letter of introduction from the Chief Rabbi, Hermann Adler, the Rumanian rabbinic hero had made his way to the Egyptian capital. Although there was no lack of things that he found objectionable, he could not resist describing it to his wife as "a glorious place, enjoying an Italian opera, French dancing masters, English administration, and Mohammetan houris." More importantly, he soon applied himself to the matter of befriending Chief Rabbi Aaron Raphael Ben Shim'on. The task was not an easy one but required both wisdom and patience. Schechter wisely smoked many cigarettes and drank innumerable cups of coffee with his rabbinic colleague, visited interesting places with him, and patiently accepted the fact that there were many days that were locally regarded as more suitable for such relaxed behaviour than for getting down to business of any sort. Ultimately, he won the confidence of both Ben Shim'on and the lay leaders of the Jewish community and was taken by the Rabbi to the Ben Ezra synagogue and shown the "windowless and doorless room of fair dimensions" at the end of the gallery which housed the congregation's Genizah collection. Having been given access by ladder

21 – Rabbi Aaron Raphael Ben Shim'on, 1848–1928, Chief Rabbi
of Cairo (J. M. Landau, *Jews in 19th-century Egypt*,
New York University Press, New York, 1969)

and introduced to the more minor synagogal officials, the Cambridge
visitor was authorized to take from the Genizah, as he himself put it,
"what, and as much as, I liked."

While Schechter's motivations are clear enough to the historian of
modern Jewish scholarship, it is rather less clear what motivated the
Cairo Jewish authorities to hand him the keys to the Genizah and to the
astonishing manuscript treasures that it contained. As far as Ben Shim'on
is concerned, he had no western educational background and may not
have appreciated the significance of the manuscript material under his
care. He did enjoy some expertise in the areas of Jewish religious law and

ritual and was learned enough in such matters to produce publications in these fields. That is, however, a very different matter from scientific and historical study and neither his early period in Jerusalem as the son of a leading Moroccan rabbi nor his mature years in Tel Aviv reveal any evidence of an enthusiasm for university learning. The more junior synagogal officials had found the Genizah a useful source of extra income and perhaps he too, as one piece of Cambridge oral tradition has it, learnt from his Jerusalem contacts how he might extract financial advantage from that source. Maybe he just succumbed to Schechter's charms. The leading families of Cattawis and Mosseris may, on the other hand, have acted the way they did precisely because of their great interest in western connections. They were anxious to educate their children in French, English and Italian schools and to establish close relations with western educational institutions whenever they could. They regarded themselves as a kind of aristocracy and conducted the affairs of the community in a somewhat dictatorial fashion. Opportunities of building close relations with distinguished visitors from Europe were always welcomed by them. They saw the Ben Ezra synagogue and its treasures as a relic of the past that played little part in their present communal life but that might provide them with future access to culture and influence in the centres of European power that were then expanding eastwards.

Whatever the reasons for his good fortune, Schechter had come upon a veritable *embarras de richesse* and quickly set to work on locating the manuscript contents of the Genizah and arranging for their transfer to Cambridge. Since there was certainly no time to examine the fragments any more than peremptorily, he left behind much of the printed matter which he regarded, not fully with justification, as late and unimportant. He removed what we now know to have been 140,000 items, doubtless eager to locate a goodly proportion of Ben Sira texts among them, and to confirm his reputation as the Cambridge scholar who had restored its Hebrew version. In order to ease his way, he had constantly to provide *bakshish* for the synagogal officials and even then lost a fair number of fragments, to which he regarded himself as fully entitled, to dealers in antiquities. Anxious to be as thorough as possible in collecting his treasure, he paid what he thought to be exorbitant prices to recover such texts. He also visited other *genizot* in the area and may have found material there too. He does, however, make it clear that his haul was primarily from the Ben Ezra synagogue. When it came to the matter of transporting the sacks of scholarly discoveries out of the country, he made use of the services of the

80

British Agent and Consul-General in Egypt, Lord Cromer, who enjoyed considerable political and military power in the area and could hardly be gainsaid.

The physical nature of the challenge to Schechter should also not be underestimated. He had to work in a dark and suffocatingly dusty atmosphere, suffering the close attentions of legions of insects and always aware that he might be damaging the very treasures that held out such hope for him. A few weeks after his arrival in Cairo, he was joined there by Agnes Lewis and Margaret Gibson, who were about to set off for another visit to Sinai. They kindly brought him various items from his wife, Mathilde, in Cambridge, including a device that would make it easier for him to breathe in all the dust. Schechter took them to the Ben Ezra synagogue to show them his place of work and source of discoveries. The two women, and a Girton College student called Miss de Witt whom Schechter had apparently brought along too, climbed into the Genizah room and were appalled by the filthy conditions. In order to assist their Cambridge friend, Agnes and Maggie took it upon themselves to clean up the manuscripts as best they could in their hotel room. They removed what dirt they could and spread the precious texts on tables and trunks to dry in the sunlight. There were other western visitors in their hotel at the time with whom the Cambridge party forged links and exchanged scholarly information and experiences.

EVENTS OF 1897

Some eighteen months later, Schechter published his recollection of the state of the Genizah when reporting on his trip and on the resultant discoveries in the London *Times* of 3 August 1897. His masterly and colourful description cannot be bettered and, though often previously cited, is well worthy of being quoted again:

> But one can hardly realise the confusion in a genuine, old Genizah until one has seen it. It is a battlefield of books, and the literary productions of many centuries had their share in the battle, and their *disjecta membra* are now strewn over its area. Some of the belligerents have perished outright, and are literally ground to dust in the terrible struggle for space, whilst others, as if overtaken by a general crush, are squeezed into big, unshapely lumps, which even with the aid of chemical appliances can no longer be separated without serious damage to their constituents. In their present condition these lumps sometimes afford curiously suggestive combinations; as, for instance, when you find a piece of some rationalistic work, in

which the very existence of either angels or devils is denied, clinging for its very life to an amulet in which these same beings (mostly the latter) are bound over to be on their good behaviour and not interfere with Miss Jair's love for somebody. The development of the romance is obscured by the fact that the last lines of the amulet are mounted on some I.O.U., or lease, and this in turn is squeezed between the sheets of an old moralist, who treats all attention to money affairs with scorn and indignation. Again, all these contradictory matters cleave tightly to some sheets from a very old Bible. This, indeed, ought to be the last umpire between them, but it is hardly legible without peeling off from its surface the fragments of some printed work, which clings to old nobility with all the obstinancy and obtrusiveness of the *parvenu*.

Schechter was intensely excited that so many thousands of items were in his hands and that such a variety of subjects was represented among the fragments. He was quickly aware of the scholarly potential of what he had found but a little worried that since he was visiting his family in Palestine during the spring the material would reach Cambridge and somehow be seen by other scholars before his return. He therefore wrote to Jenkinson and to Mathilde and diplomatically requested that the boxes be left

unopened until he was there to examine them properly himself. He indicated that he was not dictating terms, merely asking for a safe place for the documents and an assurance that they would in the meantime be regarded as his private property. The University Library would probably soon own the collection and would not be involved in making him any payment. Most poignant and significant are Schechter's estimate that "the matters I brought from Cairo contain many valuable things which make our Library as important for Hebrew literature as Oxford at least" and his communication to the Librarian that he had arranged in Jerusalem for Cambridge to be given first refusal in the case of antiquities and manuscripts being offered for sale. His feelings understood and his conditions met, he was able to relax and enjoy his pilgrimage to the Holy Land.

While Schechter was still planning his trip to the Near East, his academic competitors in "the other place" lost no time in forging ahead in the scholarly race by preparing their Ben Sira texts for publication. Their volume, published by the University of Oxford "at the Clarendon Press" was in the bookshops by January, 1897, while Schechter was still ferreting around the various Cairo synagogues and checking whether they had any treasures to compare with those of the Ben Ezra. The content of the Cowley-Neubauer edition of what the title-page confidently cites as "the original Hebrew" had much in common with Schechter's earlier work. The Lewis-Schechter fragment is included but the introduction refers to that discovery only on its fourth page, at which point it is also noted that Schechter's edition has been corrected by the writers. Even then there is something of a reluctance to set matters in an accurate chronological perspective. Far from clearly stating that they were inspired by Lewis and Schechter, the editors follow up their paragraph about Cambridge developments by reporting that "almost simultaneously the Bodleian Library acquired, through Professor Sayce, a box of Hebrew and Arabic fragments" among which they had found other texts of Ben Sira. Schechter's personal and professional relations with Neubauer had never been quite as disastrous as those of his Cambridge predecessor S. M. Schiller-Szinessy but they had always been strained. News of Neubauer's work on Ben Sira could hardly have cheered Schechter up and he is on record during his 1897 visit to Cairo as having described his Oxford rival in German as a "Lump", that is, nothing better than a scoundrel.

What then was his response to the situation on his return to Cambridge in the spring of that year? He was already aware that what he had retrieved from the Ben Ezra synagogue would grant him scholarly immortality and that no one individual or generation would ever be able to quarry more than a small proportion of the collection's rich seams of new knowledge. He could nevertheless make a start on this massive challenge to scientific Jewish study and he consequently set about the systematic sorting of the fragments, assisted by a team of Cambridge scholars, each with a particular expertise. Mrs Lewis and Mrs Gibson dealt with the Syriac; Charles Taylor with post-biblical hebraica and with palimpsests; Francis Burkitt with Greek items; Hartwig Hirschfeld with the Arabic; and Herman Leonard Pass with the Hebrew Bible. The University Librarian, Francis Jenkinson, was closely involved in all these research projects and kept the confidences of the researchers regarding their discoveries. He was particularly helpful to Schechter. The five years during which the latter applied himself with boundless energy and enthusiasm to the Genizah material were undoubtedly the most academically productive and significant in his whole life. There is hardly an area of Hebrew, Jewish and general Semitic studies that was not illuminated during his day and that has not continued to derive benefit from his work in the century since then.

THE EXCITEMENT OF GENIZAH RESEARCH

Historians of Genizah research are fond of pointing out how each generation has looked for something different among these medieval fragments and how history, like other areas of human intrest, has its changing fashions. While this is undoubtedly true, and explains why novel approaches to the same material are always possible, credit must be given to Schechter for having so soon appreciated the broad significance of his discoveries and so wisely indicated to future generations the directions their studies would take. Within a few months, he was able to summarize how Genizah research would affect the major areas of Jewish literature. He correctly predicted that unknown versions of the Bible in Greek, Aramaic and Arabic, as well as newly discovered commentaries and non-standard systems of pointing Hebrew, would contribute greatly to the history of Hebrew Bible transmission and interpretation. He had the foresight to appreciate that the talmudic and midrashic texts and commentaries that he had brought from Cairo would restore works long given up for lost, provide greatly improved editions, and explain the process of rabbinic exposition. The oldest forms of synagogal worship would be recovered and the number of known Hebrew poems greatly multiplied.

But Schechter's enthusiasm, imagination and prescience did not stop there. Consider, in the light of the work of Shelomo Dov Goitein and his school of historians many decades later, the brilliance of the following summary:

> What a rich life these long rolls unfold to us! All sorts of conditions of men and situations are represented in them: the happy young married couple by their marriage contract; the marriage that failed by its letter of divorce; the slave by his deed of emancipation; the court of justice by its legal decisons; the heads of the schools by their learned epistles; the newly appointed "Prince of the Exile" by the description of his installation; the rich trader by his correspondence with his agents in Malabar; the gentleman beggar by his letters of recommendation to the great ones in

Israel; the fanatics by their thundering excommunications; the meek man by his mild apologies; the fool by his amulet; the medical man by his prescriptions; and the patient by his will.

But had his passion for Ben Sira been replaced by these wider interests? There are certainly clear indications to the contrary. In his *Times* article in August 1897, he refers to the Lewis and "Oxford" finds of Ecclesiasticus, and expresses the hope that his recent acquisitions "will yield more remains of these semi-sacred volumes." When he wrote these words, he had probably already discovered more leaves of the same manuscript since both Taylor and Jenkinson refer to such discoveries having taken place earlier that summer. They are both very careful about chronicling the precise dates of virtually all Schechter's subsequent successes in locating Ben Sira manuscripts. The whole Cambridge team, having once been upstaged, was not again ready to permit any possibility of doubt about precedence in such matters.

The atmosphere of excitement is best conveyed in Jenkinson's diaries and in the correspondence between him and Schechter. In one instance, he records that Schechter "nearly went off his head" and in others there is evidence that the impatience of his Jewish colleague to prepare his new finds for the press, to have them conserved, and to ensure that he had checked the collection for every possible Ben Sira item, had led to some friction between the two, especially when Schechter had on one occasion rudely burst into the University Librarian's room. On the other hand, when George Margoliouth of the British Museum rushed to publish two leaves of Ben Sira that had been acquired by his institution, instead of handing them to Schechter for his projected edition, the University Librarian described him as "a self-advertising tramp". He also helped Schechter to word sharp replies to D. S. Margoliouth's continuing challenges to the authenticity of the Genizah texts of Ben Sira. When Jenkinson's brother-in-law, Hugh Fraser Stewart, was writing his biography some thirty years later, he remembered Schechter for having damaged his health by working in the dust of all the fragments and for having recovered the Hebrew Ecclesiasticus. Indeed, by the time that Schechter and Taylor published their edition of 1899, another eleven leaves had been uncovered in Cambridge, and additional material was available from the Taylor-Schechter collection for the joint Oxford-Cambridge facsimile edition of 1901, all sorted into three distinct manuscripts, referred to as A, B and C.

The period between Schechter's return from Cairo in the spring of 1897 and his departure for New York five years later was full of feverish activity and noteworthy incident. A room was set aside in the Library for work on the Genizah Collection and arrangements were made not only for the sorting and description of the material by the various experts but also for the physical treatment of the torn, stained and fragile fragments. One of the bindery staff, Andrew Baldrey, was assigned to the task and found himself still engaged on it when he reached retirement age in the 1920s. Jenkinson himself spent many a morning and afternoon supervising the conservation process which at that time amounted to cleaning, repairing and placing between glass. Much noble work was done and many precious items were preserved. There are, however, snippets of information gleaned from the Librarian's frank and informative diaries that make grisly reading for those currently devoted to the physical treatment of manuscripts. On one occasion, he notes that "Baldrey has not been careful enough with the new fragment and by bending some small pieces dry has broken them." Some fragments were simply sorted away into various drawers in the Librarian's office while others were subjected to treatment with benzine one day and chloroform the next. No sooner had some precious little pieces of sixth-century Aquila been exactly joined and placed between glass than "someone knocked it over. It fell on the iron pipes and was smashed; i.e. the glass: Ms., I hope not injured."

Reminding his readers that Schechter had once referred to the Genizah fragments as "the *disjecta membra* of the slain", a writer closely familiar with Schechter's manuscript laboratory recorded the situation as it was in 1897 (*Jewish Chronicle*, 15 October):

But these slain are coming to life again in the Cairo apartment of the Cambridge University library, which was set aside as Mr. Schechter's working-room. There he may be found at almost any hour of the day deeply engaged in sorting and examining his fragments, with an expression in his face constantly changing from disappointment to rapturous delight, just as the case of the fragment in his hand may be. Sometimes we might find him in the company of visitors – for Mr. Schechter's working-room is now one of the sights of the place, though the privilege of admittance is only granted to a few – taking them from box to box, pointing out to them the significance of this or that MS., or the peculiarity of the specimens of Hebrew writing which lie scattered about on the long tables. If he happens to be in a good humour, you may get him even to let you have a glance at the invaluable collection of autographs, in which the greatest men of Israel are represented, or at the precious palimpsests, the deciphering of which means a veritable resurrection of their authors.

22 – Solomon Schechter at work in Cambridge University Library, 1898 (Cambridge University Library)

A CO-OPERATIVE VENTURE

The University Librarian, Francis Jenkinson, was of great practical assistance, as well as a source of sound advice. He opened the Library for Schechter at unusual times and kept order among the fragments. Jenkinson also attended to all sorts of other practical matters and when formal arrangements needed to be made and reports submitted to the relevant University committees, he discussed these with Schechter and Taylor and drew up the necessary documentation. He arranged for Schechter to be re-imbursed for all his Cairo expenses (through a grant from Charles Taylor) and obtained a ticket for him to an important University function at which the distinguished Egyptologist, Flinders Petrie, was awarded an honorary degree. In addition, Jenkinson dealt with Schechter's suggestion about numbering the fragments, entrusted him with the key to the Hebrew fragment cabinet when he was scheduled to be absent from the Library, and indulged the Reader in Talmudic's cigarette addiction by arranging for a report by him to be copied at the Schechter residence so that he could smoke while he dictated its contents.

The University Librarian also read the proof of the article about the Genizah discovery that Schechter composed for the *Times* and helped Schechter to draft a letter to that journal in response to its publication of an anonymous attack on him. The attack claimed that the real credit for the discovery of the Cairo Genizah belonged to Elkan Nathan Adler who had visited it and removed material before Schechter. He even acted as a confidant not only in connection with plans for the discovery and exploitation of the Genizah material but also concerning Schechter's personal feelings about his Cambridge post and his future career. As he himself puts it in his entry for 26 August 1897: "Schechter... came to tea with me and told me many things about himself and his position here." It is interesting that Jenkinson evinces a deeper understanding of the intricacies of Genizah discovery than one might fairly expect from a non-orientalist. When Cambridge friends reported to him that they had been offered five sacks of fragments from that famous Cairo source but had declined to purchase because of a warning that Schechter had removed everything of value, he characterized that evaluation of Schechter's success with regard to the Genizah material as "rather a hasty assumption". Two additional Genizah collections did in fact come to the Library a few months after the major haul brought by Schechter. About a thousand items, ultimately to be given the classmarks "Or.1080" and "Or.1081", were purchased from the dealer W. S. Raffalovich and a smaller collection (now T-S NS 172), acquired in Cairo by Reginald Henriques, was presented by him.

But all was not sweetness and light in the relationship between Jenkinson and Schechter. Given Schechter's temperament and Jenkinson's undoubted sense of his personal and professional dignity, this would have been unlikely. At times the University Librarian contented himself with a quiet complaint to his diary concerning Schechter's angry explosions about those who had, he felt, been playing him false, or concerning crooked dealers apparently encouraged by Schechter, or in the matter of the rabbinic teacher's keenness to fill in a quiet summer Saturday by bothering Jenkinson. At others he noted his relief that Schechter had not appeared and had therefore given him the opportunity of tidying up before the next scholarly onslaught, recorded that he had simply declined to accompany his Rumanian colleague to the Library, having had too much of him already, and refused one Saturday to allow him to borrow a novel that the regulations did not make available to him. Once, at least, Schechter upset a large box of fragments in the darkest part of his room close to the pipes and begged the Librarian and his staff to set things right. This Jenkinson did but not without noting the event in his diary and adding "meanwhile, he tramples them like so much litter."

There were at least two occasions when the exchanges between the two scholars became stormy. In the first of these, Schechter had found a diamond-shaped hole in one of his fragments and angrily began to make accusations about such wilful damage. Fortunately for Jenkinson, he had noticed that the fragment had arrived in that state and was thus able to calm Schechter down, at the same time ticking him off "for his impertinence and violence". In the second incident, Jenkinson felt sympathy for Schechter but advised him to accept the situation and take no action. Burkitt had quickly prepared an edition of some sixth-century fragments of Aquila's Jewish translation of the Hebrew Bible into Greek discovered in the Genizah material at Cambridge, with a preface provided by Charles Taylor, and in the preliminary announcement of the impending publication no mention had been made of Schechter. This had infuriated him and he angrily demanded of Jenkinson that the title-page of the volume should include his name, no doubt arguing his central role in the discovery of the material. While agreeing that his name ought indeed to have appeared on the announcement, Jenkinson forcefully put it to his colleague that to *demand* the inclusion of his name on the title-page was impossible and absurd. "If you are going to be unreasonable," he mildly threatened, "the whole situation will have to be reconsidered."

The fact is, however, that when the volume appeared, credit was given to Schechter on the title-page, as well as by Taylor in the preface and Burkitt in his introduction, and it seems that Jenkinson had worked quietly behind the scenes to achieve this.

CONDITIONS OF THE GIFT

During the first half of 1898, discussions were held between Taylor, Schechter and Jenkinson about the conditions under which the Genizah Collection would be formally presented to the University. From its point of view, the Library was naturally concerned about an open-ended commitment to the expenses involved in the physical treatment of the fragments and their description. For their part, the potential donors were troubled by what they regarded as the priority given to Arabic over Hebrew in the University and the failure of the Hebraists to give sufficient attention to rabbinic Hebrew. Taylor also pressed for some remuneration for Schechter in consideration of his work on the Genizah Collection. Ultimately, Schechter was appointed Curator in Oriental Literature at the Library but this seems to have been a happy compromise (carefully engineered by Jenkinson not to affect the susceptibilities of either of them) whereby he was not specifically and embarrassingly paid for his Genizah work but nevertheless received extra income from an additional University post of standing. At the same time, Taylor and Schechter did not quite see eye to eye about making the manuscripts available to other scholars. Taylor had always been generous in this connection and although Schechter had been among the recipients of his generosity, he remained more possessive about his rights to exclusive research on particular fragments. He had no problem about the special Syriac and Arabic areas that were being covered by his Cambridge colleagues, or about leaving matters of Hebrew Bible vocalization to Paul Kahle, but was anxious to maintain control of such items as the Ben Sira texts. He also wished to reserve the right to borrow items from the Collection. When the formal document was placed before the University for its approval in June, 1898, it reflected these various considerations and one can still detect the lack of unanimity in the views of those responsible for drawing it up, as well as a rather optimistic view of how long it would take to describe the fragments. It was, however, ratified and became the basis for later developments:

> The conditions upon which the Collection is offered to the University are the following:

1. That the MSS. be kept in the University Library as a separate collection, to be called by some such name as the Taylor-Schechter collection from the Genizah of Old Cairo.
2. That the thanks of the University be given to the heads of the Jewish community in Cairo, with whose consent the MSS. were brought to England.
3. That the collection be not used without the consent of the donors for three years from the date of its acceptance by the University.
4. That Dr Schechter have the right to borrow MSS., of which facsimiles are not accessible, from the collection on giving a receipt to the Librarian for them.
5. That the University undertake to make such provision as is possible by binding, mounting, or otherwise for the preservation of the MSS., and to have them sorted, and a handlist or catalogue of them drawn up, within ten years from the acceptance of the collection.
6. That the fragments of Ecclesiasticus and those with Greek writing remain in the possession of the donors until after they have brought out complete editions of them.

It is explained in a covering letter from Dr Taylor to the Vice-Chancellor, with regard to the sixth condition, that it is intended that the fragments therein referred to would remain in the possession of the donors for two or three years.

The Syndicate are of the opinion that the Collection is of unique value, and they greatly desire that it should be secured for the Library. With a view to the fulfilment of the fifth condition they are prepared to undertake the cost of binding, mounting, and preserving the Collection; but they could not make provision out of the funds at their disposal for sorting and cataloguing the MSS. They are of opinion that for the latter purpose the sum of £500 would suffice; and they have been informed by the Vice-Chancellor that in the event of the Collection becoming the property of the University, the Council of the Senate will be prepared to recommend to the Senate that this sum be placed at the disposal of the Library Syndicate for the purpose of obtaining expert assistance in classifying and making a catalogue of the Collection

THE UNIVERSITY SAYS THANKS

It was at the same time agreed that formal documents thanking Taylor and Schechter, as well as the heads of the Jewish community in Cairo, should be sent by the University in due course. Accordingly, the University Orator's address of 15 December, 1898, thanking Schechter

91

אנשי ועד בית מדרש החכמות הכולל אשר בעיר קמבריניא
לאנשי שם ראשי חבר היהודים השוכנים בעיר מצרים שלומכם ירבה וישגה.

אנשי שם וקריאי העדה.

בנפש חפיצה הננו מגישים לכם את תודתינו לא לבד על אשר קבלתם בסבר
פנים יפות את המורה שלנו בספרת חכמי הרבנים בבואו אליכם אך גם על החסר
הרב. אשר עשיתם עמדי בהרשותכם אותו לשוב אלינו וידיו נשואות שרידי ספרים
למכביר המוצאים מבתי הגניזות אשר לכם. משמרת הקדש אשר בה שמרתם את יתר
הפליטה של הבת"י שלכם לעד היא כי משל הקדמוני "דבר שבכתב קיים" כמו חק היה
בישראל. מעם החק הזה הנשמר מאז בתוככם היתה נסבה כי מקרוב מעט שלכם על
יד נייר פישון. אשר העמיד שם לבחירי הסופרים יותר מאלף שנם. שמעו יצא בגוים
זה זמן כביר. ואנחנו תפלה כי לא יחדל לנצח. אמנם עני עדתכם צופיות ברגש קודש
להעת היותר עתיקה אשר בה הביע חוזה יה לאמר. ביום ההוא יהיה מזבח ליהוה בתוך
ארץ מצרים ומצבה אצל גבולה ליהוה : והיה לאות ולעד ליהוה צבאות בארץ מצרים :
ובכן טובי עין הנדחים בארץ מצרים תבורכו בכלל ישראל מברכותינו לארך שנים על הטובה
אשר גמלתם אותנו. הלא היא כתובה על ספר משלות להמלך החכם מכל האדם. יש
מפזר ונוסף עוד : באמונה על ידי צדקת פורוניכם אשר עשיתם עם ציר שלוח מאתנו
בתתכם לו מספריכם העתיקים יספתם על שמועתכם הטובה הנודעת מימי עולם. אך
גם צדקתכם זאת תוסיף דעת לדורשי קדמוניות ספרתכם. כי בלי ספק אף מאים
רחוקים האלה אחרי אחרי דרך מבא השמש אור מצער יסוב לאחור ויאיר פני ספרתכם. אשר
בעת מעלה על לבנו יקר תפארתה מימי קדם. נפשנו יודעת מאד כי גם עתה יאמנו
דברי החכם כי "ממזרח יחלק אור". ובכן. יהי שם יהוה מברך מעתה ועד עולם : ממזרח
שמש עד מבואו מהלל שם יהוה :

קמברינא
ב' טבת תרנ"ט לפ"ק.

---

23 – Hebrew translation of the Latin letter of thanks from the University of
Cambridge to the Jewish community of Cairo, 1898 (Cambridge University
Archives at the University Library)

on behalf of the University of Cambridge for his part in obtaining and
presenting the Cairo Genizah Collection to that institution was formally
despatched to him on 21 December, in the original Latin, duly "engrossed
and sealed", by the University Registrary, Mr J. W. Clark, no doubt at
the same time as an equivalent letter went to the Master of St. John's
College. Schechter's letter was accompanied by a handwritten note from
Clark, promising that a Hebrew version would later be appended to the
similar Latin letter sent to the Cairo Jewish community, once it had been

engrossed, and the community's address had been established. It seems that Schechter was responsible for the Hebrew translation but the assumption of Schechter's biographer, Norman Bentwich, that there was, in addition to the Latin and Hebrew texts, an official English version for the Cairo Jewish community seems unjustified. He probably had in mind the English translations of the three Latin documents from the Senate of the University of Cambridge that appeared in the *Jewish Chronicle* of 30 December, 1898, and that make interesting reading:

TO THE REV CHARLES TAYLOR

That a great number of Hebrew manuscripts found in Egypt have lately been added to our library, we owe in a very large measure to you. And, indeed, you in particular were the patron of the undertaking by which those manuscripts were found and brought to us. You, by a singular munificence, rendered the journey of our Reader in Rabbinic not only easy but agreeable. By your liberality and that of the discoverer, about 40,000 fragments of manuscripts have been presented to us, among which have been found the oldest extant example of Hebrew writing the age of which can be accurately defined; the remains of Aquila's literal translation of the Old Testament into Greek, which prove the accuracy of Origen and St. Jerome; and the Hebrew source of many chapters of the book of Ecclesiasticus, not unknown to St. Jerome, and anxiously desired by the learned until two years ago. All these, which are better known to you than to ourselves, excite no little hope that in so ample a treasure even other things worthy of mention will at a future time be found. Meanwhile to borrow the language of the book whose antique source has lately been discovered, we know there is a gift that shall not profit, and there is a gift whose recompense is double. Your gift, which is most useful to the learned, we confess we cannot recompense by aught within our power. Nevertheless, for your liberality to us we express and feel the greatest gratitude.

TO SOLOMON SCHECHTER

We congratulate you that you divined with singular sagacity that there was a treasure of Hebrew manuscripts hidden in Egypt; that near the Egyptian capital you found at once the hiding-place and the tomb of so many scrolls; that you rescued so immense, so varied a number of books, as it were warring with each other in the darkness; and that bringing them to light not without labour, not without the dust of battle, you added to the peaceful shelves of our library the spoils of your history. We congratulate ourselves, too, that by reason of your and others' liberality, so great a gift, so various, obtained with so much toil by you, expected with so much hope by the learned, has been offered on such favourable terms to us. We hope that when the varied assemblage of manuscripts has been at length brought into order and indexed, more light will daily be thrown on ancient literature. Among the sayings of your fathers it is said, that "the day is short, but the work is great, and much the wage" [Mishnah, *Avot* 2:15]; it is also said that "thou art not permitted to complete the work alone, neither art thou at liberty to leave it unfinished." [Mishnah, *Avot* 2:16] Let all who will ever be associated with you in exploring the treasure found by you, see that in searching for the truth they emulate your indomitable patience and remember the ancient precept as to the getting of Wisdom, the source of which you yourself have found: – "Search and examine, seek and find; and hold her fast, and let her not go." [Ben Sira 6:27] Whatever truth shall be found in future in so great a treasure, the name of the finder shall remain inscribed on the grateful tablets of our heart.

TO THE HEADS OF THE JEWISH COMMUNITY IN CAIRO

We offer you our thanks, not only on account of the singular goodwill with which you received our Reader in Rabbinic, but also on account of the conspicuous liberality with which you permitted him to return to us laden with so many fragments of books from your Treasury. In the faithful preservation of books the saying, "the written word remains," seems to have been as a law to you. On account of this law so long observed by you, your sanctuary, called by the name of the greatest of the scribes, the sanctuary which has been celebrated for more than a thousand years on the shore of the Nile, remains, and will long remain famous. But your congregation regards with reverence the still older words of the prophet [Isaiah 19:19–20], "In that day shall there be an altar to the Lord in the midst of the land of Egypt, and a pillar of the border thereof to the Lord, and it shall be for a sign and for a witness unto the Lord of Hosts in the land of Egypt." Therefore for your generosity to us, in the midst of the land of Egypt may your people be blessed for ages. Is it not also written in the Proverbs of the Wise King [Proverbs 11:24]: "There is that scattereth and yet increaseth"? By the generous gift of your ancient books to our envoy you have not only increased your own ancient renown but have even made a considerable addition to the history of your ancient literature. Even from our islands so far to the West, some light will doubtless be shed upon your literature, whereof, in memory of its ancient glory, we joyfully confess that day cometh from the East [Psalms 113:2–3]: "Blessed be the name of the Lord from this time forth and for evermore – From the rising of the sun to the going down of the same praised be the name of the Lord."

It has sometimes been quipped that two scholarly tragedies occurred in the life of Schechter. The first was when he discovered the Genizah and had to spend so much time working on these time-consuming documents rather than concentrating on his studies of rabbinic theology and his editions of talmudic texts. The second was when he chose to leave Cambridge and the Genizah and to devote the remaining thirteen years of his life to the reconstruction of the Jewish Theological Seminary in New York. He continued to publish what he had researched in Cambridge and to arrange for others also to do so but never again had the opportunity of such concentrated study of the fragments as he had undertaken between 1897 and 1902. He himself explains the reasons for his decision in a letter written to his friend, Herbert Bentwich, on 24 December, 1901:

> I have to tell you that I have definitely accepted the New York offer and that I have also given notice to the various institutions with which I was connected in England to take effect at the beginning of the Easter term. It was with a heavy heart that I have taken this step, but it had to be done for the sake of my family, and perhaps also for the sake of Judaism with which the future rests. Excepting you and Dr. Adler I saw no particular eagerness in the community to keep me in England. I could not bear the idea of taking money from private individuals any longer.

Whether his decision was a wise one or not, Solomon Schechter left England in the spring of 1902 and set sail for America. He did not quite leave behind the Genizah Collection since very soon afterwards 251 fragments that he had arranged to borrow joined him in New York, with every indication, soon to be proved mistaken, that they would within a short time be sent back to Cambridge.

—
—

Guide to reading

Those Genizah fragments that came to Cambridge separately from the collection presented by Taylor and Schechter bear a classmark that is prefixed with "Add." or "Or." It is possible to identify them, and those such as Chester and Wertheimer who presented or sold them to the University Library, by consulting the various indexes in S. C. Reif, *Hebrew Manuscripts at Cambridge University Library: A Description and Introduction* (Cambridge, 1997). Information on Greville Chester is fairly sparse but there are some details in J. Foster, *Alumni Oxonienses*, later series, vol. I (Oxford, 1888), p. 244;

Crockford's Clerical Directory for 1892 (London, 1892), p. 244; and the *Balliol College Register 1833–1933*, ed. I. Elliott (Oxford, 1934), p. 5. There is also considerable scope for a close study of Wertheimer. His family in Israel have various oral traditions about him and his work but the little that is published is available in the *Encyclopaedia Judaica* 16 (Jerusalem, 1972), col. 459 and in the booklet *Ktav Yad Ve-Sefer Institute* (Jerusalem, 1990). Some of the binders with Genizah material under the classmark Or.1080 at Cambridge University Library also contain original correspondence between Wertheimer and the Library.

The work done by Schechter and Singer on the talmudic Genizah fragments in Oxford was published in their volume *Talmudical Fragments in the Bodleian Library* (Cambridge, 1896) and the details of the controversy between Schechter and Margoliouth have been chronicled in S. C. Reif, "The Discovery of the Cambridge Genizah Fragments of Ben Sira: Scholars and Texts" in *The Book of Ben Sira in Modern Research. Proceedings of the First International Ben Sira Conference 28–31 July 1996, Soesterberg, Netherlands*, ed. P. C. Beentjes (Berlin–New York, 1997), pp. 1–22. The Margoliouth family was remarkable not only for converting to Christianity but for the leaders it provided for the missionary movement. General information is to be found in W. T. Gidney, *The History of the London Society for Promoting Christianity among the Jews, from 1809 to 1908* (London, 1908), pp. 16–17, 216, 247, 281, 399, 534–35 and 626 and in David S. Katz, *The Jews in the History of England* (Oxford, 1994), pp. 379–80, and there is more detailed coverage of D. S. Margoliouth in G. Murray's obituary in *Proceedings of the British Academy* 36 (London, 1940), pp. 389–97. His inaugural lecture as Oxford's Laudian Professor of Arabic was published as *An Essay on the Place of Ecclesiasticus in Semitic Literature* (Oxford, 1890) and was followed very quickly by Schechter's article "The Quotations from Ecclesiasticus in Rabbinic Literature", *Jewish Quarterly Review* 3 (1891), pp. 682–706.

Mrs Lewis and Mrs Gibson seem to have been consistently aware of the historical importance of their activities since they so often produced written accounts of aspects of these. The adventures leading up to and including the Ben Sira discovery are recounted in A. S. Lewis, *In the Shadow of Sinai: A Story of Travel and Research from 1895 to 1897* (Cambridge, 1898), especially pp. 172–78. The underlying tensions and the scholarly competition between Oxford and Cambridge become apparent from reading between the lines in the introductory essays of the two, opposing teams, as appear in A. E. Cowley and A. Neubauer, *The Original Hebrew of a Portion of Ecclesiasticus (XXXIX.15 to XLIX.11), together with the early Versions and an English Translation, followed by the Quotations from Ben Sira in Rabbinical Literature* (Oxford, 1897) and S. Schechter and C. Taylor, *The Wisdom of Ben Sira: Portions of the Book Ecclesiasticus from Hebrew Manuscripts in the Cairo Genizah Collection presented to the University of Cambridge by the Editors* (Cambridge, 1899), as well as their *Facsimiles of the Fragments hitherto recovered of the Book of Ecclesiasticus in Hebrew* (Oxford and Cambridge, 1901). On Bentwich's trip, see Margery and Norman Bentwich, *Herbert Bentwich: The Pilgrim Father* (Jerusalem, 1940), p. 105.

The most "official" account of Schechter's trip to Cairo is the one published by him in *The Times* of 3 August, 1897 and reproduced as the first part of "A Hoard of Hebrew Manuscripts" in the second series of his collected essays *Studies in Judaism* (Philadelphia–London, 1908), pp. 1–11, augmented by Norman Bentwich's treatment of that journey of discovery in the fifth chapter of his *Solomon Schechter. A Biography* (Philadelphia, 1938), pp. 126–35. There is also helpful guidance to the Cairo community of the day in Jacob Landau's *Jews in Nineteenth-Century Egypt* (New York, 1969), translated from the Hebrew original published in Jerusalem two years earlier. More personal impressions and less discreet revelations come to the surface in the correspondence involving Solomon and Mathilde Schechter, Francis Jenkinson, Mrs Lewis and Mrs Gibson, and Charles Taylor located in the manuscript collections at Cambridge University Library, indexed under these names, and in the Schechter archive at the Library of the Jewish Theological Seminary of America in New York.

These manuscripts are utilized and cited by S. C. Reif in "Jenkinson and Schechter at Cambridge: An Expanded and Updated Assessment", *Transactions of the Jewish Historical Society of England* 32 (1993), pp. 279–316, and that same article details the relationship between these two personalities and the manner in which their interaction contributed significantly to the early Cambridge work on its Genizah Collection. The results of that work may be traced in the various reports of the Library Syndicate that appear (and are indexed) in the official *Cambridge University Reporter* for these years and that same source provides the details of the gift made by Taylor and Schechter, as well as the letters of thanks sent to them and to the Cairo Jewish community. The researches of Taylor and Burkitt on the Greek texts overwritten by later Hebrew (that is, the palimpsests) resulted in F. C. Burkitt, *Fragments of the Books of Kings according to the Translation of Aquila* (Cambridge, 1897), and C. Taylor, *Hebrew-Greek Genizah Palimpsests from the Taylor-Schechter Collection* (Cambridge, 1900). That there was a less generous side to Schechter's scholarly efforts is suggested and documented in a forthcoming article by S. C. Reif in the Hebrew volume *Teʿuda* 15 being edited by M. A. Friedman and to be published in 1999 by Tel Aviv University, with the translated English title "The Cambridge Genizah Story: Some Unfamiliar Aspects".

FIVE

WHOLLY FOR BIBLE

Those with an interest in the Hebrew Bible are of course keen to understand how that remarkable source of religious inspiration was used and interpreted by the Jews at various points in their history. In meeting that aim, they have been greatly assisted by the discovery of two outstanding caches of such documents, the first made fifty years ago, and the second a century ago. The scrolls from the Judean desert near the Dead Sea shed light on many of the religious ideas and customs of Jewish groups in the years leading up to the destruction of the Second Temple in 70 c.e. during which time Christianity and Rabbinic Judaism were taking form. Their relevance to the history of biblical texts and their meaning has consequently been discussed in many publications, popular as well as academic. The thousands of manuscript fragments from the Cairo Genizah, though dating from almost a thousand years later, are equally important for our understanding of equivalent developments in the early medieval period. In the case of these fragments, strangely enough, many fewer books and articles have concerned themselves with what may be learnt from them about attitudes to the Hebrew Bible through the ages. Recently, however, all manner of questions have been asked about these manuscript treasures and there is a growing awareness of the significance of their stained, worn and crumpled folios for various aspects of biblical study.

THE TEXT AS WRITTEN, POINTED AND READ

What emerges from the latest international studies in this field relates not only to the content of the fragments but also to the manner in which the text was transmitted over the centuries. It is becoming clear that from the ninth century onwards professional Jewish scribes made significant advances with their techniques and that this had a major impact on the quality and consistency of the scrolls publicly read in the synagogue and

24 – Hebrew Bible text with masoretic notes in designs (T-S A2.7) (Cambridge University Library)

on the early development of the biblical Hebrew codex used in other less formal contexts. Differences in the physical forms of early and late Genizah material demonstrate clearly that the technical details of Hebrew Bible production were of increasing importance to Jewish custom. As far as the synagogal scroll is concerned, initial opposition by the oriental rabbinic authorities to the format used for sacred Arabic texts gradually gave way to its adoption. The methods used, which included soaking in water and lime rather than tanning, and were probably influenced by European techniques, produced a better quality of split skin. Initial examination of the Genizah evidence appears to confirm an increasing preference for the improved product.

With regard to the codex, used for purposes other than that of the synagogue ritual, the simple, even primitive folios and codices gradually gave way to altogether more elaborate and systematically produced volumes. A whole range of scribal techniques evolved, qualities of vellum began to be differentiated, and paper began to challenge the place of vellum as the primary material for the transcription of texts. Standards of illustration and illumination did not match what was to be found among the Christians but did gradually improve, making use not only of the more oriental style of micrography but also of art forms that were more typical of the west. The private and public libraries that began to spring up in North Africa, including Egypt, as early as the ninth and tenth centuries, included numerous examples of biblical texts, as well as of works relating to biblical interpretation, and there are accounts of parents buying their children biblical texts for study and benefactors purchasing such items for presentation to the community. The synagogue of Palestinian Jews in Fustat did indeed boast of its fine biblical codices and there are references to the need to repair some scrolls.

As far as the consonantal text and its layout are concerned (that is, without regard to the vowels), it is not surprising to find that most of the Genizah texts may be linked to one or other of the major medieval codices that served as models for copyists, such as those of Aleppo, St. Petersburg (Leningard) and Cairo, and that the variations, though certainly important for the specialist in textual criticism, are not therefore substantial in number or significance. Some are valuable and reflect genuine differences in readings, while others are simply the result of careless or unprofessional copying, so that they must all be individually evaluated. Where major discoveries and novel historical assessments have, however, been made has been in the area of the pointing systems used to indicate how the vowels were to be pronounced in readings texts from the Hebrew Bible.

It is now clear that the standard Tiberian system followed in the tenth century by Aaron ben Moses Ben-Asher, so sanctified since the period of late manuscripts and early prints by both tradition and scholarship, and so familiar to every current reader of Hebrew, was not unique. It was rather one of a number of such systems that were in vogue throughout the Jewish world from the period of the earliest systematic Masoretic activity (see below), say in the eighth and ninth centuries, until their almost total replacement by the standard system some five or six hundred years later. Three major systems, one supralinear Palestinian, one sublinear Tiberian, and one supralinear Babylonian are clearly documented and combinations of the various systems were also devised in an effort to create a more sophisticated reflection and record of the manner in which Hebrew vowels were pronounced. Such variant systems did

eventually give way to the Ben-Asher method before the invention of printing and that method was "codified" in the Bible produced by Jacob ben Ḥayyim and published by Daniel Bomberg in Venice in 1524–25. Nevertheless, remnants of non-standard vocalization systems may still be found in non-biblical Hebrew texts throughout the sixteenth century.

It is of course self-evident that the earliest history of traditions concerning the pronunciation and transmission of the Hebrew Bible must go back to the biblical period itself. There is clearly no way that the earliest Jews could have read Hebrew without orally attaching vowels to it. The talmudic rabbis too spoke of authoritative versions of both the text and the manner of reading it and followed a number of principles concerning the explanation of textual curiosities and their utilization in rabbinic interpretation. The definition and recording of vowel-points as such seems, however, to be a development of about the seventh century. Whether inspired by the use of points in Syriac Christian texts, by Muslim concern for the accuracy of the Qur'an, or by an internal feud with the Karaite Jews who preferred the biblical to the rabbinic traditions, a novel attention to the accurate recording of the vocalized text of the Hebrew Bible created a whole new field of Jewish learning, among both Karaites and Rabbanites.

The Genizah evidence is not early enough to shed light on the initial stages of such scholarship but it does contribute generously to our knowledge of its subsequent expansion. Schools of Masoretes (from the Hebrew root *msr* meaning "to count" and then "to transmit") flourished in the two main centres of Jewish population, Palestine and Babylon, and made it their task to surround the text of the Hebrew Bible with vowel-points that reflected their pronunciation tradition; with cantillation signs that recorded the melodies used for its synagogal chant; and with explanatory notes that inevitably testified to their understanding of the text, whether inherited or newly fashioned. Such a trend towards the canonization of an aspect of liturgical expression may well have owed a good deal to the formalization of synagogal procedures that was characteristic of developments in the geonic period, between the ninth and eleventh centuries.

Although much of the impetus for such specialized biblical study came from the biblical scholars among the Karaites, both they and the Rabbanites were active in the Masoretic process. It is indeed not always an easy matter to distinguish which of the famous personalities associated with the early history of the Masorah belonged to one group and which to the other. What is clear is that the Genizah discoveries have put us in a better position to understand the identifying features of each method and the basic differences between the various schools. Treatises and scholars, hitherto unknown or given scant recognition in later manuscripts, have been more clearly identified and new sets of vocabulary and terminology have been uncovered. Such an interest in the text read and translated before the congregation in the synagogue naturally had an effect not only on exegesis (as will shortly be noted), but also on the development of Hebrew philological studies. Once texts and their interpretation became more consistent and authoritative, the way was open for comparisons to be made by keen linguists of the features of the various Semitic languages known to them. It hardly required a genius to see a connection between Hebrew *rosh*, Aramaic *resh* and Arabic *ra's*, all meaning "head", and to make similar sense of many hundreds of such examples. Grammatical rules were consequently drawn up, text-books and dictionaries compiled, and the literal interpretation of the biblical verse given a boost by such systematic approaches. It should not be forgotten that such grammatical and philological studies provided the foundations on which was built much of the translation and interpretation of the Hebrew Bible, by both Christians and Jews, in the later medieval and modern times.

In the earliest years of Genizah research, now over a century ago, the discovery of the Palestinian triennial cycle for both the pentateuchal and prophetic weekly readings generated great excitement. Having identified a system that took over three years to complete the reading of the Pentateuch rather than one, and was used in the Holy Land rather than in Babylon, experts in the field believed that they were now in a position to reconstruct what precisely had been read in the synagogue on particular sabbaths of the year from as early as the time of Jesus. Attempts were therefore made to relate the sermons of both the New Testament and the rabbinic midrashim to the Palestinian cycle and to establish the precise time of the year in which it commenced. The truth is, however, that such attempts are not convincingly supported by the evidence. More recent work has therefore moved away from such theories and demonstrated that the primary sources bear witness not to one Palestinian cycle of readings, and one Babylonian, but to a number of possible variations in Eretz Yisrael and to the possibility that each influenced the other from the talmudic to the medieval period. Although the Babylonian cycle as it emerged from the Iraqi talmudic centres in and around the tenth century came to dominate Jewish synagogal practice worldwide, its victory was not so easily or swiftly achieved. The reports of the traveller Benjamin of Tudela in the twelfth century and Genizah material from the thirteenth testify to the continuing struggle waged by the community of Palestinian emigrés in Cairo to maintain their own traditions and to withstand the pressure to conform to the customs of the Babylonian academies. The relevant section of Benjamin's itinerary, as translated in the edition of Marcus Nathan Adler, describes two of the Cairo synagogues and their customs:

> Two large synagogues are there, one belonging to the men of the land of Israel and one belonging to the men of the land of Babylon. The synagogue of the men of the land of Israel is called Kenisat-al-Schamiyyin, and the synagogue of the men of Babylon is called Kenisat-al-Irakiyyin. Their usage with regard to the portions and sections of the Law is not alike; for the men of Babylon are accustomed to read a portion every week, as is done in Spain, and is our custom, and to finish the Law each year; whilst the men of Palestine do not do so, but divide each portion into three sections and finish the Law at the end of three years. The two communities, however, have an established custom to unite and pray together on the day of the Rejoicing of the Law, and on the day of the Giving of the Law.

25 – Palimpsest showing 10th-century Hebrew poetry imposed on 6th-century Greek translation of the Bibl
(T-S 20.50) (Cambridge University Library)

SYRIAC AND GREEK OVERWRITTEN

It is not, however, only the liturgical traditions of the synagogue that are represented in the Genizah Collection since Syriac and Greek versions are to be found there, albeit lurking under later Hebrew texts in a number of palimpsests ("writing material on which an earlier text has been erased and replaced by a later one") dating back as early as the fifth or sixth century. Those redoubtable women who inspired Schechter's trip to Cairo and then worked enthusiastically with him on sorting his finds at Cambridge University Library, Mrs Agnes Lewis and Mrs Margaret Gibson, were given responsibility for the Syriac texts and edited thirty-four of these. They count among the earliest set of Palestinian (and one Edessene) texts of the Syriac Bible, covering four books each in the Old and New Testaments. Quite how they came to be used by rabbinic Jews as second-hand writing material, on which they could record their legal, homiletical and poetic compositions, is an intriguing question. Did Muslims capture Christian monasteries and sell the contents of their libraries to Jews as scrap? Were there Christian converts to Judaism who brought their religious texts with them into their new communities, to be used for the promotion of their adopted faith? Or was used vellum and paper simply available in the scribal market? The problem awaits its solution until further evidence is uncovered.

Other palimpsests dating from between the fifth and ninth centuries contain Greek texts of the Gospels, Acts and 1 Peter, of Origen's *Hexapla* on Psalms 22 and of Aquila's renderings of parts of Psalms 90–103 and Kings. Aquila's version, written in the second century probably under the influence of Rabbi Akiva, was profoundly literal, no doubt for good theological reasons, and was widely used by Jewish communities in the Greek-speaking diaspora; hence its inclusion in the columns of the *Hexapla*, originally compiled by the Church Father, Origen, in the third Christian century and recording the Hebrew and Greek texts of the Bible. Since the Genizah fragments are derived from an independent text of Aquila and not from the *Hexapla* and have been dated to the fifth or sixth century, it is possible to regard them as evidence that these Jewish communities continued to use his version until the conquest of the Near East by the Arabs in the seventh century and the subsequent linguistic takeover of the area by Arabic. On the other hand, unless such Jewish communities were more theologically liberal than has hitherto been supposed, the presence of palimpsests of New Testament texts is again perhaps more convincingly explained as the result of the acquisition by

Jews (through Muslims?) of second-hand writing material from Christian sources. The nearest Jewish Aramaic equivalent to Aquila is the authoritative and synagogal translation ascribed to a contemporary of his, the proselyte Onqelos. Whether or not Aquila is, as has sometimes been suggested, identical with Onqelos, is not clarified by the Genizah texts, but they do have much to add to our knowledge of the development of that popular genre of Aramaic translation known simply as *targum*.

TRANSLATIONS AND INTERPRETATIONS

Numerous examples of the Onqelos, Jonathan, Palestinian and fragmentary targums that were widely used in the post-talmudic centuries are to be found and are naturally important for the textual (and perhaps pre-textual) history of these versions. It is, however, in the area of more diverse targumic material that surprising discoveries are still being made. Some items are directly related to festivals or other special occasions and to the relevant synagogal readings from the Bible, while another variety constitutes homiletic expansions often inserted into Onqelos texts. One genre provides poems on themes such as the death of Moses, the praiseworthiness of Jonathan ben Uzziel or indeed, as in the following Genizah text, translated by Michael Klein, the glories of the month of Nisan (with an opening word that is an Aramaic version of the Greek *eleson*):

> O save us! How glorious is this month, in which fathers and sons were redeemed.
> At midnight, the Lord was revealed, and His right hand was spread over Israel.
> The mighty of the Egyptians became a ruin, because they had enslaved the people.

In addition, there are texts that abbreviate Onqelos, provide Masorah for the same version, offer a Judaeo-Arabic translation of Palestinian targum, or incorporate interpretations of verses that run counter to the Jewish religious law found in the Talmud. Sometimes, a collection of targums reflects a particular lectionary cycle – pentateuchal or prophetic – which may turn out to be novel for records of either Babylonian or Palestinian traditions. A recently published description of the targumic manuscripts in the Cambridge Genizah Collection lists over 1,600 items, dating from the ninth to the fourteenth century, and this would indicate the likelihood that there are from Cairo, in the various Genizah collections around the world, well over 2,000 pieces of targum. Since it may confidently be asserted that these are generally older than any other manuscript attestations to medieval targumic traditions, they must by definition be of profound significance to the latter's textual as well as exegetical study.

The custom of translating the Hebrew Bible into Aramaic was an ancient one, prescribed by Jewish religious law (*halakhah*), and one that had acquired a significance above and beyond its linguistic usefulness. It was therefore not abandoned when Arabic replaced Aramaic and Greek as the predominant Jewish vernacular but was incorporated with an Arabic rendering into a trilingual version. Such Judaeo-Arabic renderings of the biblical readings, written in Hebrew characters and reflecting the popular Arabic dialect of the Jewish communities, appear to have come into existence at least as early as the ninth century. They provided the inspiration for the tenth-century leader of the Babylonian Jewish community, the Egyptian scholar Saʿadya ben Joseph of Fayyum (882–942), to compose his own Judaeo-Arabic version, the text and spelling of which were destined to become the standard translation for the oriental Jewish communities for the remainder of the medieval period. But Saʿadya was not only a translator of the Hebrew Bible; he also composed a commentary, more and more of which has recently come to light and has demonstrated how, as a philosopher, he struggled to rationalize much of Scripture but without overdoing the degree of literalness. The exegetical work of his successor as head of the Sura *yeshivah*, Samuel ben Ḥofni, has also been rescued from the Genizah and is characterized by his desire to impose systems of classification on his treatment of the biblical texts.

Of other exegetical material in Hebrew and Arabic from that same Egyptian source, some is extended, some brief. There are commentaries that make use of the latest syntactical and philological theories while others prefer traditional midrashic methods. Philosophy inspires one expounder of Scripture, kabbalah another. New discoveries reveal for the first time how scholars such as Judah ibn Balaam and Moses ibn Gikatilla handled difficult verses from the Hebrew Bible in the intellectual atmosphere of eleventh-century Spain. By then, the tensions between the literal and applied senses of Scripture had grown and the cause of the former was then carried forward in Spain and France, while the latter tended to recover an honoured place as the situation of Jews in the Orient deteriorated after the period of the Fatimid dynasty.

The move towards the literal interpretation had been championed by the Karaites, whose linguistic interest and textual orientation in the golden age of their biblical studies in tenth and eleventh century Jerusalem led to a high level of lexical and syntactical exegesis. Suspicious as they were of the rabbinic traditions, they produced their own word-for-word translations, alternate renderings, and interpretations, amounting to what a recent researcher has defined as "scientific literalism". There is no doubt that the Karaites and Rabbanites exercised both positive and negative influences on each other and that the Rabbanites were torn between a desire to steal the copyright of the devil's best tunes and the need to avoid betraying what they saw as the authentic nature of the talmudic-midrashic interpretation of Scripture. The Karaites too were not without their polemical intent, as is indicated by the strange phenomenon of surviving folios of their Bibles from Palestine and Egypt in the eleventh and twelfth centuries that record the text of the Hebrew Bible in Arabic characters with Hebrew vowel-points. According to one plausible theory, such an idiosyncratic system was employed as a means of retaining an independent religious identity in the face of Rabbanite influence and incursion. That being the case, one wonders precisely what kind of religious identity is presupposed by the existence of texts of the Qur'an written in the Arabic language but in Hebrew script. Had they been prepared by converted Jews anxious to bring others to know and embrace Islam? Were they transcribed in that

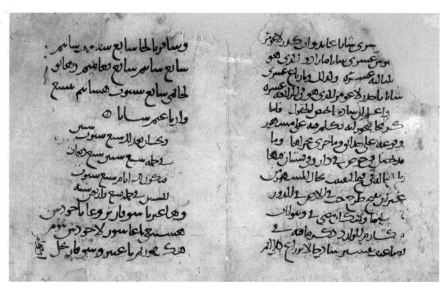

26 – Biblical Hebrew text written in Arabic characters (T-S Ar.41.18)
(Cambridge University Library)

way so that Jews could respond theologically to their content and in that way defend their own religious stance? Was the culture of the day simply broad enough to encourage the understanding of another faith? Other strange combinations of languages that occur in the Genizah include Judaeo-Greek, Judaeo-Persian, Judaeo-Spanish and Judaeo-German and a number of texts in these Jewish dialects written in Hebrew characters testify to the manner in which their speakers understood and approached the Hebrew Bible.

No less strange is the phenomenon of a scholar of the Hebrew Bible who was in a sense a whole millennium ahead of his time in his scepticism about its authenticity and reliability. The communal origins of the ninth century Bible critic, Ḥiwi al-Balkhi, are yet to be established but even before the discovery of the Genizah his searching questions about the Bible were known from their citation in the work of Scripture's defenders. God's characteristics seem totally unimpressive, the Bible's religious ideas are unreasonable and not truly monotheistic, and there is much inconsistency in the commandments and the stories. From Genizah fragments, the rabbinic response to these attacks as composed by Sa'adya Gaon has been reconstructed and demonstrates just how seriously the challenge was taken. It was clearly part of a wider tendency in the Islamic, Christian and Jewish world of the day to call into question the religious ideas and literature of the three major religions, a tendency that is remarkably "liberal" and "modern" and that clearly disturbed the spiritual mentors of the various faiths.

MIDRASHIM

Rabbinic commentaries on the Bible, or midrashim, are greatly varied in their ideological intent and their literary structure, as well as in their geographical and chronological origins. What they all have in common is that they represent in one way or another important links in the historical chain of Jewish commentary on the Hebrew Bible. It is therefore not surprising that contemporary understanding of the development of such a significant rabbinic genre in the post-talmudic period also owes much to Genizah research. Hitherto, the earliest manuscripts were medieval, from the early periods of major Jewish settlement in European countries, while now there are thousands of fragments written at a much earlier date in the oriental countries from which such literature emerged, and representing older textual traditions. Such traditions are more likely to preserve the authentic form of the midrash since later editions and copyists tended to treat anything unusual as erroneous and to harmonize it with what had already become standard or authoritative for them. While such a statement may be made about all the well-known midrashim of the "classical" talmudic period, for which the Genizah provides useful textual variants, it is especially true of the halakhic midrashim dating from then, such as the *Mekhilta of Rabbi Ishmael* on Exodus, *Sifra* on Leviticus and *Sifrey* on Numbers and Deuteronomy, the original halakhic statements of which were not always permitted to survive. Halakhic midrashim for which no complete codices survive have also surfaced in the Genizah collections and considerably expanded the horizons of the Hebrew literary historian. Fragments have been identified of the *Mekhilta of Rabbi Shim'on bar Yoḥai* on Exodus, of the *Sifrey Zuṭah* on Numbers and of the *Mekhilta* on Deuteronomy, and these have been or are being exploited for the creation of new scientific editions.

In the standard aggadic (non-legal) field too, discoveries of new midrashim, particularly of the *Tanḥuma Yelammedenu* homiletical variety on the Pentateuch and of the exegetical treatments of the hagiographical books such as Proverbs and Ecclesiastes, have added greatly to our knowledge of developments during the post-talmudic and early medieval ages. At the same time, the identification of new anthologies from the last period of midrashic activity have demonstrated how use was made of earlier material to build up a Jewish exegetical overview of biblical texts. Here and there, in various midrashic contexts, the Genizah has thrown up previously unknown interpretations of verses. When, for example, in 1976, Zvi Meir Rabinovitz published a selection of midrashim that he had discovered in the Genizah, he could find no parallel in rabbinic literature for a significant number of them. One of them will suffice for citation and translation here and concerns the comments of David to Saul, after he had spared his life, as narrated in 1 Samuel 24:11–12:

Another interpretation: LOOK, MY FATHER, LOOK CAREFULLY [AT THE CORNER OF YOUR CLOAK THAT I HAD IN MY HAND]: David said to him, "LOOK, if I had fallen into your hand, you would not have shown me such compassion. LOOK CAREFULLY at how you fell into my hand and I showed you compassion. And what was it that led to your being spared? It was the fringe [*ha-ṣiṣit*] that I had in my hand. Instead of saying HE WANTED TO KILL YOU BUT I SHOWED YOU COMPASSION, the scriptural verse [v. 11] says HE WANTED TO KILL YOU BUT *IT* SHOWED YOU COMPASSION [that is, the presence of the *ṣiṣit* encouraged me to show you compassion].

110

27 – Scribal colophon dating from 924 c.e. with a liturgical note (T-S A42.2)
(Cambridge University Library)

Perhaps more important than anything else, there are a whole fresh set of
new or little-known midrashim that testify to the fact that medieval
Jewish interpretation of the Hebrew Bible could be distinctly colourful
and heterogeneous, if not downright weird. Fanciful expansions of
biblical accounts, apocalyptic visions and mystical works were among
the earliest midrashim acquired from the Genizah and quickly published
by such equally colourful personalities as Solomon Wertheimer in
Jerusalem and Moses Gaster in London. As such a variegated approach
to the Bible gave way to the more linguistic and philological
commentaries of the tenth, eleventh and twelfth centuries, so the
written evidence from the Genizah also records the influence of the
centralized Babylonian authorities in inspiring the change. They thereby
achieved their intention of thwarting some of the Karaite efforts to
discredit rabbinic interpretation as lacking the serious, literal dimension.

THE PRACTICAL DIMENSION

Since the Genizah contains not only literary items but also mundane
documentary material, it is not surprising to find fragments relating to
the place of the Hebrew Bible in everyday Jewish life. Since an ability to
read simple biblical and rabbinic Hebrew was a prerequisite for active

participation in synagogal worship, most of the male community was introduced to the Bible at an early age and it was not uncommon to commit lengthy sections to memory. Many were literate enough to employ biblical verses in their correspondence while the more lyrically minded were able to intertwine the Hebrew of the *Tanakh* with its later rabbinic equivalent in the florid introductions that they composed for their various compositions. Some Jews requested rabbinic decisions about the permissibility of recording biblical verses on the *ṭallit* (prayer-shawl), while others were not averse to using the Hebrew Bible as a magical means of predicting the best course of action. Simple texts, sometimes in alphabet primers, were used by children and girls were sometimes educated in the Bible, particularly bright ones becoming teachers of the subject. In one sad little Genizah fragment, a father bewails the loss of such a daughter, recalling her intellect, her knowledge of Torah and her piety, as well as the lessons he used to give her. Items from the Genizah are also significant in writing the history of both the illumination of the Hebrew Bible and the melodies used for chanting it. Incipits and colophons are on occasion colourfully treated in an oriental style while the famous eleventh- and twelfth-century Jewish proselyte from Christianity, the Catholic priest John Oppidans, converted as Obadiah Ha-Ger, took the trouble to record for posterity the music to be used for particular parts of the contemporary Jewish liturgy, including biblical verses. Fragments of incunables and early editions of the printed Hebrew Bible (but not only of the Hebrew Bible), some of them on vellum and others not yet with vowel-points, are another feature, albeit a limited one, of Genizah collections. Many of them represent rare remnants of texts that were produced on the printing presses of Spain and Portugal just before the expulsion of the Jews from the Iberian peninsula and that were among the belongings brought to North Africa and Egypt by refugees from these anti-Semitic persecutions. There is little doubt that the Hebrew Bibles later printed in other countries took some time before they could match the quality of their predecessors.

SURPRISING DISCOVERIES

It remains only to make brief reference to items that are either already widely familiar or are only indirectly related to biblical studies. The recovery of the Hebrew text of Ben Sira or Ecclesiasticus from the Genizah is a well-rehearsed story. The first such fragment to come to light, brought to Cambridge from their travels in Egypt and Palestine by

Mrs Lewis and Mrs Gibson, was enthusiastically identified by Solomon Schechter and acted as a catalyst for his expedition to Cairo and for other identifications elsewhere, particularly in Oxford, London and Paris. Indeed, it is now clear that some such fragments had been retrieved from the Genizah in earlier years and there was considerable competition between various academic institutions, particularly Oxford and Cambridge, in the matter of prior claims and publication. A whole set of fragments, some of them from as early as the tenth century, surfaced in Cambridge during Schechter's initial sorting of his Cairo material and were published by him and Charles Taylor as a new Hebrew edition, followed by a handsome portfolio of facsimiles two years later. In his introduction to their edition, *The Wisdom of Ben Sira*, which appeared in Cambridge in 1899, Taylor told the story of the discovery and had the following remarks to make, substantially still valid, about the importance of the Hebrew Ben Sira for biblical studies:

> By a surprising series of discoveries in recent years, much of the Hebrew of Ecclesiasticus, a book which had been known to the modern world only through Versions and some Rabbinic Quotations, has now again been brought to light. The Revision of the Authorised Version of 1611, undertaken in 1870, having at length been accomplished, it was said in the Preface to the Apocrypha (1895), of the book Ecclesiasticus: "Considerable attention was paid to the text; but the materials available for correcting it were but scanty."...
>
> Ben Sira's book is of unique interest to the scholar and the theologian as a Hebrew work of nearly known date, which forms a link between the Old Testament and the Rabbinic writings. The first step to its right appreciation is to note its discursive use of the ancient Scriptures, and the author's free way of adapting their thoughts and phrases to his purpose. The Hebrew restores allusions which were lost or obscured in the Versions.

If the Genizah evidence was insufficient to prove that there had been an original Hebrew in the second century b.c.e. and that much of it had survived in rabbinic circles, the further work of M. H. Segal and J. Schirmann in the late 1950s and Yadin's discovery soon afterwards at Masada of texts that tallied with the oldest Genizah version completed the process of the book's rehabilitation to the Hebrew literature of the Second Temple period.

A less immediate fame was achieved by the Zadokite Fragment or Damascus Document (= CD). It is greatly to his credit that Schechter

28 – Damascus or Zadokite Document, found in the Genizah 50 years before the discovery of other literature of the Dead Sea (T-S 10K6) (Cambridge University Library)

recognized the importance of the two Genizah manuscripts of this work when little was known about its literary and historical background. On the basis of a close examination of the history, constitution, law, theology and calendar of the sect who wrote it, and some ten years' consideration and discussion of the issues, he was able to offer, in his introduction to *Fragments of a Zadokite Work* (pp. xxv–xxvi), an interesting summary of its significance:

114

We may, then, formulate our hypothesis that our text is constituted of fragments forming extracts from a Zadokite book, known to us chiefly from the writings of [the tenth-century Karaite] Kirkisani. The Sect which it represented, did not however pass for any length of time under the name of Zadokites, but was soon in some way amalgamated with and perhaps also absorbed by the Dosithean Sect, and made more proselytes among the Samaritans than among the Jews, with which former sect it had many points of similarity.

Other students of Jewish history and literature preferred to identify the work as Christian, Karaite or Pharisaic and Schechter's colleague in New York, Louis Ginzberg, opted for a purer and earlier form of Pharisaism than that later familiar to the Rabbis. No scholar was able to place it in its precise historical and theological context until the discovery of the Dead Sea Scrolls exactly fifty years after the arrival of the Genizah pieces in Cambridge. Once fragments of the same work had been identified among the Qumran treasures, it became possible to trace the origin of CD and its use by a sect identified by many as Essene. And now more material has come to the fore from among the Qumran manuscripts that show the Genizah version to be a reliable copy of the earliest texts; a little less than half of an original tract that constituted an admonition and corpus of Torah interpretation and sectarian rulings; and a composite work belonging to a Qumran legal corpus, at times also related to Sadducean and proto-rabbinic traditions. The scholarly wheel has come full circle and Schechter's theories have to an extent stood the test of time. In addition, the Genizah provides us with texts of Tobit in Hebrew and the Testament of Levi in Aramaic. It also includes many copies of the Scroll of Antiochus, a popular Aramaic account of the Hasmonean wars and the origins of the festival of Ḥanukkah, dating from the talmudic period.

How is one to account for the survival of such material, in some sort of context, from Second Temple Judea to tenth-century Cairo? It is possible that the rabbinic tradition was central through these centuries and was lukewarm about such items, which found greater acceptance among Karaites, fringe groups and non-Jewish communities and made only occasional, haphazard appearances in the more normative synagogues. Alternatively, the rabbinic tradition was less central than it later imagined itself to have been, and historians should be seeking to uncover major Jewish religious trends during the first Christian millennium that manifest themselves in a variety of ideologies that were, for their part, unenthusiastic about rabbinic developments.

115

Whatever the nature of such alternative "Judaisms", it would have been natural for talmudic Judaism to have played down their importance and condemned their literature, perhaps not always with success. At periods of literary expansion, such as the one represented by the classic Genizah texts, the drive towards the adoption of written, and therefore authoritative versions (and broader, syncretistic vistas?) may have been one of the factors leading to the temporary acceptance within the talmudic communities of a greater variety of compositions than that sanctioned in some earlier or later contexts. For some historians, the answer is even simpler and is to be found in the fact that texts were hidden away in caves and surfaced from time to time. But would Jewish communities indiscriminately embrace such texts as part of their sacred literature?

Finally, it should be noted that neither Jesus nor Christian liturgy escape mention among the Genizah fragments. The rather uncomplimentary and folkloristic account of the life of Jesus known as *Toledot Yeshu*, some of it originating in talmudic times, is well represented and no doubt made the persecuted Jews of the Middle Ages feel a little better. In response to the New Testament accounts of a divine fatherhood, a virgin birth and miraculous acts, they were able to counter with a set of stories that referred to an unscrupulous father, rape and adultery, and deceptive trickery. While such polemics are not difficult to explain, no wholly satisfactory reason can be offered for the existence in the Cairo Jewish community of parts of a Nestorian Syriac hymn-book. Perhaps these thirteenth- or fourteenth-century texts belonging to a feast of the Virgin Mary were sold as scrap when the Nestorian community faded out of existence in Cairo at that time or shortly afterwards. Such a surprising find should alert us to the fact, if it is not already patently obvious, that there is hardly any area of medieval Near Eastern studies that is not illuminated by the fragments from the Ben Ezra synagogue of medieval Fustat.

Guide to reading

Much of the text of this chapter tallies with an article by S. C. Reif entitled "The Cairo Genizah and its Treasures, with Special Reference to Biblical Studies" in *The Aramaic Bible . Targums in their Historical Context*, edited by D. R. G. Beattie and M. J. McNamara (Sheffield, 1994), pp. 30–50. Fuller documentation for the information and conclusions offered above may be found in the notes that accompany that article. The history of the biblical Hebrew scroll and codex has been closely examined by M. Haran in various articles, especially "Bible Scrolls in Eastern and Western Jewish Communities from Qumran to the High Middle Ages", *Hebrew Union College Annual* 56 (1985), pp. 21–62, while its textual history is covered in E. Tov's volume *Textual Criticism of the Hebrew Bible* (English translation, Minneapolis–Assen/Maastricht, 1992). The more technical side of Hebrew codicology has in recent years received substantial attention from M. Beit-Arié, particularly in his volumes *Hebrew Codicology* (second edition, Jerusalem, 1981), and *Hebrew Manuscripts of East and West. Towards a Comparative Codicology* (London, 1993), and another article to be consulted is I. M. Resnick's "The Codex in Early Jewish and Christian Communities", *Journal of Religious History* 17 (1992), pp. 1–17. Details of the use of the Hebrew Bible in the Genizah communities are provided throughout S. D. Goitein's *A Mediterranean Society* (5 volumes, plus index volume, prepared by Paula Sanders, Berkeley, Los Angeles, London, 1967–93). M. Ben-Sasson refers to the volumes available in the synagogues of medieval Cairo in his article "The Medieval Period: The Tenth to Fourteenth Centuries" in the volume edited by Phyllis Lambert, *Fortifications and the Synagogue. The Fortress of Babylon and the Ben Ezra Synagogue, Cairo* (London, 1994), pp. 201–23.

The complicated story of the Masoretes and their work on the text and pointing of the Hebrew Bible is not easily understood by non-specialists but there is an excellent and up-to-date treatment of the subject by A. Dotan in the *Encyclopaedia Judaica* 16 (Jerusalem, 1971), cols. 1401–82. Those with an appetite for more should consult I. Yeivin's *Introduction to the Tiberian Masorah* (English translation of a Hebrew original, Missoula, 1980), and precise details of manuscripts found in the Genizah are available in E. J. Revell's *Hebrew Texts with Palestinian Vocalization* (Toronto, 1970) and M. C. Davis, *Hebrew Bible Manuscripts in the Cambridge Genizah Collections*, (two volumes; Cambridge, 1978 and 1980; and another two being prepared for the printer). The talmudic statement about the authoritative traditions concerning the reading and writing of the biblical text is in BT *Sukkah* 6b while the role of the Karaites is touched on by J. Mann in his two works, *The Jews in Egypt and in Palestine under the Fatimid Caliphs* (reprinted with an introduction by S. D. Goitein, New York, 1970) and *Texts and Studies in Jewish History and Literature* (Cincinnati–Philadelphia, 1931–35). As to the Genizah's relevance to the development of the grammatical analysis of biblical Hebrew, see, for example, the articles by D. Becker, "Traces of Judah Ibn Quraysh in Manuscript, particularly in Genizah Fragments" and I. Eldar "Mukhtaṣar (an abridgement of) Hidāyat al-Qāri': A grammatical Treatise discovered in the Genizah" in the volume edited by J. Blau and S. C. Reif, *Genizah Research after Ninety Years. The Case of Judaeo-Arabic* (Cambridge, 1992), pp. 14–21 and 67–73.

The scholarly theories concerning the reading cycles (lectionaries) covering the Pentateuch and the Prophets are neatly summarized and briefly analysed by J. J. Petuchowski in the volume edited by him entitled *Contributions to the*

Scientific Study of the Jewish Liturgy (New York, 1970), pp. xvii–xxi and by B. Z. Wacholder in the reprint of J. Mann's *The Bible as Read and Preached in the Old Synagogue* (New York, 1971), first prolegomenon. Benjamin of Tudela's comments on this matter are here cited from the edition of Marcus Nathan Adler, *The Itinerary of Benjamin of Tudela* (London, 1907), Hebrew section, pp. 62–63, English section, pp. 69–70. The Syriac, Greek, Aramaic and Judaeo-Arabic versions to be found in the Genizah are dealt with by A. S. Lewis and M. D. Gibson, *Palestinian Syriac Texts from Palimpsest Fragments in the Taylor-Schechter Collection* (London, 1900); M. Sokoloff and J. Yahalom, "Christian Palimpsests from the Cairo Geniza", *Revue d'Histoire des Textes* 8 (1978), pp. 109–32; F. C. Burkitt, *Fragments of the Books of Kings according to the Translation of Aquila* (Cambridge, 1897), and C. Taylor, *Hebrew-Greek Genizah Palimpsests from the Taylor-Schechter Collection* (Cambridge, 1900); M. L. Klein, *Genizah Manuscripts of Palestinian Targum to the Pentateuch* (two volumes; Cincinnati, 1986), especially vol. 1, pp. 190–91 and *Targum Manuscripts in the Cambridge Genizah Collections* (Cambridge, 1992); J. Blau, "On a Fragment of the Oldest Judaeo-Arabic Bible Translation Extant" in the volume *Ninety Years of Genizah Research* (see end of previous paragraph), pp. 31–39; and C. Baker and M. Polliack, *Arabic and Judaeo-Arabic Manuscripts in the Cambridge Genizah Collections* (Cambridge, 1999). On the Karaite versions, see G. Khan, *Karaite Bible Manuscripts from the Cairo Genizah* (Cambridge, 1990) and M. Polliack, *The Karaite Tradition of Arabic Bible Translation* (Leiden–New York–Köln, 1997). Ḥiwi's biblical heresies are covered in J. Rosenthal's *Ḥiwi Al-Balkhi. A Comparative Study* (Philadelphia, 1949).

Two helpful and reliable English guides to the whole midrashic field, as background to the relevance of the Genizah texts, are R. Kasher's article "Scripture in Rabbinic Literature" in the volume *Mikra: Text, Translation, Reading and Interpretation of the Hebrew Bible in Ancient Judaism and Early Christianity*, eds. J. Mulder and H. Sysling (Assen/Maastricht–Philadelphia, 1988), pp. 547–94 and G. Stemberger's *Introduction to the Talmud and Midrash* (Edinburgh, 1996). M. Gaster's midrashic pieces were reprinted in his three volumes *Studies and Texts in Folklore. Magic, Mediaeval Romance, Hebrew Apocrypha and Samaritan Archaeology* (London, 1925–28). For examples of the treatment of Genizah fragments of midrashim, see M. Sokoloff, *The Geniza Fragments of Bereshit Rabba* (Jerusalem, 1982), and S. C. Reif, "A Midrashic Anthology from the Genizah" in the volume edited by J. A. Emerton and S. C. Reif, *Interpreting the Hebrew Bible. Essays in Honour of E. I. J. Rosenthal* (Cambridge, 1982), pp. 179–225. B. Narkiss has described children's Hebrew exercises in his article "Illuminated Hebrew Children's Books from Mediaeval Egypt", *Scripta Hierosolymitana* 24 (1972), pp. 58–71 and many of the Genizah incunables are listed in David Goldstein's *Hebrew Incunables in the British Isles: A Preliminary Census* (London, 1985).

The whole story of the Cambridge Genizah fragments of Ben Sira is told in S. C. Reif, "The Discovery of the Cambridge Genizah fragments of Ben Sira:

Scholars and Texts" in the latest volume to cover research in the whole field, edited by P. C. Beentjes, *The Book of Ben Sira in Modern Research. Proceedings of the First International Ben Sira Conference, 28–31 July 1996, Soesterberg, Netherlands* (Berlin–New York, 1997), pp. 1–22. Schechter published the Zadokite or Damascus Document (CD) in the first volume of his *Documents of Jewish Sectaries* under the sub-title *Fragments of a Zadokite Work* (Cambridge, 1910). The literature relating to CD is helpfully summarized in the excellent bibliography provided by F. García Martínez in Magen Broshi's *The Damascus Document Reconsidered* (Jerusalem, 1992) and the issue of the relationship between the Dead Sea Scrolls and the Genizah texts is summarized in S. C. Reif's entry "Cairo Genizah" in *The Encyclopaedia of the Dead Sea Scrolls*, edited by L. H. Schiffman and J. C. VanderKam (Oxford and New York, 1999). A symposium on CD, organized by Michael Stone and Esther Chazon for the Orion Institute, was recently held in Jerusalem and the proceedings, including an article by S. C. Reif on the discovery and early study of CD, will no doubt be published in the near future. For a detailed bibliography relating to *Toledot Yeshu*, see R. Di Segni's Italian monograph *Il Vangelo del Ghetto* (Rome, 1985), and S. P. Brock has edited and published the Syriac liturgies from the Genizah in his articles "East Syrian Liturgical Fragments from the Cairo Genizah" and "Some Further East Syrian Liturgical Fragments from the Cairo Genizah" in *Oriens Christianus* 68 (1984), pp. 58–79 and 74 (1990), pp. 44–61.

The reader of modern Hebrew may also wish to consult M. Haran's article "The Codex, the Pinax and the Wooden Slats", *Tarbiz* 57 (1988), pp. 151–64, with his additional note in 58 (1989), pp. 523–24, as well as the fifth chapter on Genizah literature in the first part of his study *The Biblical Collection* (Jerusalem, 1966), pp. 276–303 and S. Z. Havlin's "From Scroll to Codex", *Alei Sefer* 16 (1989–90), pp. 151–52 and 160–61. David Téné has an important article on the comparative study of Semitic languages by medieval Jewish grammarians (with no English title) in *Hebrew Language Studies presented to Professor Zeev Ben-Hayyim*, eds. M. Bar-Asher, A. Dotan, G. B. Sarfati and D. Téné (Jerusalem, 1983), pp. 237–87. On the matter of the historical development of the reading cycles, see the somewhat iconoclastic views of E. Fleischer in his articles "Inquiries concerning the Triennial Reading of the Torah in Ancient Eretz-Israel", *Hebrew Union College Annual* 62 (1991), pp. 43–61 and "Annual and Triennial Reading of the Bible in the Old Synagogue", *Tarbiz* 61 (1992), pp. 25–43, and the Genizah texts T-S H12.11 and Erzherzog Rainer 96 that report on the Palestinian synagogue's customs in medieval Cairo, as edited at the end of his volume *Eretz-Israel Prayer and Prayer Rituals as Portrayed in the Geniza Documents* (Jerusalem, 1988).

As far as rabbinic commentaries are concerned, M. Perez has, for example, published important fragments of the work of Judah Ibn Balaam and Moses ibn Gikatilla in the *Proceedings of the American Academy for Jewish Research* 57 (1991), pp. 1–16; *Sinai* 108 (1991), pp. 7–17; *Leshonenu* 55 (1992), pp. 315–22; *Hebrew Union College Annual* 63 (1993), pp. 1–17; and *Sinai* 113 (1994), pp. 262–76. M. Zucker did important work on Saʿadya's biblical scholarship in his *Rav Saadya Gaon's Translation of the Torah* (New York, 1959) and *Saadya's Commentary on Genesis* (New York, 1984) and Y. Ratzaby has published many additional fragments of Saʿadya's commentaries, as in *Sinai* 109 (1992), pp. 97–117, 193–211; and *Sinai* 111 (1993), pp. 1–26. Another important edition is that of A. Greenbaum, *The Biblical Commentary of Rav Samuel ben Ḥofni Gaon according to Geniza Manuscripts* (Jerusalem, 1979). Hebrew volumes on Genizah midrashim include S. A. Wertheimer's *Batei Midrashot*, ed. A. J. Wertheimer (Jerusalem, 1954); J. Mann's *The Bible as Read and Preached in the Old Synagogue* (Cincinnati, 1940 and 1966, with I. Sonne; with a reprinted edition by B. Z. Wacholder, New York, 1971); L. Ginzberg's *Genizah Studies in Memory of Doctor Solomon Schechter. I. Midrash and Haggadah* (New York, 1928); Z. M. Rabinovitz's *Ginzé Midrash* (Tel Aviv, 1976); and M. Kahana's *Manuscripts of the Halakhic Midrashim: An Annotated Catalogue* (Jerusalem, 1995). There is an interesting exchange between Y. Erder and H. Ben-Shammai in a section entitled "Discussion: Karaism and Apocryphic Literature" in *Cathedra* 42 (1987), pp. 54–86 and articles on *Toledot Yeshu* by Z. Falk and D. Boyarin in *Tarbiz* 46 (1977), pp. 319–22 and 47 (1978), pp. 249–82.

SIX

IN RABBINIC GARB

The sacred and authoritative texts of the rabbinic Jewish communities in the Genizah period consisted not only of the Hebrew Bible, which had come to be known as the Written Torah, but also of the Oral Torah, which was made up of the talmudic, midrashic and related literature. Aspects of the concept of a broader Torah already existed as early as the Second Temple period but it was in the early Christian centuries that the rabbinic leadership nurtured and extended the theological notion that they and their system of beliefs (broadly, *aggadah*) and practices (broadly, *halakhah*) had become the guardians of Jewish religious authority. The idea was that the revelation to the Jewish people at Sinai, and the later religious messages of the prophets and other inspired writings – the biblical books – had been complemented from the outset by a set of traditions that had been orally transmitted but that also enjoyed the status of divinely revealed teaching, namely, the rabbinic corpus.

Both elements of Torah provided the guidance needed for the required Jewish lifestyle, as the rabbis saw it, and although the degree of authority did in certain contexts vary between the written and oral versions, and within each, the foundations of authentic rabbinic Judaism were regarded as firmly set in a combination of the two. The Hebrew Bible was best and most reliably explained by one or other, or indeed perhaps by all of the varied rabbinic interpretations (*midrashim*) that had been offered, and were being offered, for it, as the time and circumstance required. Whenever possible, the rabbinic teaching was traced to the written biblical source. In those cases where such an explicit link could not be made, the authority of the tradition was seen to be grounded in the implicit link presupposed by the idea of the Oral Torah. The written Torah had given authority to the elders, the prophets, the sages and the rabbis to transmit and expound its divine message in an inspired fashion. Among the rabbis, and within their communities, that authority found

121

expression in practical decisions concerning the implementation of Jewish religious law. It also led to the formulation of a broad Jewish culture and a whole ideology of Judaism that touched on a great variety of areas that were not strictly controlled by *halakhah*.

THE TALMUD AND ITS EARLY DEVELOPMENT

To appreciate what the Genizah material contributes to our understanding of rabbinic law and lore in the early Middle Ages, it is first necessary to summarize what came into existence in the first seven centuries of the current era, before the Genizah period, and what the situation had become by, say, the thirteenth century, which is widely regarded as marking the end of the time-span covered by most of the fragments from Cairo. Being careful not to make any suppositions about the manner in which it was memorized, redacted and transmitted, we may confidently state that the Mishnah and the Tosefta represented the traditions of the rabbinic teachers (*tanna'im*) of the first two centuries and that they had achieved some sort of edited format within a further century. The discussions concerning these and other tannaitic traditions (*beraitot*) that had not found a place in such a format, and touching on many relevant and less relevant topics, were formulated into a *Talmud*

Yerushalmi, or Palestinian Talmud, in the Holy Land around 400 c.e., and into a *Talmud Bavli*, or Babylonian Talmud, in the Mesopotamian Jewish centres in a process that may have taken at least two centuries longer. The Babylonian interpretation of the Hebrew Bible found a place in the Babylonian Talmud while its equivalent among the communities of Eretz Yisrael was given expression in a whole genre of midrashic literature, some of it halakhic and some of it aggadic. The earliest of such literature, or at least its essential content, may safely be dated from the tannaitic period, while its production was still under way when the Islamic conquest of the whole Near East in the seventh century brought so many political, religious and cultural changes to the area.

All historical divisions are somewhat arbitrary but it is convenient to categorize the period from the seventh until the eleventh century as the geonic era, after the *ge'onim*, or outstanding rabbinic leaders, that held sway over their communities after the Babylonian Talmud had achieved a fairly final format. Perhaps at this point some indication should be given of the degree to which the talmudic and midrashic literature that they inherited was limited in its nature. The first, and perhaps the most important question is the manner in which it was then being transmitted. It appears from the limited evidence available that the system of transmission was still predominantly an oral one. While other Jewish groups had opted for the written form, the rabbis preferred to pass on their traditions by word of mouth, perhaps in an effort to distinguish the Oral Torah from the Written Torah, perhaps to retain a unique and powerful educational experience. This is not to say that there was no process of editing. Textual interpretations and legal discussions had for centuries been acquiring an increasingly formal structure but there is no reason to suppose that such a structure could not be adopted and developed without recourse to writing. Oral transmission was seen as a special feature of the revelation to Israel and there was a serious suspicion that a commitment to writing was a betrayal of the authentic historical experience. It therefore follows that there was a considerable degree of fluidity in all the texts being orally transmitted. It is then erroneous to imagine that the date of the composition of a particular talmudic or midrashic corpus is by definition either the date of all its content, or the date at which it was first copied, letter by letter, on to writing material.

Given the absence of a written and "canonized" form, it is hardly surprising that the Babylonian Talmud had yet to develop tendencies that characterize the acquisition of such a status. There were accretions that offered expansions, summaries, mnemonics and halakhic conclusions but these were incorporated within the oral text and did not have an independent existence. Satellite texts were still a development of the future, as were the specific genres of talmudic commentary and digest. As far as statements of halakhic procedure are concerned, these were *ad hoc* rather than in any way systematic, local rather than central, and consequently not prone to overall consistency. Jewish communities were scattered around the known world, were functioning in different milieux, and being influenced by a variety of cultures, especially the Byzantine and the Parthian. Midrashic and targumic compilations had been made but those that stood at the centre of the talmudic tradition appear to have been somewhat straitlaced, restricting themselves to standard halakhic or homiletical interpretation of the pentateuchal books. Other, more peripheral material was either given less attention or was yet to develop to any serious degree. Certainly, no attempt had yet been made to separate the literal from the applied sense of Scripture, at least not in the categorical manner in which such a separation later came to be expressed.

THE BEGINNINGS OF SYNAGOGAL LITURGY AND POETRY

On the liturgical front, similar considerations applied. The reading of the morning and evening *shema'*, with their attendant blessings, was well established, and it was certainly the custom to recite the *'amidah* at least twice, if not three times a day. Biblical passages were read and expounded and collections of Psalms were particularly central to the services. The synagogue was well on the way to becoming a formal centre of communal worship, as the Temple had once been, but the academy and the home still functioned as important settings for some prayers and ceremonies. There is no doubt that, as far as the Dead Sea Scrolls are concerned, prayers, hymns and benedictions on the one hand, and supplicatory formulas and

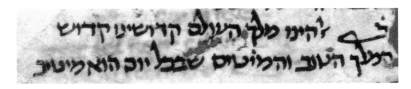

incantations on the other, were already structured, communal, and an integral part of religious duties. Some items were intended for daily, sabbath and festival use while others were more closely related to social and political contexts, or to apocalyptic and angelological themes The linguistic and contextual parallels with rabbinic prayer are striking, but the precise formulation is unique to each group, and it is an open question whether the rabbis followed the Qumran practice and committed their prayers to writing. It is also yet to be clearly established whether there was a general uniformity of text and custom in the talmudic period, or a considerable variety of options in the different communities and synagogues. What is beyond doubt is that there was no prayer-book as such and that the way that prayers were formulated, recited and transmitted still left a great deal of room for development.

Perhaps the most novel development in the rabbinic synagogue at the end of the talmudic period was the introduction of the *piyyut*, or liturgical poem, into the services by way of its inclusion in the various sections of the *shema'* and the *'amidah*. The custom undoubtedly arose in the land of Israel, at about the same time as similar developments in the Syriac

Church, and there are some scattered references to the new literary phenomenon in the talmudic literature. In its earliest and anonymous format, the *piyyuṭ* enjoys an elevated style and a lyrical structure but there is as yet no rhyme. In the sixth and seventh centuries, before the Islamic conquest, the Palestinian communities produced a number of outstanding composers of synagogal poetry, the most famous of whom were Yose ben Yose, Yannai, Eleazar b. Qallir and Simeon ben Megas. While in its earliest and anonymous form, the language of the *piyyuṭ* was a combination of biblical and rabbinic style, vocabulary and ideology, the situation changed drastically during the period of the named poets. They took great pride in coining linguistic forms, in creating their own words and idioms, and in introducing vague allusions to Jewish personalities, events and ideas that could be understood only by the learned and the initiated. Those who were expert in the field could take particular pleasure in the synagogue from such sophisticated compositions, just as their Christian contemporaries enjoyed the religious art forms of their houses of worship, while the remainder of the community could enjoy the sound of the poetry and appreciate how it generally related to the central prayers and embellished their content and message.

REVOLUTIONARY CHANGES

If we make a jump of some six centuries, the situation looks manifestly different. Texts of the Babylonian Talmud are available in complete volumes and there are widely disseminated digests and commentaries. Authoritative codes of Jewish law, with their own form and structure, have come into existence and there are many collections of responsa, containing rabbinic discussions and decisions in problematic matters. The whole field of Jewish Bible commentary has taken on a new look, with distinctions being carefully drawn between what is and what is not the strict sense of the revealed text, and attempts are being made to respond, even aggressively, to non-rabbinic interpretations. The standard rabbinic prayers are now included in the *siddur*, which is attracting to itself all manner of additional material, both liturgical and halakhic, and has acquired an almost canonical status. There are clear views about what has to be recited and when, communal prayer is undoubtedly the norm, and activities, many of them of a ceremonial type, are centred in the synagogue.

There is concern about the correct kind of Hebrew to be used in the standard prayers but many of the *piyyuṭim*, however novel they once were, have now found respectable places for themselves in the fixed liturgy.

Indeed, such poetic literature has outgrown its liturgical origins and become a literary genre in its own right, ready to expand in all manner of directions, some of them not entirely to the satisfaction of the rabbinic authorities. How did all these changes come about? What were the factors that played a major part in such developments? Do we possess the necessary data for describing and explaining the history of rabbinic literature in the geonic and early medieval centuries? Thanks to the Genizah discoveries, we now do. Before these fragments came to light, historians were faced with a kind of dark age and could only guess whether what applied to the talmudic or medieval periods did or did not apply to the intervening period. Now, via the manuscripts originating in Cairo a thousand years ago, we can offer plausible answers to many intriguing questions.

First, two general statements need to be made about Jewish cultural history in the geonic period, one relating to intellectual development and the other to literacy. While under Parthian and Byzantine hegemony, the Jewish communities of the Near East and the Mediterranean area had been prone to periods of tolerance interchanging with times of persecution, and had been unable to rely on any degree of political stability. With the conquest of that mass of territory by the Arabs, and its resultant domination by Islam, their position in general society underwent a considerable revolution. Jews remained second-class citizens but their status was legally established. The religio-political system under which they lived held sway as far east as Afghanistan and as far west as Spain. The Arab absorption of the finest achievements of the peoples they conquered led to a flourishing of what was perhaps the broadest culture yet known to humanity. This not only led to the emergence of a variety of religious and heretical trends from both within Islam and outside it, but also provided a remarkable example of centralization, authority, standardization and educational progress. The Jews were not slow in following such an example and adapting it to their own communal, religious and literary requirements.

With regard to written material pre-dating the ninth century, the remarkable fact is that we lack any Hebrew manuscripts (excluding a few inscriptions) from the time of Bar Kokhba in the second century until the earliest Genizah fragments. It is of course possible that this absence of manuscripts is historically fortuitous and that evidence will at some future date become available. On the other hand, it is more tempting to suggest that it reflects the predominantly oral nature of rabbinic literature, as already described. In this case too, the impetus for the Jewish community to adopt the codex may have come from the example set by Islam. Its motivation may have been to match the cultural and religious encroachments being made by that powerful empire. As the codex became fashionable, at first with the use of papyrus or vellum but later exclusively with vellum, it contained a few gatherings simply stitched together and tended to be of a small and manageable size, perhaps originally written only on one side. The Arabic term for the bound volume containing such gatherings, namely, *muṣḥaf*, was adopted by the Jews of the Orient as *maṣḥaf* in Hebrew and *maṣḥafa* in Aramaic. It would be strange if such a revolutionary development in the transmission of texts had no effect on the literature for which it was used. As such a medium expanded and developed, so did the whole gamut of rabbinic literature become better arranged and recorded, and more open to expansion. Once such material was disseminated, it attracted notation and commentary, and its contents tended to be regarded as standard and authoritative.

TEXTUAL DEVELOPMENTS

Rabbinic literature, ranging from talmudic and midrashic texts and commentaries to halakhic decisions, collections and codes, accounts for as much as fifteen per cent of the Genizah material and has been greatly enriched by the latter's discovery and analysis. As far as the talmudic text itself is concerned, the first point to be made is that most of the Genizah fragments are three or four centuries older than the one extant manuscript of the whole Babylonian Talmud, to which reference is so often made and with which the printed editions are regularly compared.

29 – Text from the Palestinian Talmud (*Yerushalmi*) (T-S F17.20) (Cambridge University Library)

While the Munich manuscript dates from 1334, many of the talmudic folios from the Genizah are no later than the eleventh and twelfth centuries and a minority are undoubtedly earlier. They therefore reflect a text that is nearer its origins both geographically and chronologically and that has not yet been interfered with in the Christian west. If this is true in the case of the Babylonian Talmud, which was widely studied and disseminated, how much more is it applicable to the textual history of the *Yerushalmi*, which was more neglected and much of which was barely preserved in the Middle Ages. From the initial days of Genizah research, talmudists have therefore been intrigued and excited by every discovery of an early *Yerushalmi* fragment. It is not rare to find among Genizah fragments talmudic sections that were later lost or removed, or to discover that post-Genizah texts have attracted all manner of adhesions. Sometimes the text is early enough to shed light on the origins of an expression that puzzled later generations. An unusual linguistic usage, a word of Greek or Persian origin, the exchange of one letter for another, a forgotten place name, or an unexpected abbreviation – such phenomena often led to corruptions in the text and it is not unusual for Genizah versions to uncover authentic readings. Fragments of incunables and early editions of talmudic texts, some of them on vellum, are another feature, albeit a limited one, of Genizah collections. Many of them represent rare remnants of editions that were produced on the printing presses of Spain and Portugal just before the expulsion of the Jews from the Iberian peninsula and that were among the belongings brought to North Africa and Egypt by refugees from these anti-Semitic persecutions. While such outstanding rabbinic text-critics as Joel Sirkes in seventeenth-century Poland and the Gaon of Wilna in eighteenth-century Lithuania could only offer hypothetical corrections to the text, today's experts in talmudic fragments from the Genizah can sometimes categorically confirm the brilliance of their proposals.

Such versions also contribute to a better understanding of linguistic developments. A clearer distinction between the Western Aramaic of Palestinian texts and the Eastern Aramaic of their Babylonian counterparts has become possible, with the result that the relevant dictionaries and grammars have been improved or, indeed, created from scratch. Glosses on the text, some of them in Judaeo-Arabic or Judaeo-Greek, have helped to restore long-lost meanings, while the use in some manuscripts of vowel-points, following a variety of systems, has enabled experts in Hebrew linguistics to explain how different communities pronounced the Hebrew of their rabbinic texts. It has even become apparent from Genizah evidence that there was a custom not only to chant mishnaic texts in a particular way but to ensure that the practice was recorded for future generations by way of cantillation signs. Better and earlier versions have also made it possible to trace how rabbinic Hebrew was able to maintain for many centuries a separate identity from its biblical equivalent, despite a definite trend towards their equalization on the part of many transmitters of the texts.

This is not of course to say that all talmudic Genizah texts are old and reliable. A significant number are late or are crude and unprofessional copies, and it should not be forgotten that a hundred folios may represent, say, no more than ten or twenty original manuscripts. Until fairly recently, little work was done on the identification, description and evaluation of such "run-of-the-mill" items, since researchers were on the hunt for more sensational finds. As such prominent literary treasures have become rarer, so the tendency has increased to give attention to the overall picture of textual history that can be restored through a close examination of the many mundane, rather than the few exceptional items. There are now therefore ongoing projects to produce scholarly catalogues of all the Genizah talmudica and rabbinica. As such projects reach completion, so will it become possible to describe how talmudic texts moved from the oral to the written format, how their use in a variety of literary contexts and in different centres of study influenced their evolution, and how fluidity changed to canonicity.

THE INTERPRETATION OF TALMUD

Two major effects of those changes, that are certainly reflected in the Genizah evidence, were the creation of supplements to the talmudic text, in the form of brief, additional tractates in the earlier geonic period, and the compilation of commentaries at a later date. Themes that are briefly treated in the standard tractates of the talmudic and immediate post-talmudic periods, or are dealt with there in scattered statements attached to various contexts, are expanded upon in the so-called "minor tractates". By way of examples of such *masekhtot qeṭanot, Avot de-Rabbi Nathan* provides a commentary on the mishnaic tractate *Avot; Soferim* offers further details of scribal and liturgical practices, as these became more standardized in the geonic period; and *Semaḥot* sums up the laws relating to bereavement and mourning. If these tractates constitute the first stage of the process of commentary, the second stage is to be located in the statements made by various geonic authorities about the meaning of individual talmudic passages and preserved in their responsa, that is, in the authoritative replies given by them to enquiries addressed to them from Jewish communities all around the Islamic empire. It was obviously necessary for them to deal with such passages not only for their own sake but also in the course of discussing wider problems of Jewish religious practice that had been referred to them. The third stage is that of the compilation of running commentaries, such as that which appears to have been undertaken in the Babylonian centre by Hai Gaon of the Pumbedita school in the tenth and eleventh centuries but most of which has been lost, and that of his later contemporary, Hananel ben Hushiel, in Qayrawan, one of the most important Jewish communities in North Africa.

While investigative Genizah scholarship has played a role in the reconstruction of these earlier developments, it has made nothing short of a massive contribution to the recovery of the later work of Nissim ben Jacob ibn Shahin. As Hananel's successor in eleventh-century Qayrawan, Nissim was the leading talmudic teacher and authority who succeeded in transplanting into the fertile soil of his contemporary North Africa the rabbinic culture that had been nurtured in Babylon. Thanks to a lifetime of research on the man and his work by Shraga Abramson, an important link in the chain of rabbinic literary history has been reforged. On the basis of Abramson's close manuscript studies, many of them dependent on Genizah sources written in the original Judaeo-Arabic, a much clearer picture has emerged of the books that Nissim ibn Shahin compiled and of their importance to the talmudic field. In a work that might justifiably be translated "A Key to the Talmudic Treasure-Chest", he assisted the student of the vast talmudic literature by providing sources and parallels for many statements, as well as explanations of many recurrent themes. For more popular use, the same Nissim wrote a collection of Hebrew stories and folklore that offered religious inspiration and encouragement to his fellow Jews. He also drew up commentaries on some tractates, compiled a set of halakhic rulings, and provided general religious guidance on many topics that had a major impact on leading rabbis throughout the Jewish world for many generations.

QUESTIONS AND ANSWERS

That inseparable connection between talmudic text and halakhic ruling, that was so well established by the time that these North African scholars were dominating the field, had been fused in the course of the geonic period, as talmudic traditions became more authoritative and clearcut halakhic guidance to the wider (and commercially developing)

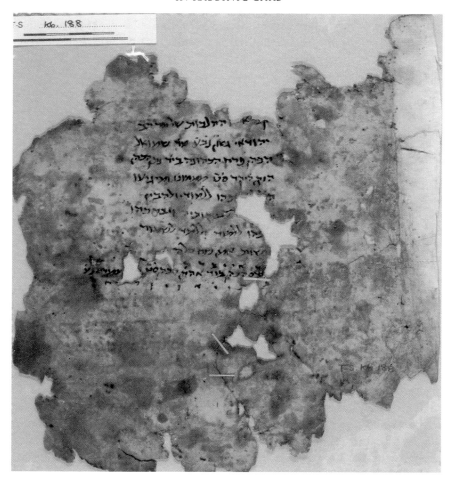

30 – A note attributing *Halakhot Pesuqot* to R. Yehudai Gaon (T-S K6.188)
(Cambridge University Library)

Jewish community more desirable. The expansion of that system of
guidance has also been illuminated by a centenary of Genizah study. The
earlier distinctions between the Babylonian talmudic traditions and their
equivalents in Eretz Yisrael also found later expression in the
formulation of their respective laws and customs. As the Babylonian
teachers and institutions between and around the Tigris and the
Euphrates began to grow in stature and influence, so it became necessary
for the Palestinian communities to put on record those instances
(*ma'asim* in Hebrew) in which they differed. A body of literature thus

131

came into being, perhaps early in the seventh century, the purpose of which was to clarify, recall and maintain these differences. It is not yet clear whether the particular corpus of *She'iltot* ("questions"), compiled by the Pumbedita scholar, Aḥai of Shabḥa, in the eighth century, reflects a purely Babylonian background or also incorporates Palestinian elements. Its author certainly left Babylon to settle in the Holy Land but he and others of a like mind who made *'aliyah* may well have imported their Babylonian traditions with them. Certainly, the Palestinian experts in talmudic and halakhic traditions were much less prolific than their counterparts in Mesopotamia.

The questions raised and answered in that Aramaic work related to the text of the Pentateuch and were intended to link the Written and Oral Torah. Possibly originating in extempore synagogal sermons but later developing a more formal structure, they used the biblical text as the point of departure for a halakhic journey that ended in the secure haven of a religious decision. The Genizah has supplied important additions and improvements to the questions and the homilies of the *She'iltot*, as it has contributed better texts to later compilations of Jewish religious law from the geonic period, such as the *Halakhot Pesuqot* and the *Halakhot Gedolot*. Both of these collections, the first possibly made by Yehudai in the eighth century and the second probably by Simeon Qayyara a century later, still incorporated Palestinian traditions but a serious attempt was made by a student of the school of Yehudai to discredit, and indeed to bring into total disrepute, the rabbinic teachings of the Holy Land. From many fragments preserved in the Genizah, it emerges that a certain Pirqoi ben Baboi, whose name is either of Persian origin or perhaps represents some sort of *nom de plume*, decided that the time had come to usher in a new halakhic era and to put an end to any influence that the talmudists of the Holy Land might still have.

With those purposes in mind, he wrote an epistle to the Jewish communities of his day, perhaps especially aimed at North Africa, in which he strongly attacked the customs and practices of the Palestinian communities. Since they lacked authentic foundations and had arisen out of ignorance and persecution, they should in no way be followed by other centres of rabbinic Judaism. The *Talmud Bavli* and the halakhic decisions arising out of it were authoritative, the Babylonian academies were superior to all others, and their interpretation of the Oral Torah was the correct one. This approach undoubtedly became the dominant one and the communities in Egypt and North Africa became the halakhic successors of the Babylonian *ge'onim*. The later Genizah material includes hundreds of fragments of the halakhic digest of the Babylonian

Talmud that Isaac Alfasi prepared in the eleventh century. There, the *Yerushalmi* is used only when there are no Babylonian rulings. It is also the Babylonian tradition that lies behind the first fully comprehensive code of Jewish law, the *Mishneh Torah* of Maimonides, completed in Cairo in 1180 and, not surprisingly, well represented among the medieval fragments from the Ben Ezra synagogue. Equally unsurprising is the fact that many of these fragments cover such themes as ritual slaughter and marital matters, both of which issues were of major concern to the daily lives of the community. In the case of the latter, there are important remnants of Palestinian religious practice which demonstrate that in matters of personal status the emigrés from the Holy Land succeeded in maintaining their halakhic individuality for some time.

Another medium for the formulation and transmission of halakhic decisions that dates from the middle of the geonic period was the responsa literature. Sometimes individuals or communities as far away from the major centres as Spain were troubled by a particular problem of Jewish religious practice. In such circumstances, they took advantage of the excellent systems of communication that existed in the Islamic empire to address their questions to leading authorities, particularly in Babylon. To encourage a response, or to ensure that a future approach would be welcome, they might forward a financial contribution to the expenses of the institution that was headed by the expert being approached. Before the discovery of the Genizah, there were no direct sources for such Jewish legal responsa from that early period. The texts that were available had been copied in places and periods far distant from their original provenance. They had been abbreviated by some scribes and adapted by others. They were cited in other works and the decisions of different rabbis were not preserved as discrete statements but were blended together within the treatment of a particular theme.

Via the Genizah, hundreds or maybe even thousands of authentic and original halakhic responses have now been recovered. The original groups of decisions sent by the authority by way of guidance to a number of questioners have surfaced. They have retained the original formulation, with the prefaces and conclusions of the author, and they often provide us with his name. Many texts can now therefore be traced to their composers and many decisions that had been lost or forgotten have come to light. It should not be forgotten that there are also Genizah responsa that date from the post-geonic periods, say, the twelfth and thirteenth centuries, many of them emanating from Moses Maimonides himself or his son Abraham, occasionally in their own hands. The themes covered in enquiries to such scholars are not restricted to the

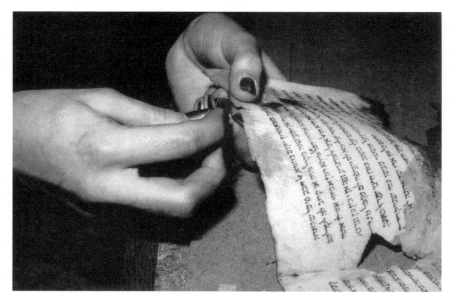

31 – Repairing a vellum fragment of the *Sefer ha-Sheṭarot* of R. Saʿadya Gaon (882–942)
(T-S Ar.50.221) (Cambridge University Library)

technicalities of religious rituals and customs; they are just as likely to relate to mundane matters such as financial arrangements, women's status, family life and social problems.

LEGAL MONOGRAPHS AND RABBINIC EXEGESIS

In the matter of *halakhah*, it is not only collections and codes on the one hand, and individual decisions on the other, that have been restored to us by way of the Genizah finds. It is now clear that monographs on halakhic themes were composed from at least as early as the tenth century. Saʿadya may have been one of the innovators in this field; he is certainly among those whose works on Jewish legal themes appear among the fragments. What has been recovered of his study of the laws of inheritance does not include any references to sources and may therefore be a remnant of an abbreviated format. As far as his practical guide to Jewish rules on testimonies and deeds (*Sefer Ha-Sheṭarot*) is concerned, fifty Genizah fragments (forty of them in Cambridge) have produced some 200 folios, amounting to over ninety per cent of the original work. Part of the novelty of the work was in its preference for a thematic rather than the talmudic order. Its composition in Judaeo-

Arabic rather than Aramaic represented an attempt to reach the user who was not so *au fait* with the talmudic sources but still needed to know the law. Like all attempts to be up-to-date and "relevant" it suffered, together with many other examples of the genre, from the fact that fashion moved on and later halakhic literature left Arabic behind and returned to Hebrew. Since the first scientific edition of Sa'adya's prayer-book was published, almost sixty years ago, many more fragments of the work have been located and the time has come for a new edition that will incorporate all these new finds.

Some of Sa'adya's successors in the Babylonian academies followed his example and produced their own halakhic monographs. Samuel ben Ḥofni of Sura, whose scholarly profile is becoming progressively sharper as more and more of his prolific work is revealed to us, dealt with the liturgical benedictions, as well as with the laws relating to ritual slaughter and to the inspection of carcasses. Hai Gaon is again to the forefront of developments with a treatise on oaths and a study of commercial transactions. These works were translated into Hebrew but, as the Genizah versions in the original Judaeo-Arabic now make clear, the renderings were loose, unreliable, and subject to alterations. With the rediscovery of a number of such treatises, written by these and other authors, it has emerged that what is being viewed is perhaps only the tip of the historical halakhic iceberg. Some monographs survived only in the Genizah; some are known only by name and others only by quotation elsewhere; others are no doubt yet to be revealed.

As far as rabbinic commentary on the Hebrew Bible is concerned, Naṭronai ben Hilai, head of the Sura academy in the ninth century, expressed criticism of the relative neglect of this subject in his circles and the trend to correct this alleged inbalance has been traced among his successors and summarized in an earlier chapter. Scholars as early as Sa'adya ben Joseph and Samuel ben Ḥofni, and as late as Tanḥum ben Joseph Ha-Yerushalmi in the thirteenth century, wrote commentaries that demonstrated how one could remain faithful to the biblical source, and at the same time provide rational and philosophical responses to the problems raised by the texts. They were able to offer sound linguistic explanations of difficult words and passages, while also absorbing many aspects of Islamic culture. No doubt, they were partly inspired by the existence of challenges from within and outside their faith to the authenticity of the biblical message, particularly as interpreted by the rabbinic tradition. As the Genizah makes clear, that tradition not only included halakhic and exegetical midrashim but also produced a welter of aggadic items that are closer to mysticism, magic and folklore than to

ברכת מזון לחול

ברוך אתה ה׳ א׳ינו מלך העולם בורא עולם
ויזר אדם מכין מזון לכ׳ בריותיו כאמור
פותח את ידיך ומשביע לכל חי רצון כ׳
הזן את הכל · ⟨ ⟩ ארץ עשיתה שולחן ערוכה
תורה ובריתך חלקינו נתתה ועל כן נודך ונברך
לשמך כאמור ואכלת ושבעת וברכת את ה׳א׳
להיך על הארץ הטובה אשר נתן לך כ׳ ⟨ ⟩
על הארץ ועל המזון · ⟨ ⟩ עירך תבנה שלם
תכונן ובית מקדשך ברחמים תפקוד בימינו
ומלכות משיחך מהרה תחזירה למקומה
כי לך ה׳ מיחלות עינינו ותבנה עיר קדשך
בימינו כאמור בונה ירושלם ה׳ נדחי ישראל
יכנס שם שצמיח קדן לדוד עריך למש׳
ב׳ ⟨ ⟩ ה׳ בונה ירושלם ·
⟨ ⟩ א׳הינו מלך העולם קדושיעקב קדוש
המלך הטוב והמיטיב שבכל יום הוא מיטיב ·

154

32 – 10th-century Palestinian version of the grace after meals (Or.1080 15.4) (Cambridge University Library

the more sober comments of leading codifiers and rationalists. In addition, new discoveries have shown the existence of all sorts of mini-anthologies of midrashim, tailor-made, as it were, for special days, for particular passages, and for linguistic matters, and sometimes attributed to rabbinic figures.

NOVEL LITURGY

From the very first Genizah discoveries, especially those made in Oxford and Cambridge in the 1890s, one of the fields that has held the greatest fascination for historians of rabbinic literature and in which they have therefore been most prolific, has been that of Jewish liturgy. The reason for this is simple. Unlike the Hebrew Bible which was in parts more than two thousand years old, and the Talmud, which had been compiled many centuries before, the Hebrew prayer-book, or *siddur*, had barely come into existence when the oldest Genizah scraps were written. Sa'adya's version dated only from the tenth century and although that of Amram was earlier, neither yet represented the normative practice in the Egyptian communities of the early Genizah period. Indeed, what the fragments from that source have demonstrated is that one can no longer speak of one correct and original text, at least not at that time, if at all, since there was then considerable variety. There is an ongoing discussion as to whether that variety was a fresh creativity inspired by the liturgical poets in the post-talmudic period, or the continuation of a situation that already applied in the talmudic period. Either way, what researchers have found particularly exciting has been the sheer novelty of so much of the liturgical material. Some have tried to reconstruct a broad historical picture and to seek the origins of each part of that picture in the different communities of the period. Others have been content to collect and record more and more detailed manuscript evidence about words, expressions and formulations, and how they evolved over the centuries and were preserved within the various rites.

It now emerges that some new blessings, such as those used on the kindling of the sabbath lights and on reciting collections of psalms, were introduced during the geonic period and managed to survive, in spite of their non-talmudic origin. Other such novelties, including benedictions for the *shema'*, the Yom Kippur confession, the recitation of the second chapter of the mishnaic tractate *Shabbat*, and for three sets of hand-washing in the Passover *seder*, met with halakhic objection and were abandoned, sometimes without trace. Unknown versions have been

33 – Passover Haggadah from 14th-century Spain (T-S K10.1) (Cambridge University Library)

uncovered of such central and popular prayers as the 'amidah, the qaddish, the blessings on rising in the morning, and the grace after meals. There is now documentation about broader uses of psalms and verses, about some forgotten ceremonies involving the Torah scrolls and others that were conducted at the walls of Jerusalem, and about a variety of cycles of Torah and prophetic readings that were once in use. Occasionally, approaches were made to non-Jewish rulers with requests for rulings on matters relating to controversial synagogal practices, as, for instance, when the mystical tendencies of Abraham Maimonides aroused the ire of some of his fellow Jews. Indeed, it was not only the leading rabbis of the day for whom special prayers were offered, in their case by way of invocations at the beginning of the service and insertions made in the qaddish. Prayers were also composed and recited by the Jews on behalf of the Muslim Caliph. One of these called on God to bless the twelfth-century Imam, al-Amir bi-'ahkam Allah, and read as follows:

> And we pray for the life of our distinguished sovereign lord and Muslim leader ... commander of the faithful, and for the royal princes and for all the royal family, and for those who devotedly assist the king and for those who do battle for him against his foes. May Almighty God come to their assistance and to ours, subdue those who arise against us and against them, and inspire them to deal kindly with us and with all his people, the house of Israel, and let us say Amen.

The inclusion of the Ten Commandments and the Song at the Sea were greatly favoured by some worshippers while others took every opportunity of making mystical and messianic insertions into the standard prayers, even when their content was not strictly relevant to the liturgical topic. The language of the prayer-book was not exclusively Hebrew but sometimes drifted, for reasons that are not entirely clear, into Aramaic, the scholastic medium, and Arabic, the vernacular. Perhaps most important of all, a large number of siddurim used in Eretz Yisrael before the Crusaders put an end to its many communities have been discovered in the Genizah, enabling historians of Jewish prayer to reconstruct an essential but long-lost link in the chain of liturgical transmission. It is now possible to compare the prayer texts used in Babylon and Palestine and to reach some concrete conclusions. After many literary and theological battles ranging over a number of centuries, with some leaders and communities taking maximalist positions, and others opting for compromise, the Babylonian prayer-book won the liturgical war and dictated terms to most Jewish communities. Only here and there were remnants left of the alternative versions and they can now be explained in the light of the original Palestinian rite.

THE EXPANSION OF POETRY

In the matter of synagogal poetry, the issue is once again one of transmission. Those who initiated the study of the medieval Jewish poets and poems, some 150 years ago, knew of many compositions and authors, but neither the texts nor the attributions they had before them were in any way complete or accurate. In the course of being incorporated into the prayer-book, they had lost the link with their original provenance, and many times and places had left their marks. There were manuscripts in European libraries that could be consulted but they themselves often post-dated the authors by many centuries and reflected the world of Europe rather than the Orient. The thousands of folios and hundreds of authors that the Genizah has restored to us have effectively created a whole new field of study. While they once had 40,000 compositions available to them, the enthusiasts for medieval Hebrew poetry now have 150% additional material to contend with. Earlier texts – some on papyrus, perhaps as early as the eighth century – are now available, authorship is better established, and whole new schools of poets have been added to the history of Hebrew verse. We have been made aware of the degree to which the whole literary genre blossomed in geonic Palestine and it has even been suggested that it represented the primary Jewish entertainment of the time. It is possible to uncover the emergence of a Saadyanic school in Babylon and to identify the linguistic and structural innovations that it daringly made. Comparisons may be made between the style and content of such poems and those composed in places as far away as Byzantium, Italy, North Africa and Spain. What is even more significant is that there are now sufficient data to plot an accurate graph that traces the chronological and geographical development of Jewish poetic theory, structure and style. Anthologies of medieval Hebrew poetry need no longer concentrate exclusively on "the golden age of Spanish Jewry" but can offer examples and surveys of broader literary treasures.

Not that medieval Jewish Spain has lost its importance through the Genizah discoveries. On the contrary, there is now even more to say about its contribution to Hebrew poetry. The close association between

Spain, North Africa and Egypt in the classical Genizah period ensured that many manuscripts from the Iberian peninsula, and even some from other parts of Europe, made their way to Cairo. As a result, we can see more clearly how the Sefaradi authors revolutionized the language, structure and content of their poems. They preferred the biblical style, adopted many Islamic formats, and opted for subjects much less dominated by rabbinic texts and ideology. Indeed, their greatest claim to fame is perhaps the fact that they developed a whole new genre of secular Jewish poetry. This could centre on topics such as wine, women and song and, given that the rabbinic authorities were not too enthusiastic about such a concentration, it is hardly surprising that we need to look to the Genizah rather than to the *siddur* for remnants of such verses. Many examples of Hebrew poems in praise of physical beauty are now revealed and, since some of them appear to be addressed to young men, they raise questions not only about heterosexual activity at the time but also about the possibility of homosexual tendencies. One of the most exciting of recent finds does however relate to a married couple, none other than the famous tenth-century linguist and poet, Dunash ibn Labraṭ, and his wife. When he left Spain soon after the birth of their son, his wife wrote him a poem expressing her sadness and questioning his loyalty. His lyrical reply assured her of his faithfulness:

She:

> Will her beloved remember the graceful hind
> On the day of separation, her only son on her arm...
> On the day she took his mantle as a keepsake
> And as his keepsake he took her veil

He:

> But how shall I betray a clever woman like thee
> Surely God bound us to the wife of our youth
> and if my heart had plotted to abandon thee
> I would have cut it into a thousand pieces

Whether the poems were artificially created for literary effect, or represent the record of a genuine romantic exchange, is open to question. What is beyond doubt is their ascription to the Dunash couple. In that case, what we have before us here and in many other Genizah pieces is clear evidence of the extent to which rabbinic literature had developed in a period of a few centuries. Talmudic and midrashic traditions concerned with Bible and *halakhah* and somewhat scholastic in nature had first

141

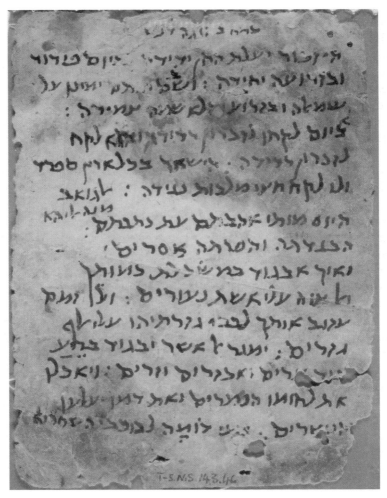

34 – Poems written by Dunash ibn Labrat and his wife, dating from the 10th century
(T-S NS 143.46) (Cambridge University Library)

found themselves more popular roles in the broader life and interests of structured and flourishing Jewish communities and then gone on to inspire the development of what may to a degree be regarded as aspects of secular culture.

If some Jewish literature preserved in the Genizah represents a preoccupation with rabbinic law and lore that ultimately found expression in the composition of both scholastic and popular poetry, there is also evidence that the field of more intense spirituality was not neglected. There is a whole range of mystical material in the Genizah that is called *hekhalot* literature because it purports to describe the celestial palaces. Much of it originated in pre-Christian times and it contains hymns about the attributes of God and his angels, as well as prayers to inspire the pious in their pursuit of the heavenly. There are narratives about those specially holy personalities who have achieved closeness to the divine spheres, and guidance on the use of secret magic for religious purposes. The rabbinic Hebrew and Aramaic used in these texts are characterized by elevated style, lyrical expression, and figurative language. Repetition and rhythm may have been employed to induce trances in those reciting the formulations and this whole genre of literature may have been part of a mystical way of life devoted to fasting, purity and other spiritually uplifting exercises.

There is undoubtedly a significant presence of such material in what became the standard rabbinic prayer-book and no shortage of early Genizah texts that contain a variety of *hekhalot* content. There is, however, considerable difficulty in dating the origins of these traditions, establishing the precise context in which they were used, and defining how they related to what are regarded as more standard rabbinic works. It is therefore by no means clear whether what is found in the Genizah is a mere remnant of a religious expression once much more powerful and influential or is a move towards the more mystical and spiritual in reaction to the growing centrality of the halakhic voice. Some have argued that these texts represent the devotions of pious individuals and small mystical groups while others prefer to give them a greater communal relevance within the rabbinic practice of the early medieval period. What also remains to be clarified is whether what we are seeing is evidence of borrowings by one set of traditions from another or overlaps within a rabbinic Judaism that was broader than is sometimes credited.

Guide to reading

As far as sound scholarly description of the extensive talmudic and halakhic literature is concerned, there is, unsurprisingly, considerably more reference material in Hebrew than in English. For general guidance in the latter language, see the details in the newly revised English version of Emil Schürer's *The History of the Jewish People in the Age of Jesus Christ (175 B. C. – A. D. 135)* by Geza Vermes and Fergus Millar, vol. 1 (Edinburgh, 1973), pp. 68–118; the richly informative volume *The Literature of the Sages. First Part: Oral Tora, Halakha, Mishna, Tosefta, Talmud, External Tractates*, ed. S. Safrai (Assen, Maastricht and

Philadelphia, 1987); and G. Stemberger, *Introduction to the Talmud and Midrash* (Edinburgh, 1996), originally an updated version of Hermann Strack's classic, but now an important work in its own right, with the latest scholarly data.

Recent years have seen notable disagreements between scholars on the earliest history of the rabbinic liturgy, particularly concerning whether there are precedents in earlier Jewish literature for the developments among the teachers of the second century, and whether the texts remained fluid from then until Genizah times. It is always useful to consult I. Elbogen's classic work, now fully available in an English version based on the updated Hebrew edition of 1972 and entitled *Jewish Liturgy: A Comprehensive History* by R. Scheindlin (Philadelphia, Jerusalem and New York, 1993), but it should be borne in mind that most of Elbogen's study was completed early in the century, when Genizah research was in its infancy. For a more current historical survey, see S. C. Reif, *Judaism and Hebrew Prayer* (Cambridge, 1993) and in the matter of the liturgical items in the scrolls from the Dead Sea, most helpful studies are C. Newsom, *Songs of the Sabbath Sacrifice: A Critical Edition* (Atlanta, 1985), B. Nitzan, *Qumran Prayer and Religious Poetry* (Leiden, New York and Köln, 1994) and E. G. Chazon, "Prayers from Qumran", *Dead Sea Discoveries* 1 (1994), pp. 265–85. An updated bibliographical summary is appended to S. C. Reif's contribution to the third volume of the *Cambridge History of Judaism*, scheduled for publication in 1999. The origins, development and content of liturgical poetry have been extensively covered in Hebrew publications and the English reader is best advised to consult, as an introductory volume, T. Carmi's *Penguin Book of Hebrew Verse* (Harmondsworth, 1981), at the beginning of which the editor rightly notes that "scholars are still engaged in the arduous task of processing thousands of manuscripts from the hoard of the Cairo Genizah." A fine example of the treatment of Genizah poetry is J. Yahalom's *Palestinian Vocalised Piyyuṭ Manuscripts in the Cambridge Genizah Collections* (Cambridge, 1997).

The overall literary achievements and cultural developments of the Jewish world in the Middle Ages are themselves also in the process of being traced and assessed. In the meantime, one can view the broader canvas by consulting a number of works. S. W. Baron, *A Social and Religious History of the Jews*, vols. 6–7 (New York, London and Philadelphia, 1958) and M. Waxman, *A History of Jewish Literature*, vols. 1–2 (second edition; New York, 1960) provide the background to the literary history while the set of essays entitled *Communication in the Jewish Diaspora: The Pre-Modern World*, edited by Sophia Menache (Leiden, New York and Köln, 1996) deals with how Jews were in literary contact. Important papers are to be found in *The World History of the Jewish People. Medieval Period. Dark Ages*, edited by Cecil Roth (Tel Aviv, 1966) and there is impressive, illustrative material, as well as helpful text, in *The Jewish World: Revelation, Prophecy and History*, edited by E. Kedourie (London, 1979) and in T. and M. Metzger's *Jewish Life in the Middle Ages* (London and New York, 1985). The cultural symbiosis between Islam and Judaism is covered in S. D. Goitein, *Jews and Arabs: Their Contacts through the Ages* (London, Melbourne and Henley, 1955); E. I. J. Rosenthal, *Judaism and Islam* (London, 1961); Bernard Lewis, *The Jews of Islam* (Princeton, 1984); see also Norman A. Stillman, *The Jews of Arab Lands: a History and Source Book* (Philadelphia, 1979).

The history of the Hebrew book in general is an intriguing subject and the emergence of the codex is of special interest and relevance here. For the overall topic, see D. Diringer, *The Hand-Produced Book* (London, 1953) and *The Hebrew Book: An Historical Survey*, eds. R. Posner and I. Ta-Shma (Jerusalem, 1975). For more detailed studies, see C. Sirat, *Les papyrus en caractères hébraïques trouvés en Egypte* (Paris, 1985) and her brief note on the early liturgical papyrus, T-S 6H9–21, in *Genizah Fragments* 5 (April, 1983), pp. 3–4; S. Lieberman, *Hellenism in Jewish Palestine: Studies in the Literary Transmission, Beliefs and Manners of Palestine in the I Century B. C. E. – 4 Century C. E.* (2nd edition, New York, 1962), pp. 203–9; C. M. Roberts and T. C. Skeat, *The Birth of the Codex* (2nd edition, London, 1983); R. H. Rouse and M. A. Rouse, "Codicology, Western European" in *Dictionary of the Middle Ages*, vol. 3 (New York, 1983), pp. 475–78; M. Beit-Arié, "How Hebrew Manuscripts are Made" in *A Sign and a Witness: 2,000 years of Hebrew Books and Illustrated Manuscripts*, ed. L. S. Gold (New York and Oxford, 1988), pp. 35–46; and I. M. Resnick, "The Codex in Early Jewish and Christian Communities", *Journal of Religious History* 17 (1992), pp. 1–17.

There are many English volumes that may serve as introductions to the history of the talmudic text and its interpretation. In addition to the works of Safrai and Stemberger earlier cited, see also the essays edited by J. Neusner, *The Formation of the Babylonian Talmud* (Leiden, 1970) and by A. Corré, *Understanding the Talmud*, as well as H. Maccoby, *Early Rabbinic Writings* (Cambridge, 1988) and A. Steinsaltz, *The Talmud: The Steinsaltz Edition: A Reference Guide* (New York, 1989). On the matter of the Aramaic used in the rabbinic tradition, ample literature is cited by M. Sokoloff in the collection of essays that he edited entitled *Arameans, Aramaic and the Aramaic Literary Tradition* (Ramat Gan, 1983) and in his *A Dictionary of Jewish Palestinian Aramaic of the Byzantine Period* (Ramat Gan, 1990). For the history of *halakhah* and of responsa literature, see Louis Ginzberg, *Geonica*, 2 vols. (New York, 1909); S. B. Freehof, *Responsa Literature* (Philadelphia, 1955); J. Newman, *Halachic Sources from the Beginning to the Ninth Century* (Leiden, 1969); A. M. Schreiber, *Jewish Law and Decision-Making: A Study Through Time* (Philadelphia, 1979); E. E. Urbach, *The Halakhah: Its Sources and Development* (E. T., Jerusalem, 1986); Mendell Lewittes, *Principles and Development of Jewish Law* (New York, 1987); E. N. Dorff and A. Rosett, *A Living Tree: The Roots and Growth of Jewish Law* (Albany, 1988); and Gideon Libson, "Halakhah and Law in the Period of the Geonim", in *An Introduction to the History and Sources of Jewish Law*, eds. N. S. Hecht, B. S. Jackson, S. M. Passamaneck, D. Piattelli and A. M. Rabello (Oxford, 1996), pp. 197–250; see also N. Danzig, *Introduction to the Halakhot Pesuqot* (Hebrew; New York, 1993). On Samuel b. Ḥofni, see David E. Sklare, *Samuel ben Ḥofni Gaon and his*

145

Cultural World: Texts and Studies (Leiden, New York and Köln, 1996). The latest information in English about Genizah fragments in the talmudic and halakhic fields appears in Robert Brody's essay on the Cairo Genizah included in Benjamin Richler's *Hebrew Manuscripts: A Treasured Legacy* (Cleveland and Jerusalem, 1990) and in Brody's *A Hand-list of Rabbinic Manuscripts in the Cambridge Genizah Collections* (Cambridge, 1998). On Pirqoi ben Baboi, see the useful summary and bibliographical details in *Encyclopaedia Judaica* 13, cols. 560–61, and the work of M. Ben-Sasson and R. Brody on Sa'adya's *Sefer Ha-Sheṭarot* is discussed in *Genizah Fragments* 19 (April, 1990), p. 2. Neil Danzig's volume *A Catalogue of Fragments of Halakhah and Midrash from the Cairo Genizah in the Elkan Nathan Adler Collection of the Library of the Jewish Theological Seminary of America* (New York and Jerusalem, 1997), which has a summarized English introduction, is also important for the study of rabbinic literature in the Genizah.

Some of the history of Jewish biblical exegesis is covered in S. C. Reif, "Aspects of the Jewish Contribution to Biblical Interpretation" in *The Cambridge Companion to Biblical Interpretation*, ed. J. Barton (Cambridge, 1998), pp. 143–59 and there are important essays in this field as well as other Genizah topics in *Genizah Research After Ninety Years*, eds. J. Blau and S. C. Reif (Cambridge, 1992). In the areas of liturgy and poetry, see in addition to the volumes already cited above, the reprinted essays edited by J. J. Petuchowski in *Contributions to the Scientific Study of Jewish Liturgy* (New York, 1970); L. A. Hoffman, *The Canonization of the Synagogue Service* (Notre Dame, 1979); Geoffrey Khan, "Twenty Years of Genizah Research", *Encyclopaedia Judaica Year Book 1983/5* (Jerusalem, 1985), pp. 163–70; and S. C. Reif, "The Genizah and Jewish Liturgy: Past Achievements and a Current Project", scheduled for publication in the proceedings (*Medieval Encounters* 5) of a conference on *'Avodah and Ibada* held in the Institute for Islamic-Judaic Studies at the University of Denver and organized by Professor Seth Ward in March, 1998. The approaches to the Muslim authorities concerning the liturgical practices of Abraham Maimonides, recorded in T-S Ar.41.105 and T-S AS 182.291, have been published by Geoffrey Khan in his *Arabic Legal and Administrative Documents in the Cambridge Genizah Collections* (Cambridge, 1993), pp. 291–94 and the prayers for the Fatimid Caliphs, as in T-S NS 110.26, have been discussed by S. D. Goitein in his contribution to *Studies in Judaism, Karaitica and Islamica Presented to Leon Nemoy*, ed. S. R. Brunswick (Ramat Gan, 1982), pp. 47–57. An English summary of the poems written by and in response to Mrs Dunash in T-S NS 143.46 appears in *Genizah Fragments* 7 (April, 1984), p. 3. On the need to create a better balance between the scholarly treatments of Ashkenazi and Sefaradi cultures in the Middle Ages, see I. Schorsch, "The Myth of Sephardic Supremacy", *Leo Baeck Institute Year Book* 34 (1989), pp. 47–66.

The mystical constituent of Jewish liturgy also continues to attract attention although many of the notions to be found there are notoriously difficult to date. They may appear in substantial form only in the post-talmudic and medieval periods but they are now widely considered to have originated many centuries earlier. Those interested in establishing the nature of the relationship between Jewish mysticism and Jewish liturgy from as early as the axial age should now consult P. Schäfer, *Geniza-fragmente zur Hekhalot Literatur* (Tübingen, 1984); P. B. Fenton, *The Treatise of the Pool* (London, 1981) and *Deux traités de mystique juive* (Lagrasse, 1987); M. Idel, *Kabbalah: New Perspectives* (New Haven and London, 1984); R. Goetschel (ed.), *Prière, Mystique et Judaïsme* (Paris, 1987), especially P. S. Alexander's "Prayer in the Heikhalot Literature" on pp. 43–64 ; M. Bar-Ilan, *The Mysteries of Jewish Prayer and Hekhalot* (Hebrew; Ramat Gan, 1987); and M. D. Swartz, *Mystical Prayer in Ancient Judaism: An Analysis of Ma'aseh Merkavah* (Tübingen, 1992).

For the Hebrew reader, there is a vast literature relating to the development of rabbinic literature up to and including the Genizah period, recent examples of which may be found in the various volumes of the *Index of Articles on Jewish Studies* published annually in Jerusalem, beginning in 1969. The projects of the Israel Academy of Sciences to describe all the fragments from the Genizah in the talmudic and midrashic fields (directed by Professor Jacob Sussmann of the Hebrew University) and in the poetic field (directed by Professor Ezra Fleischer of the Hebrew University) have made extensive progress and are already much consulted. These projects had their earliest origins in the work of B. M. Lewin and J. N. Epstein in the talmudic field and in the work of the Schocken Institute in the sphere of poetry. In addition to what has been cited above, examples of significant Hebrew publications would have to include S. Assaf, *Gaonic Responsa* (Jerusalem, 1928), *Gaonica* (Jerusalem, 1933), *Responsa Geonica* (Jerusalem, 1942), *Texts and Studies* (Jerusalem, 1946) and *Tequfat Ha-Geo'nim Ve-Sifrutah* (Jerusalem, 1955). Also central are the works of Shraga Abramson, including his *Essa Meshali* (Jerusalem, 1943); *Ba-Merkazim Uva-Tefuṣot* (Jerusalem, 1965); *R. Nissim Gaon Libelli Quinque* (Jerusalem, 1965); and *'Inyanot Be-Sifrut Ha-Ge'onim* (Jerusalem, 1974); see also M. Margaliot, *Hilkhot 'Ereṣ Yisra'el min Ha-Genizah* (ed. I. Ta-Shma; Jerusalem, 1973), and the essays and bibliography in the memorial booklet produced by the Israel Academy *Le-Zikhro shel Shraga Abramson* (Jerusalem, 1997). There is a Hebrew essay by S. Spiegel on Pirqoi ben Baboi, citing Cambridge Genizah fragment T-S NS 275.27, in the third volume of the *Harry Austryn Wolfson Jubilee Volume*, eds. S. Lieberman, S. Spiegel, L. Strauss and A. Hyman (Jerusalem, 1965), pp. 243–74. On the matter of talmudic incunables, see H. Z. Dimitrovsky, *S'ride Bavli* (2 vols.; New York, 1979). J. Blau's edition of *R. Moses b. Maimon: Responsa*, 4 vols. (Jerusalem, 1957–61 and 1986) is an essential reference tool and Robert Brody has offered an important estimate of the importance of the Genizah for rabbinic literature in his essay "Terumatah shel Ha-Genizah Le-Ḥeqer Sifrut Ha-Ge'onim", scheduled for publication in *Te'uda* 15, edited by M. A. Friedman, probably in 1999, and has also written on *The Textual History of the She'iltot* (New York and Jerusalem, 1991). Neil Danzig's important volume *A Catalogue of Fragments of Halakhah and Midrash* (already mentioned above) also contains useful information about the rabbinica in the Cairo Genizah and those who have written about it. See also the essays included in *Meḥqere Talmud: Talmudic Studies*, edited by J. Sussmann and D. Rosenthal (Jerusalem, 1990–93). By way of historical background to all developments in the Genizah period, Moshe Gil's studies are essential reading, particularly his *Palestine During the First Muslim Period (634–1099)*, 3 vols. (Tel Aviv, 1983) and his *In the Kingdom of Ishmael*, 4 vols. (Tel Aviv and Jerusalem, 1997).

As far as Hebrew poetry from the Genizah is concerned, the subject has expanded beyond recognition especially since the 1930s and through the pioneering work of the late M. Zulay, A. M. Habermann, J. Schirmann, S. Spiegel and N. Allony. An excellent introduction to the whole subject, with an extensive bibliography, is Ezra Fleischer's *Hebrew Liturgical Poetry in the Middle Ages* (Jerusalem, 1975) and his own list of publications, prepared by T. Beeri and S. Ben-Ari, is to be found in the *Festschrift* edited for him by S. Elizur, M. D. Herr, G. Shaked and A. Shinan entitled *Knesset Ezra: Literature and Life in the Synagogue: Studies Presented to Ezra Fleischer* (Jerusalem, 1994). Fleischer's full treatment of the poem by Mrs Dunash was published as "On Dunash Ben Labraṭ, his Wife and his Son: New Light on the Beginnings of the Hebrew-Spanish School", *Jerusalem Studies in Hebrew Literature* 5 (1984), pp. 189–203. Outstanding Genizah research on poetry is also currently being done by J. Yahalom; see, for example, *A Collection of Geniza Fragments of Piyyuṭe Yannai* (Jerusalem, 1978); *Liturgical Poems of Shimʿon Bar Megas* (Jerusalem, 1984); and *Maḥzor Eretz Israel: A Genizah Codex* (Jerusalem, 1987).

The edition of Saʿadya's prayer-book currently available is that of I. Davidson, S. Assaf and B. I. Joel, *Siddur R. Saadja Gaon* (Jerusalem, 1941, 2nd edition, Jerusalem, 1963) and the fullest study of the Palestinian rite to date is that of E. Fleischer, *Eretz-Israel Prayer and Prayer Rituals as Portrayed in the Geniza Documents* (Jerusalem, 1988). A detailed study of prayers for dignitaries, including T-S NS 110.26, has been produced by P. Fenton, "Tefillah Beʿad Ha-Rashut U-Reshut Bʿad Ha-Tefillah", *Mi-mizraḥ Umi-Maʿarav* 4 (1984), pp. 7–21, and M. A. Friedman has dealt with the special invocations in "R. Yeḥiel b. Elyakim's Responsum Permitting the Reshut" in *Masʾat Moshe: Studies in Jewish and Islamic Culture Presented to Moshe Gil*, eds. E. Fleischer, M. A. Friedman and J. A. Kraemer (Jerusalem, 1998), pp. 328–67. On liturgical ceremonies around Jerusalem, see E. Fleischer, "Pilgrims' Prayer at the Gates of Jerusalem" and H. Ben-Shammai, "A Unique Lamentation on Jerusalem" in the Gil *Festschrift* just noted, pp. 298–327 and 93–102. For a thorough guide to the bibliography on Jewish liturgical matters, see J. Tabory, *Jewish Prayer and the Yearly Cycle: A List of Articles*, supplement to *Kiryat Sefer* 64 (Jerusalem, 1992–93), and a substantial collection of *addenda* to that publication that appeared together with his facsimile edition of the Hanau prayer-book of 1628 (eds. J. Tabory and M. Rapeld, Ramat Gan, 1994). Tabory has also surveyed the latest developments in the whole field in a Hebrew article entitled *"Tefillah"* in supplementary volume 3 of the *Encyclopaedia Hebraica* (Jerusalem and Tel-Aviv, 1995), cols. 1061–68.

SEVEN

POLITICS, PLACES AND PERSONALITIES

The Jews of the Genizah period were no less influenced by the Islamic environment in which they lived than the American or European Jewries of today are swayed by the Western culture that surrounds them. It is not therefore surprising to find that Arabic language played a major role in Jewish life and that Jews built and furnished houses, wore fashionable jewellery, and pursued general commercial and cultural interests much in the same way as their Muslim neighbours. They even visited each other's homes on the occasion of religious festivals. What is more, their religious ideas and practice also took account of what was going on around them, sometimes producing parallel developments, as, for instance, in the matter of the adoption of mystical ideas similar to those of the Sufis, while at others creating an opposite reaction, as, for example, in the defence of Jewish interpretation of Scripture or Jewish religious philosophy against non-Jewish challenges.

MUSLIMS, CHRISTIANS AND JEWS

As far as their status in Islamic society was concerned, Jews and Christians were formally recognized as the next best thing to Muslims. They were *dhimmi* peoples, that is, tolerated monotheistic minorities living under the protection of Islam, and as long as they agreed not to give offence to Muslims by any pretence at equality, they could, when the Muslim rulers tended towards tolerance, enjoy a reasonably good lifestyle. They simply paid their special poll-tax, wore their distinctive Jewish clothes, built no synagogues higher than mosques, and went about their ordinary business. There were occasionally times when rulers decided to take a maximalist position. A national leader might object to the existence of all non-Muslim houses of worship; local leaders might ban Jewish ritual slaughter, demand more taxes, or refuse access to water wells. In the reign of the Fatimid caliph, al-Ḥakim (996–1021), the Jews

149

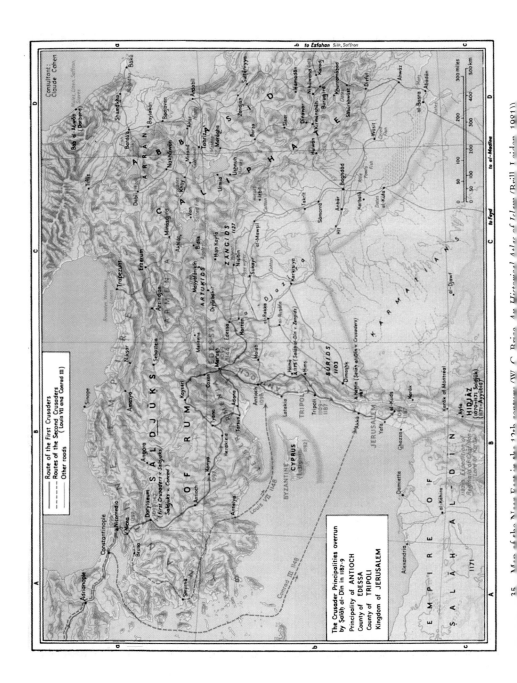

35. Map of the Near East in the 12th century. (W. C. Brice, *An Historical Atlas of Islam* (Brill, Leiden, 1981))

of Cairo compiled a chronicle (*megillat miṣrayim*) in which they praised him for saving them from the mob and from judicial execution on tax charges but it was that same ruler who ordered the destruction of all the synagogues and churches, and whose troops engaged in an orgy of murder, rape and plunder in Cairo and Damascus. Generally, however, what has been referred to as a cultural symbiosis, the productive blending of various cultures, was the dominant theme, particularly during the Fatimid period, from the tenth to the twelfth centuries.

Contrary to what is sometimes thought, it is now clear that Muslims, Christians and Jews in the East did not live intellectually ghettoized lives. They were aware of each other's religious texts and traditions, sometimes recording these in their own languages and literatures, and at other times subjecting them to criticism and even derision. In a religious debate with Rabbanites and Karaites conducted at the end of the tenth century, the Fatimid vizier, Ya'qub ibn Killis, a convert from Judaism to Islam, cited the content of the prayer-book of Sa'adya ben Joseph in order to heap ridicule on the Jewish liturgy. Religious thinkers took account of what was being said and written by the theological opposition, so much so that it is at times possible to reconstruct that opposition by way of the views of such thinkers. Although there was the occasional romantic tryst between a man and woman of different religious allegiance, intermarriage was not a phenomenon of the time. Conversion, however, certainly was. Just as in Christian Europe, there were Jews who were so anxious to climb the social and political ladder that they felt constrained to convert to the dominant faith. Some of them made life difficult for their former co-religionists while others retained a certain sympathy for them, even engaging them in religious dialogues. But the movement was not always in one direction and there are accounts of Muslim and Christian anger at conversions to Judaism. The records of rabbinical courts make reference to approaches made by non-Jews wishing to throw in their religious lot with the Jews. As was the talmudic custom, they were initially rebuffed but there were a number, some of them women, who were determined enough to repeat their applications until they were finally accepted and even married into the Jewish community. One convert missed only one thing from his former life – the Jews could not make bread like the non-Jews!

The Genizah's most famous example of a Christian convert is Obadiah Ha-Ger (=the Proselyte). John Oppidans was born late in the eleventh century in Italy, into an aristocratic Norman family, the twin brother of Roger, who went on to become a knight. He was the son chosen to enter the priesthood but had early doubts about where he

151

36 – The verses set to music by Obadiah the Proselyte (T-S K5.41)
(Cambridge University Library)

belonged religiously. Young John took to studying the Hebrew Bible and was attracted by the way in which its traditions were continued in daily Jewish life. His interest was so intense that he circumcised himself and began to observe Jewish customs. When as a youth he heard that Andreas, the Archbishop of Bari, had converted to Judaism and moved to Egypt, he knew that this was a sign for him to follow a similar path. He moved to Constantinople, progressing with his studies of Judaism and Hebrew literature, and even writing pamphlets challenging

Christian beliefs. He knew that his Christian companions would not be pleased but he never imagined that they would wound, threaten and imprison him, as they did, and force him to lead the life of a fugitive. Constantinople to Baghdad; Baghdad to Aleppo; Aleppo to Banias, at the foot of Mount Hermon, where the River Jordan rises – his travels in search of religious identity and security were many and varied, involving him in much poverty and pain. It was in Aleppo in 1113 that Rabbi Barukh ben Isaac, head of the Yeshivah, verified John's conversion to Judaism, and after a period of residence in Tyre, the newly-named Obadiah Ha-Ger settled in Cairo. Obadiah was a popular raconteur and writer, with many tales with which to entertain his fellow Jews. Although he wrote a brief autobiography and some poetry, his first love was music. He was responsible for committing to writing the texts and the musical notes of liturgical poems and biblical verses used in the synagogue. It may well be the case that he also imported into such music what he had absorbed in his previous existence.

There is one remarkable Cambridge Genizah document, from the late eleventh century, in which reference is made to a Jewish husband and a Muslim wife. Although the man is engaged as an administrator of the Sultan's estates in Palestine, it would seem, as Goitein has suggested, that his marriage to the Muslim woman had taken place earlier in a Christian country, since Muslim law would not otherwise tolerate such a relationship. His wife had apparently left him and taken their daughter with her but she had fallen on bad times and the husband now writes to his daughter from Jerusalem, offering her a choice of future. He explains how successful and powerful he has become and strongly criticizes her mother for her behaviour. He indicates that he will assist her if she clarifies where she stands but that he cannot support her ("one other thing which I cannot do") while she remains in the Muslim community. He concludes with a note about his impending return to Byzantium, perhaps hinting that if she now throws her lot in with him, he will take her with him and look after her:

> Now, my daughter, I do not know with whom you are, with the Jews who are the stock of your father, or with the stock of your mother, the Muslims. But this I wish you to know: even if they wanted to sell you to me, who are my own daughter, I would buy you and rescue you from their hands, except one other thing which I cannot do.

ARABIC SCRIPT

The close contact between Jews and Muslims is also expressed in the number of items written in Arabic script to be found in the Genizah. They amount to about 5% of the total and include legal documents, scientific and religious literature, and folklore. In the legal field, Jews usually settled matters within their own system of jurisprudence but there are instances in which they applied to Muslim courts. They may have done so by way of appeal after losing in their own courts or because a non-Jew was involved. Alternatively, they were in need of the kind of notarization of a contract, a gift or a debt that could be provided only by a government court. Certainly, negative rabbinic attitudes towards the use of such courts softened during the geonic period, when they even left their mark on the organization of Jewish law. Remarkably, the best source of information about the activities of the Fatimid chancery is also the Genizah. Petitions and reports requiring the attention of the caliph, the vizier or some other high official, sometimes with the response attached, cover a great variety of topics. The return of a church to the Christian community; the investigation of a murder on a Nile boat; an enquiry about the payment of poll-tax; and a formal account of battle with the Crusaders – these are only a few of the subjects covered by these official texts. Clearly, not all these documents were either addressed to the court by Jews or in any way affected Jews. Their presence in the Genizah may have come about by way of Jewish court officials, through their sale as scrap, or because of the Jewish content of something scribbled on them; whatever the reason, the circumstance again points to close Muslim-Jewish relations.

Also pointing in the same direction are other Arabic items. Some Jews, such as the Karaites, may have maintained their separate identity by writing their letters or accounts, and indeed their copies of the Hebrew Bible, in Arabic script. Others may have preferred to utilize that language when reporting to Muslim authorities, or as an indication of their professional and administrative competence. Those specializing in medicine, mathematics and the physical sciences, for instance, were accustomed to using Arabic as the medium of broader education. Jews with such educational leanings may have been responsible for the Arabic poetry, philosophy and grammar to be found in the Genizah, although one does wonder about the presence of Qur'ans and other religious literature of Islam. Perhaps the mutual religious awareness already referred to was even more extensive than sometimes thought. Less surprising is the fact that Jews were comfortable with Arabic astrology,

37 – Petition to the 11th-century Caliph al-Mustansir about a murder on a
Nile boat (T-S Ar.42.158) (Cambridge University Library)

magic and folklore, since they were just as likely as their Muslim
counterparts to look for guidance at times of uncertainty and for
entertainment at times of relaxation. There are even examples of Arabic
translations of Jewish biblical and liturgical texts that are written in
Arabic script.

155

THE KARAITE WAY

If the Karaites did write their Hebrew Bibles in Arabic script in order to stress their separate religious identity, such a policy may justifiably be regarded as part of their general efforts over a number of centuries to promote their own brand of Judaism, in opposition to the talmudic variety. Contrary to what is sometimes imagined, they were no minor sect that broke away from the rabbinic norm and soon declined. Far from it. Many Genizah texts testify to the considerable success of their religious philosophy, practice and communal life. Starting with Schechter's discovery of the law-book of Anan ben David, the earliest proponent of the movement, a century of research has demonstrated the major role played by the Karaites in the social, economic, cultural and religious development of the Jewish communities of the Near East from the eighth to the twelfth century. Firstly, it is clear that they had a number of doctrines, traditions and linguistic terms that are in tandem with those recorded in the literature uncovered in the Dead Sea scrolls. It therefore seems unlikely that their religious commitments were totally novel and revolutionary. Their identity in the first century or two of their documented activity was by way of smaller groups, sometimes at theological loggerheads, but gradually these anti-talmudic sects joined forces. This ultimately led to a blossoming of Karaite culture from the tenth to the twelfth centuries, precisely the period best represented in the Genizah texts. Such texts testify to close social relations and even intermarriage, as well as religious differences, between Karaites and Rabbanites.

Karaite communities flourished from Iraq to Spain and were especially strong in Egypt and Eretz Yisrael. Commercial successes led to the emergence of powerful and influential families, some of whose members even held important positions at the Muslim court. Such families founded and supported communal institutions and synagogues, where the stress was on the use of verses from the Hebrew Bible, particularly from the Psalms. Devotion to Zion and a love of the Hebrew language became the characteristic features of many adherents to the faith and large settlements were built up in the Palestinian cities of Jerusalem and Ramla. Groups of such settlers followed the custom of bewailing the loss of the Temple, the Holy City and the homeland, referring to themselves as "the mourners for Zion". The "holy tongue" and the "holy books" were of course their alternatives to the Aramaic language and the talmudic texts beloved of the rabbis and they emerged as champions of both biblical study and Hebrew grammar. They moved

38 – The law-book of Anan, the "founder of Karaism" (T-S 16.364)
(Cambridge University Library)

from Aramaic to Arabic and from Arabic to Hebrew, as they strove to establish a linguistic and literary identity, and in the process they made a major contribution to the Jewish interpretation of Scripture. One of their most outstanding leaders, Daniel al-Qumisi (9–10th centuries), was a prolific Bible commentator who rationally explained away the existence of angels and contemptuously dismissed the views and criticized the activities of both Karaite and Rabbanite predecessors. The rabbinic leadership was ultimately shamed into demonstrating that they too had a love for Zion, for Hebrew, and for the Hebrew Bible. One of the results was an increase in the quantity and an improvement in the quality of biblical exegesis. Even in the area of religious law, the Karaite concern for fixing their own calendar, for kosher food, for ritual impurity, for avoiding marriages between relatives, and for maintaining a fire-free sabbath were strong enough to leave an impact on rabbinic behaviour. Sometimes, the talmudic Jews felt under pressure to intensify

157

their own strictness while in other cases they positively flaunted their own interpretations.

A JEWISH KHAZARIAN KINGDOM

Another remarkable group made its appearance on the Jewish historical scene at about the same time as the earliest Karaites and some historians have even suggested that its cultural remains should be sought among what is today left of the Karaite communities of eastern Europe. Beginning in about the sixth century, a Turkic people called the Khazars made their presence felt in the area between the Black Sea and the Caspian Sea and were in contact and conflict with the Persians, the Byzantines and the Muslims. They established a kingdom which in its heyday held sway over territories and peoples ranging from Armenia to Russia and acted as a kind of political buffer between Islamic power in the south and Christian authority in the north. Jewish lore had long claimed that this kingdom converted to Judaism in about the eighth century and Judah Ha-Levi made use of the tradition in his work popularly known as the *Kuzari*. In this philosophical justification of Judaism that he wrote in the twelfth century, he chose, as the historical and literary peg on which to hang his theology, the account of how the king of the Khazars opted for the Jewish religion. Similarly early is the first account of the tenth-century correspondence between Joseph, King of the Khazars, and Ḥisdai ibn Shapruṭ, the distinguished Jewish politician at the Muslim court of 'Abd al-Rahman III in Cordova, and texts of these letters were transmitted and printed over the centuries. As more critical views began to dominate in the modern period, historians tended to question the authenticity of such sources and expressed doubt about the possibility of separating simple fact from embellished legend.

The evidence about the Khazars recovered from manuscripts found in the Genizah has given a jolt to such scepticism. Again, there is an account of how Jews settled among the Khazars and influenced them to adopt such customs as circumcision and the sabbath. Here too, the Khazarian king is reported to have been influenced by his wife and his Jewish minister to convert to Judaism and to have been criticized by the Christian and Muslim rulers for contemplating such a move. In a text at least a century older than Judah Ha-Levi's *Kuzari*, the tale is told of how leading teachers of Judaism, Christianity and Islam were summoned by the Khazarian king to debate the relative merits of their religions and how the Jewish view was confirmed by sacred texts discovered in a cave. What is more, the correspondence between King Joseph and Ḥisdai the diplomat is no longer restricted to one letter from the Spanish Jewish nobleman enquiring about the origins of this strange Jewish kingdom, the nature of its religious practice and any information it has about the future of the world, and a reply from the Khazar ruler that covers the conversion, the nature of local Judaism, the royal family and what is to be expected in the coming age. There is now a set of correspondence that has recently been interpreted as relating to Ḥisdai and touching on the Khazars as well as on various other aspects of the contemporary Jewish world.

One letter is addressed to the Empress Helena of Byzantium, indicates an interest in travel to the land of the Khazars, and appeals for the welfare of the Byzantine Jews, while a second is more difficult to decipher but may be another example of diplomatic correspondence between the Spanish court and another leading power. Two other letters, also perhaps directed to Ḥisdai in the hope of enlisting his support for local Jewish communities, detail the persecutions suffered by the Jews in Otranto and other towns in southern Italy, and in Toulouse. In the Provençal city, they were forced to bring a tribute to the bishop each Easter and their representative was publicly assaulted for his trouble. Another document is even more intriguing and is of interest not only to those engaged in the study of Jewish history but also to those anxious to recover details of the earliest cultural developments in Russia and Ukraine. It constitutes a letter that apparently made its first appearance in Kiev and that appeals to Jewish communities to assist a Jew named Jacob ben Ḥanukkah who had been imprisoned by non-Jews for his murdered brother's debts but had recently been ransomed by his co-religionists. The ransom had been paid only in part and Jacob was sent on a mission from the Dnieper river as far as Cairo to drum up the necessary financial support in order to clear the balance. Not only is Kiev mentioned but the signatories have Khazarian as well as Hebrew names, and there is one word written in the Khazarian script and language. Perhaps what has been uncovered here is the earliest settlement of Khazar Jews in eastern Europe, one that predated the arrival there of Jews after their emigration and expulsion from western European countries.

JEWS IN PALESTINE

If the Genizah discoveries have illuminated obscure corners of Khazar and Karaite history, they have aimed brilliant flood-lights at what were once the dark expanses of Palestinian Jewish history. From knowing virtually nothing about how the Jews of the homeland conducted their personal, public and intellectual lives in the centuries immediately before and after the Crusader invasion that began in 1099, we now have access to a welter of data about people, places and events. It turns out that the Jews were encouraged to resettle Jerusalem after the Arab conquest of the seventh century and that, despite the difficult economic conditions and political upheavals brought about by competing Muslim claims to the territory, communities grew and flourished. Fragments relate to Ramla as the capital city and to the havoc wreaked there by the terrible earthquake of 1033, to Tyre and Acre as busy sea ports, to Tiberias as a centre of Torah and textiles, and to Ashkelon as a particularly strong fortress. It was perhaps as a result of the earthquake that part of the synagogal premises of the Palestinian Jews in Ramla was still in a state of ruin in 1039. To obtain funding for repairs and maintenance, the leaders leased part of the property to a private individual, Ṣedaqah, son of Yefet, at an annual rental of half a gold piece. There were of course even more miserable times. During the first half of the eleventh century, for instance, letters refer to the battles between Bedouin insurgents and the Fatimid rulers and provide gruesome details of the robbery, rape and crippling overtaxation suffered by the local Jews.

Later, Jews fought alongside Muslims in a desperate effort to defend the Holy Land against the Christian attacks and, when they failed, those unable to flee suffered massacres or capture. As some eye-witness accounts relate, major fund-raising efforts had to be made in other Jewish centres to pay the ransoms demanded by some Christians for the release of Jewish prisoners. Those who did escape made their way northwards to the cities of the Lebanese coast or southwards to Egypt and many documents testify to their resilience in maintaining their

traditions and their identity for two or three centuries. Contrary to what was previously thought, there was a significant Jewish presence in Palestine during the Crusader kingdom. Although only a few Jews lived in and around Jerusalem, there were active and sometimes even prosperous communities in the other cities where they had earlier lived. Following the recapture of the Holy City by Saladin in 1187, Jews rebuilt their community there and, although their situation remained precarious, they were strengthened by the arrival of immigrants from western Europe. The deteriorating situation in England and France in the late twelfth and early thirteenth century, coupled with the spiritual attractions of settlement in the land of Israel, encouraged a number of eminent rabbis and their flocks to make this ideological emigration, or 'aliyah.

Throughout the centuries of the classical Genizah period, the spiritual and intellectual dimension was by no means less significant for oriental Jewry than the political circumstances in which they found themselves. At the same time, it has to be admitted that as the social and economic conditions improved in particular countries, so did the ability of their Jewish communities to influence the broader situation relating to their brethren. Whatever the religious status of a specific centre, it could not retain the reins of spiritual leadership for very long if other areas of Jewish population were larger, better served by communication possibilities, and more affluent. In this connection, one of the most intriguing subjects uncovered by the Genizah is the competing claims of Palestine, Babylon, Egypt, North Africa and Spain to be the arbiters of religious and scholarly standards from the ninth to the thirteenth centuries.

COMPETING CENTRES

As is well known, the ge'onim or heads of the yeshivot that functioned as the leading religious and educational institutions of the Babylonian Jewish communities made every effort in the early centuries of Muslim hegemony to impose their will and authority on the whole Jewish world. As part of a centre that was fast achieving high standards of intellectual and religious development, as well as unprecedented levels of political, administrative and judicial independence, these rabbinic leaders saw standardization of Jewish religious activity as one of their primary objectives. They took advantage of their talmudic and halakhic expertise, and of their comfortable and well respected position in the Jewish world, to issue directives to all and sundry. Not satisfied with their control of the communal life of the Jewish diaspora, they attempted to discredit the religious leadership and practice current in the land of Israel and many a document reflects the tensions that arose as a result. For its part, the Palestinian community fought to protect its traditions against this encroachment and the best example of its rearguard action is perhaps the calendar controversy of the early tenth century. Not only did it argue that it should fix the Jewish calendar; it also took such practical steps in this connection that led to the celebration of the Jewish New Year of 922 on different dates in the two centres. Although the Holy Land ultimately failed in its battle with Babylon, such figures as Aaron ben Meir, Nathan ben Abraham and Solomon ben Judah fought hard for power within Palestine and Egypt and resolutely faced the Karaite challenge. As a result, they succeeded in maintaining their authority over both Jewries during the tenth and the first half of the eleventh centuries and their position was formally recognized by the Fatimid rulers in Cairo.

Interestingly, neither Mesopotamia nor the Holy Land could retain authority over the expanding communities of Egypt, North Africa (including the "bridging" Mediterranean island of Sicily) and Spain. They left indelible marks on the fabric of Jewish religious life there but, after the political deterioration in Palestine and the decline of the Babylonian gaonate, the situation underwent considerable change. While allegiance had previously been owed to the Babylonian and Palestinian academies and no move had been made without reference to their spiritual mentors, the western or Maghrebi communities came of age during the classical Genizah period and developed enough confidence to make their own decisions. Documents relating to such centres as Qayrawan in Tunisia and Andalusian Spain, and making mention of their personalities and institutions, demonstrate without doubt their new powers not only in the social, economic and political fields but also, concomitantly, as Jewish religious trend-setters. This is not to say that these communities themselves were free from persecution and could enjoy unhampered development. The rising power of Muslim fanaticism in Spain and North Africa brought their golden ages to an end in due course but not before they had left a remarkable literary and documentary heritage. Fortunately for lovers of Jewish history, the movement of the relevant populations, in the case of both the Palestinian and the Maghrebi centres, was in the direction of Egypt, where Cairo was ready to become the new hub of Jewish activity and the Genizah depository was waiting to absorb their remarkable records.

Between the eleventh and twelfth centuries, the community of Egypt was transformed from being a satellite of the Palestinian religious authority to being the leader of the Jewish communities in the whole area. At first, the rabbinical academies of Eretz Yisrael sought better conditions in Tyre and Damascus but by doing so initiated an inevitable process by which they lost their spiritual and educational pre-eminence. By 1127, they understood that their place had been taken by the Egyptian community and they acknowledged this fact by moving to Cairo. Meanwhile, the Crusader conquest of the Holy Land had also propelled another significant Jewish emigration in the same direction. For its part, the Tunisian community also contributed to the emergence of the new Egyptian centrality when the Bedouin invasion of 1057 emptied its cities and sent many of its Jewish inhabitants eastwards, a fair number of them to join the synagogue of the Palestinian emigrés in Fustat. The history of the institution of the *nagid*, the head of the Egyptian Jewish community and its representative in the Islamic world, also bears witness to such developments. Although some Jewish literary accounts favour the view that the office was created by the Fatimid authorities when they conquered Egypt in the tenth century, the documentary Genizah evidence appears to point to a gradual emergence in the eleventh century. Responding to internal developments in the Jewish community and external changes in the broader Muslim context, Egyptian Jewry, with a strong Karaite as well as Rabbanite presence, made the necessary adaptations to its infrastructure that gave greater strength and authority to its system of self-government. Between 1082 and 1126, the leadership provided by David ben Daniel, Mevorakh ben Sa'adya and Moses ben Mevorakh ensured the successful completion of the process, as well as leaving future generations a rich source of documentation that testifies to detailed and controversial developments.

PILGRIMAGES

The land of Israel stands at the centre of another type of text to be found in the Genizah, namely, those items relating to pilgrimage. The Jewish custom of visiting holy places, particularly Jerusalem, is of course of biblical origin and was an aspect of religious practice that came to be adopted and adapted by Christianity and Islam. Whatever the reasons, and whichever religion most promoted the idea, the Middle Ages saw an expansion of the custom into a virtual industry and Judaism was affected no less than its daughter faiths. Holy cities, sacred sites and the tombs of venerable sages and saints were among the attractions for the pious pilgrim visiting the land of the Bible and there were those who recorded their experiences for their contemporaries and for posterity. In doing so,

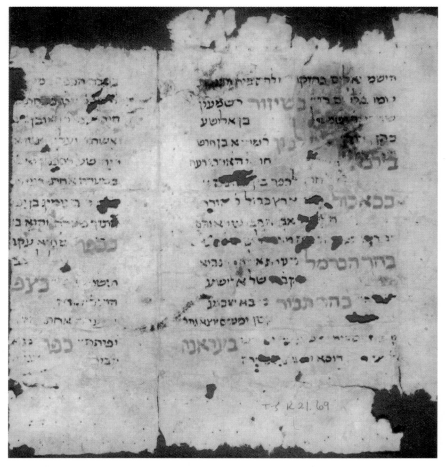

39 – List of burial sites to be visited in the 15th-century Holy Land (T-S K21.69)
(Cambridge University Library)

they also preserved information about more mundane matters, making it possible for later generations to reconstruct details of personalities and populations long since forgotten. In some cases, they described in detail their journeys across Palestine, noting the names of each of the places visited and recalling what had often been unpleasant adventures. Special prayers came to be composed for recitation at particular shrines and the whole exercise gradually developed more formalized patterns for the guidance of its participants.

By the fifteenth century, lists of places, their names boldly written in red ink, had been drawn up, and to each were attached details of which tombs were to be found there. One particular such list from the Genizah, mentioning such places as Safed, Mount Tabor, Kefar Ḥares, Shechem, Shiloh and Ashkelon, and describing the annual pilgrimage and celebration at the tomb of the prophet Samuel in Ramah, was pieced together by various scholars in Cambridge and led to the rediscovery of a lost Galilean town mentioned by the first-century Jewish historian, Josephus. On the basis of its occurrence in the Genizah list, a search was made for Kefar Marus (= Marus=Marut=Merot) by the archaeologist, the late Zvi Ilan, and its ruins were located four kilometres west of Tel Ḥasor, north of Lake Tiberias. The subsequent excavations uncovered the remains of a Jewish community that had continued to exist there through the Byzantine, Islamic, Crusader and Mamluk periods.

For those visiting the Holy Land in the sixteenth century, there were the major Jewish settlements of Jerusalem and Safed to include, and Genizah correspondence between the homeland and Egypt provides an insight into the lives and work of more than a dozen leading scholars, mostly of Spanish origin, who were then active in the Palestinian Jewish communities. One of the rabbinic leaders of the Jerusalem community, known for his participation in the great debate between its sages and those of Safed regarding rabbinic ordination and the possible re-establishment of the Sanhedrin, was Moses de Castro. In a letter written in 1513/14 to a prominent dignitary in Egypt, Abraham ibn Sanji, de Castro requests financial assistance for the completion of a communal building for the Jews of Jerusalem. He also mentions his step-father, the well-known rabbinic visionary, Abraham ben Eliezer Ha-Levi, and his maternal uncle, the famous astronomer and historian, Abraham Zacuto, author of the *Sefer Ha-Yuḥasin*. Concerning them, he writes: "There is nobody in Jerusalem who is poorer and more needy than they are." Moses de Castro also indicates the presence in Jerusalem of his teacher, Rabbi Levi ibn Ḥabib, thus providing a corrective to the prevalent view that the latter had settled in the Holy City only in 1523.

Other such letters make it clear that affluent Egyptian Jews were at that time supporting the Jerusalem community and that particular assistance had been received by both the Ashkenazi and the Sefaradi *yeshivot*, or rabbinic academies. There is also evidence not only of scholarly contacts between Egypt and the land of Israel but also of more mundane matters concerning famous scholars. The signature of one of history's most famous codifiers of Jewish law, Joseph Karo, appears at the foot of one letter, penned in a beautiful Sefaradi hand of the sixteenth century and probably written by a professional scribe. The subject of the correspondence has nothing to do with *halakhah* but concerns a debt owed to the famous rabbi by an Egyptian Jewish dignitary and his most polite request for repayment. There is also a text with a reference to "our honoured teacher and rabbi, Joseph Karo" in connection with a precious stone and in the general context of goods and their prices. Another leading figure from Safed, the distinguished kabbalist, Isaac Luria Ashkenazi (the "Ari") is also mentioned in a letter and again the topic is far from a spiritual one. In this case, the discussion revolves around a consignment of pepper and demonstrates that at least some mystics were obliged to concern themselves with the practical matter of making a living as salesmen.

SA'ADYA'S CONTRIBUTION

Many centuries earlier, the leading *ge'onim*, or institutional heads of Babylonian Jewry, and their successors had also left their personal marks on literature that eventually found its way into the Cairo Genizah. As a result, clearer and more personal accounts of their lives and their literary activity have emerged and one of the best examples of a figure who is now much better known and understood is the leader of the academy of Sura in the tenth century, Sa'adya ben Joseph. Although no Genizah fragment has been identified as containing the actual handwriting of Sa'adya, there are hundreds that record his work and clearly demonstrate that he was the leading rabbinic figure of his day in a number of fields. He offered new translations and commentaries for the Hebrew Bible and composed the first comprehensive anthology of Jewish prayer and poetry. He introduced a new type of literature that devoted single monographs to individual subjects and he was responsible for pioneering developments in the use of Hebrew language, the study of Hebrew grammar, the presentation of Jewish religious thought, and the systematic chronicling of Jewish legal procedure. Above all, the few inaccurate pieces of information about Sa'adya's life that circulated among the learned in the nineteenth century have now been replaced by more reliable data from the Genizah. Already in 1921, a new biography was possible and its author, Henry Malter, made it clear how indebted he was to such data:

> After repeated study of certain Genizah fragments, hitherto partly ignored, and partly misinterpreted, new points of view gradually revealed themselves and fresh combinations appealed for consideration. Finally, after much sifting and analyzing, grouping and classifying of the collected details, the subject of our investigation stood out in relief. For here was

166

Saadia, the *man*, with his human faults and virtues, his passions and convictions, his sufferings and rejoicings, victories and defeats. His entire life opened before us and we could follow his career almost without interruption. At times we were also granted a glimpse into his family affairs and his personal relations with his pupils.

His date of birth could be fixed at 882; his move from Egypt, his birthplace, to Babylon, via Palestine and Syria could be plotted; and his struggles to establish himself as the outstanding authority of his day throughout the Jewish world could be described in detail. Sa'adya emerges as a powerful polemicist who engaged in controversies not only with the local Babylonian leadership but also with the Jews of Eretz Yisrael in the matter of the calendar, with the Karaites on the subject of Jewish theology, and with sceptical intellectuals regarding the validity of the Hebrew Bible. Given the rich texture of his life, and the prolific nature of his literary productivity, it is not surprising that hardly a month passes without the discovery of some new Genizah text relating to his personal and scholarly activities.

Many such texts also relate to the work of other *ge'onim* in Babylon but it is a rare occurrence to find a document in the handwriting of any one of them. This adds to the excitement of one fragment identified as having been personally written by Hai ben Sherira in Baghdad on 9 February 1007, and closely studied by Moshe Gil. The letter is addressed to Abraham and Tanḥum, the sons of Jacob, in the Moroccan city of Fez, and mentions queries sent with a caravan of Muslim pilgrims on their way to Mecca, probably to be left in Egypt for further dispatch. Hai expresses his sadness at the death of the distinguished talmudist, Jacob ben Nissim ibn Shahin of Qayrawan, describes the mourning for him in Baghdad and notes how he himself had lost his father only a short time earlier:

> ... the quire containing your other queries was sent with the pilgrims' caravan... A few days ago, a letter reached us, from our beloved sage Abu'l Faraj, may God grant him everlasting honour, in which he wrote to us about the demise of Abu Yusuf, our lord and master, Jacob the sage, ibn Shahin, may the memory of this righteous one be blessed... This was one of the most distressing disasters and blows that we have suffered ... and I eulogized him at our meetings and gatherings, and the community wept over him... This was a sorrow added to the sorrow over the demise of our diadem, the Gaon, our father...

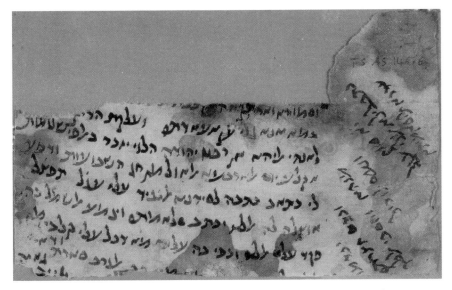

40 – Letter describing the departure of Judah Ha-Levi from Egypt to Israel in 1141
(T-S AS 146.6) (Cambridge University Library)

A POET OF ZION

Another distinguished medieval Jew whose life has been remarkably illuminated by the manuscripts from Cairo is the poet and philosopher from Muslim Spain, Judah Ha-Levi. More than a thousand Genizah fragments provide not only additional texts of his poetry but also details of his stay in Egypt towards the end of his life. It was always well known that he set out from his native Andalusia on a pilgrimage to the Holy Land, where he expected to spend his last days, but it has now become clear that he stopped off in Egypt for a few months early in 1141 and enjoyed a remarkable period of local acclaim and poetic productivity. He was the guest of honour at many soirées and he penned a number of lyrical compositions in honour of his patrons.

Judah Ha-Levi was enjoying himself so much that there were those who believed he would never fulfil his intention of leaving for the land of Israel. Indeed, the difficulties of undertaking the trip by land, and the winter storms that were making the sea journey impossible, kept him in Egypt, and the Genizah material uncovered in the first half of this century about his experiences there seemed to confirm a sad conclusion already reached by some. Despite the longstanding tradition that told of

168

his death under the hooves of a galloping horse as he recited his poems before the walls of Jerusalem, it appeared more likely that he never actually reached his sacred destination. Might he perhaps have ended his days in Egypt in a dizzy spell of parties and paeons? Thanks to the eagle eye of Shelomo Dov Goitein, the story is now known to have a more romantic ending. In a small fragment of a few lines that he found in Cambridge in 1975, Goitein was able to decipher the name of the famous poet and the information that he set sail eastwards from Alexandria on 14 May, 1141, presumably arriving in Palestine within ten days. That would have given him a month to visit the holy sites before his death in July, a pilgrimage by him that is hinted at, if not clearly spelt out, in another Genizah text. Apparently, then, his Zionist ambitions, so clearly expressed in his writings, were finally realized.

MAIMONIDES AS SCHOLAR AND LEADER

Undoubtedly, some aspects of the Genizah discoveries appeal to scholars in their quest to dot another "i" and cross one more "t" in the rewriting of Jewish history, while others excite the imagination of those with no specialized knowledge but with a genuine interest in people and events of the past. There is one topic, however, that attracts universal fascination and that is the life and work of a twelfth-century Cairene rabbi who excelled not only in talmudic studies but also in medicine, philosophy and communal leadership. Known to the Muslims as Abu 'Imran Musa ben Maimun ibn 'Abd Allah, to the Christians as Maimonides, and to the Jews as Rambam, Moses ben Maimon of Cordova ("the Sefaradi" as he called himself) settled in Fustat in the 1160s and in a period of some forty years built himself a reputation as one of Jewish history's greatest figures. That such a reputation was well deserved has become clearer as some sixty fragments in his own handwriting and others closely relating to him have surfaced among the Genizah treasures. Folios from draft copies of his three most famous works on the Mishnah, rabbinic law, and Jewish philosophy show him at work and reveal some of his thought-patterns, particularly concerning the order in which he presented his material, the degree to which he justified his views, and the terminology that he employed. Unlike most of his predecessors and contemporaries, he did not neglect the *Yerushalmi*, the Palestinian version of the Talmud, but also prepared a summary of the religious decisions arising out of that work, a small part of which survived in the Genizah.

What never ceases to amaze those who consult what Rambam succeeded in writing, in a lifespan that barely reached the biblically allotted "three score and ten", is the degree to which he found time not only for composing three of Judaism's major text-books but also, as is convincingly demonstrated by the fragments from the Ben Ezra synagogue, for so much else besides. As a medical expert who ran clinics in the Islamic court of what was then new Cairo as well as teaching medicine, he was much in demand for specialist opinion, as well as consultations and prescriptions, and there are even a few survivors from his medical library. One lengthy letter contains many compliments about Rambam's skill as a physician and begs him to agree, regardless of the amount of fees involved, to take on as a student the writer's own son. When asked by one of the Ayyubid rulers to write on sexual matters, Maimonides prepared a draft text in Judaeo-Arabic before forwarding his definitive text in Arabic. The surviving fragments of that draft contain advice on how best to achieve sexual potency. One should avoid foods such as cucumber, melons, lettuce and most spices, since they cool one down. The opposite effect is said to be achieved by wine and iron water (prepared from iron filings), which are regarded as the best aphrodisiacs.

The majority of enquiries addressed to him were of course on matters of Jewish law. They opened with a welter of epithets that referred at some length to his distinguished learning, his outstanding leadership, and his unique reputation, before finally coming to the controversial point. Was a marriage permitted between *a* and *b*? Who should properly inherit the wealth of *x*? Was it permitted to lengthen the synagogal service by adding lots of liturgical poetry to the statutory prayers? Rushed off his feet with professional, literary and communal commitments, Rambam could rarely do more than append a brief decision to the foot of the enquiry but the survival of hundreds of such responsa indicate that he dealt efficiently with many of the questions addressed to him. He also found the time to provide references for rabbinic colleagues who were travelling to unfamiliar places. In one such case, he introduced a friend, Isaac al-Dar'i, and his son to a colleague of his in another Egyptian city, Minyat Zifta, and pleaded that the poll-tax which was due from them should be paid by that community so that they could continue their journey to Damietta to undertake some business on his behalf.

Other letters and documents relate even more closely to Maimonides the man. It had always been a puzzle how an immigrant to Fustat in the middle of the twelfth century could so quickly make himself indispensable to the community and win their recognition as a leader. Now it turns out that it was his success in mounting a major fund-raising campaign that played an important part in his rise to fame. On

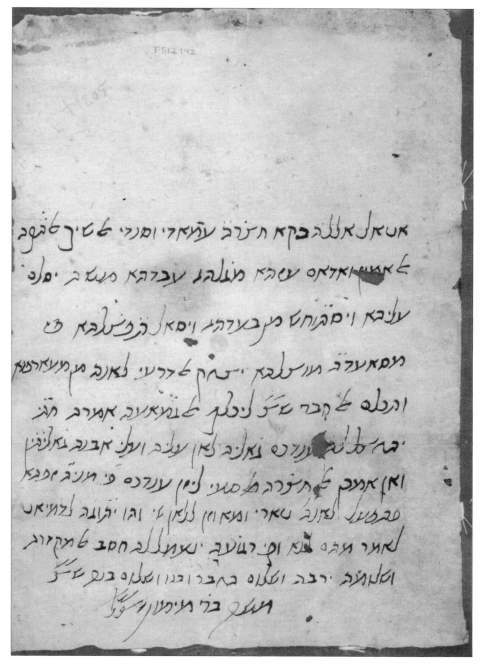

41 – Letter of recommendation written by Moses Maimonides (1138–1204) for his friend Isaac al-Darʿi (T-S 12.192) (Cambridge University Library)

3 November, 1168, the Crusader king of Jerusalem, Amalric, captured the town of Bilbays and took many of its inhabitants, including a large number of Jews, as prisoners. As was the custom of the Christian knights, he sought ransoms for these unfortunate individuals from their co-religionists but at the enormous rate of one hundred gold pieces for every three Jews. Intensive efforts were required to raise the money and it was Rambam who enlisted the support of many communal leaders, cajoled the public to associate themselves with the appeal, and undertook the administration of the finances. As various Genizah documents make clear, this was not the first and last time that he engaged in such charitable work. Having also married (at the same time as one of his sisters) into a local Jewish family and gained recognition as the leading religious authority, it remained for him only to be appointed as the *ra'īs al-yahūd*, the official head of the Jewish community, a year or two later. In a draft copy of the letter of appointment, it is made clear that the purpose "of this blessed, auspicious, fortunate and apposite document is the installation, as communal head, of our glorious, esteemed, great and holy master and teacher, our lord Moses, the great rabbi of the Jewish people." Like all such communal appointments, the leadership was not held without controversy, and after five years Maimonides was replaced by Sar Shalom Ha-Levi, to return to that office only in the last few years of his life.

MOSHE THE MAN

Although we do have correspondence between Maimonides and his sister, Miriam, who had remained in the Maghreb when he emigrated east, it is the detail of his relationship with his brother, David, and how it ended tragically, that makes for the most moving reading. Long before the discovery of the Genizah, it was known that Rambam had a close relationship with his brother, David; that David undertook business trips to maintain the family; and that the drowning of David in the Indian Ocean had brought his brother years of misery and depression. There was always the possibility that further details would be added to the historical picture and in 1954 the distinguished talmudist, Saul Lieberman, at a meeting with Shelomo Dov Goitein in New York, expressed the hope that a fragment might be found of relevance to the sad tale.

Remarkably, during Goitein's next trip to Cambridge, he discovered just such a fragment. It was badly damaged, with large sections of text missing, but Goitein's brilliant decipherment and reconstruction made it possible to correct and refine the information about Moses and David.

Rambam was not the closeted scholar but had a hand in the family's business activities. He had warned his younger brother about the dangers of trips across the desert and voyages by sea. David's last and fatal trip was beset with unfortunate incidents but he optimistically thought that these were over when he reached the Sudanese port of 'Aydhab in the spring of 1169. Unaware that this would prove to be the last communication he would have with his brother, he addressed him affectionately and longingly and reported his plan, together with a number of companions, to set sail for India where he hoped to find the business that had until that time eluded him. He also told the story of his journey from the Nile and how he and one fellow Jew had been separated from the caravan and therefore completed the trip without the safety of numbers or of local tribal protection. An excerpt from the letter, in Goitein's translation, brings the tale to life:

> So we travelled alone out of fear of him. No one has ever dared to embark on such a disastrous undertaking. I did it only because of my complete ignorance. But God [saved] us after many frightful encounters, to describe which would lead me too far afield. When we were in the desert, we regretted what we had done, but the matter had gone out of our hands. Yet God had willed that we should be saved. We arrived in 'Aydhab safely with our entire baggage. We were unloading our things at the city gate, when the caravans arrived. Their passengers had been robbed and wounded and some had died of thirst... We were saved only because we had taken upon ourselves those frightful experiences... So I thought about what I had endured in the [des]ert [and how I was saved;] then it appeared to me an easy matter to embark on a sea voyage... Now despite all of this, do not worry. He who saved me from the desert ... will save me while at sea... Anyhow, what has passed is past, and I am sure this letter will reach you at a time when I, God willing, shall already have completed most of the journey.

Sadly, of course, he never did, and Rambam was left to regret the loss of such a close personal relationship. It seems from much of what he wrote, and from what was written about him, that he was not the kind of man with whom it was easy to have such a relationship and that his contemporaries were somewhat in awe of him. It is consequently exciting to come across in the Genizah, as did Paul Fenton in Cambridge in about 1980, the description of a meeting with the great leader that was singularly friendly. When, in the late 1190s, two envoys were entrusted with the task of delivering an important message to Maimonides, one of

173

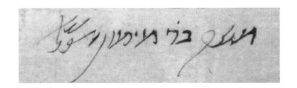

them was reluctant even to seek an audience and left it to his companion, accompanied by his young son, to enter the august premises. He was not only received warmly by the distinguished rabbi but also asked to sit down with him and with his son, Abraham, and entertained to lemon cakes. Rambam expressed his pleasure at the message and the gifts brought to him and chatted intimately with his visitor. Meanwhile, Abraham taught the messenger's son a term with which to address Rabbi Moses and, far from being offended by this lack of formality, medieval Jewry's most outstanding writer and representative was highly amused and played with the child. Politics and places have their central roles and serious functions but revelations about people and their personal contacts and feelings, such as these concerning Maimonides and others that abound in the Genizah, add a welcome dimension to historical analysis.

Guide to reading

The cultural symbiosis between Islam and Judaism is covered in S. D. Goitein, *Jews and Arabs: Their Contacts through the Ages* (London, Melbourne and Henley, 1955); E. I. J. Rosenthal, *Judaism and Islam* (London, 1961); Bernard Lewis, *The Jews of Islam* (Princeton, 1984); Mark R. Cohen and A. L. Udovitch (eds.), *Jews among Arabs: Contacts and Boundaries* (Princeton, 1989); see also Norman A. Stillman, *The Jews of Arab Lands: a History and Source Book* (Philadelphia, 1979). For more detailed examination of the social and political status of Jews and Christians under Islam, see Bat Ye'or, *The Dhimmi: Jews and Christians under Islam* (E. T., London, 1985) and *The Decline of Eastern Christianity under Islam: From Jihad to Dhimmitude Seventh–Twentieth Century* (E. T., London, 1996), and P. B. Fenton, "Interfaith Relations as Reflected in the Genizah Documents", *Bulletin of the Israeli Academic Center in Cairo* 21 (1997), pp. 26–30. The Cairo chronicle from the reign of al-Ḥakim (T-S 8K10) and its aftermath are dealt with by J. Mann, *The Jews in Egypt and in Palestine under the Fatimid Caliphs* (reprinted edition with preface and reader's guide by S. D. Goitein; two volumes in one; New York, 1970), vol. 1, pp. 30–38, vol. 2, pp. 35–37 and 432–37, while the ibn Killis document is at the Jewish Theological Seminary in New York, ENA 3734, f. 12 and ENA 2643, f. 12, and is fully discussed by M. R. Cohen and S. Somekh, "In the Court of Ya'qūb ibn Killis: A Fragment from the Cairo Genizah", *Jewish Quarterly Review* 80 (1980), pp. 283–314.

H. Ben-Shammai has made interesting studies of the intellectual interchanges between Jews and Muslims, as in his article "Mediaeval History and Religious Thought", to be published in the forthcoming volume *Fragments Found and Fathomed*, ed. S. C. Reif (Cambridge, 2000), and a remarkable account of a love affair between a Jew and a Christian is to be found in Or.1080 J93. The theological tensions between Jews and Christians are well exemplified in the excellent edition of *The Polemic of Nestor the Priest* by D. J. Lasker and S. Stroumsa (2 vols., Hebrew and English; Jerusalem, 1996). On the matter of conversions, see Norman Golb, "Notes on the Conversion of European Christians to Judaism in the Eleventh Century", *Journal of Jewish Studies* 16 (1965), pp. 69–74, especially concerning T-S 12.732, and S. D. Goitein, *A Mediterranean Society*, vol. 2 (Berkeley, Los Angeles and London, 1971), pp. 299–311. The fragment containing a proselyte's comments on bread is T-S 12.244 and is cited by Goitein on p. 129 of that volume. Most of the relevant publications on the famous proselyte Obadiah are cited by Golb in his important article "The Music of Obadiah the Proselyte and his Conversion", *Journal of Jewish Studies* 18 (1967), pp. 43–63 and the Cambridge Genizah fragments central to the story are T-S K5.41, T-S Misc.35.31, T-S 10K21 and T-S 8.271. The document relating to the Jewish husband and the Muslim wife is Or.1080 J21, published in English translation by S. D. Goitein in his "Parents and Children: A Geniza Study on the Medieval Jewish Family", *Gratz College Annual of Jewish Studies* 4 (1975), pp. 55–57.

The Arabic material in the Genizah is described by Geoffrey Khan in his articles "The Arabic Fragments in the Cambridge Genizah Collections", *Manuscripts of the Middle East* 1 (1986), pp. 54–60 and "Arabic Documents in the Cairo Genizah", *Bulletin of the Israeli Academic Center in Cairo* 21 (1997), pp. 23–25. A wealth of such texts are carefully edited, translated and annotated in his volume *Arabic Legal and Administrative Documents in the Cambridge Genizah Collections* (Cambridge, 1993). The specific items here mentioned are to be found in T-S Ar.7.38, T-S Ar.42.158, T-S Ar.42.177, and T-S 16.114 together with T-S 24.57, T-S AS 11.383 and T-S AS 146.95, described in Khan's volume, pp. 321–23, 330–31, 359–60 and 428–30; see also Gideon Libson, "Halakhah and Law in the Period of the Geonim", in *An Introduction to the History and Sources of Jewish Law*, eds. N. S. Hecht, B. S. Jackson, S. M. Passamaneck, D. Piattelli and A. M. Rabello (Oxford, 1996), pp. 197–250. The remarkable texts of the Hebrew Bible transcribed in Arabic script also receive the important attention of Khan in his volume *Karaite Bible Manuscripts from the Cairo Genizah* (Cambridge, 1990) while the material relating to the medical field is dealt with by H. D. Isaacs, assisted by Colin Baker, in *Medical and Para-Medical Manuscripts in the Cambridge Genizah Collections* (Cambridge, 1994), where there are brief descriptions of 1,616 items. The complicated linguistic situation documented in the Genizah material, and the particular uses of Hebrew, Arabic and Aramaic, are discussed in the ninth chapter below under the title "Bookish and Lettered".

The subject of the Karaites and Karaism is so central to Genizah research that there is hardly a single study relating to these manuscripts that does not touch on it. For general guidance, examples of texts and bibliographical details, see S. Schechter, *Documents of Jewish Sectaries, vol. 2: Fragments of the Book of the Commandments of Anan* (Cambridge, 1910); J. Mann, *Texts and Studies in Jewish History and Literature* (2 vols., Cincinnati and Philadelphia, 1931–35; and the reprint of Philadelphia-New York, 1991, with Gershon Cohen's important essay on "The Reconstruction of Gaonic History"); *Karaite Anthology: Excerpts from the Early Literature*, ed. L. Nemoy (New Haven and London, 1952); Z. Ankori, *Karaites in Byzantium: The Formative Years 970–1100* (New York and Jerusalem, 1959); N. Wieder, *The Judean Scrolls and Karaism* (London, 1962); *Karaite Studies*, ed. P. Birnbaum (New York, 1971); *Studies in Judaica, Karaitica and Islamica presented to L. Nemoy*, ed. S. R. Brunswick (Ramat Gan, 1982); G. Khan, *Karaite Bible Manuscripts from the Cairo Genizah* (Cambridge, 1990); Michael Corinaldi, "Karaite Halakhah" in *An Introduction to the History and Sources of Jewish Law*, eds. N. S. Hecht, B. S. Jackson, S. M. Passamaneck, D. Piattelli and A. M. Rabello (Oxford, 1996), pp. 251–69; and M. Polliack, *The Karaite Tradition of Arabic Bible Translation* (Leiden–New York–Köln, 1997). A study of the Hebrew style of Karaite marriage documents found in the Genizah is shortly to be published by Judyta Olszowy-Schlanger. The first Cambridge Genizah document to be published in connection with the Khazarian correspondence was T-S Misc.35.38, treated by S. Schechter, "An Unknown Khazar Document", *Jewish Quarterly Review*, N. S., 3 (1912–13), pp. 181–219. P. Kokovtsov made a major contribution to the field in his Russian publications but there are comprehensive studies in English of the various manuscripts, also including T-S 12.122 (on Kiev), T-S J2.71 and T-S Misc.35.45, by D. M. Dunlop, *The History of the Jewish Khazars* (Princeton, 1954) and by Norman Golb and Omeljan Pritsak, *Khazarian Hebrew Documents of the Tenth Century* (Ithaca and London, 1982). A more popular and controversial study of the subject is Arthur Koestler's *The Thirteenth Tribe* (London, 1976). As pointed out in chapter 5 above, when reference was made to the Damascus Document, scholars have sometimes linked Karaism and Samaritanism. The Genizah material contains a few scattered remnants of Samaritan items, such as the Targum to the Pentateuch in T-S 16.317, liturgy in T-S 8.267 and Hebrew Pentateuch in T-S Ar.1a.136, as has been pointed out in books and articles by A. D. Crown, A. Tal and B. Tsedaka; see, for example, *A Companion to Samaritan Studies*, eds. A. D. Crown, R. Pummer and A. Tal (Tübingen, 1993), p. 46, and A. Tal, *The Samaritan Targum of the Pentateuch: A Critical Edition* (3 vols.; Tel Aviv, 1980–83), vol. 3, pp. 50–51.

For many years, Mann's *The Jews in Egypt and in Palestine*, mentioned in the first paragraph of this reading list, was the most informative guide in English to the history of Palestinian Jewry in the Genizah period. It has now, however, been overtaken by the remarkably comprehensive treatment of the sources produced by M. Gil in *A History of Palestine 634–1099* (Cambridge, 1992; based on the original 3-volume Hebrew edition, Tel Aviv, 1983). On the Crusader aspect, see J. Prawer, *The Latin Kingdom of Jerusalem* (London, 1972), and for the overall military and social situation, see the collection of essays *War and Society in the Eastern Mediterranean, 7th–15th Centuries*, ed. Y. Lev (Leiden– New York–Köln, 1997), especially Elinoar Bareket's contribution "Personal Adversities of Jews during the Period of the Fatimid Wars in Eleventh Century Palestine", pp. 153–62. A brawl in Ramla is described in T-S 8J22.25 and details of an earthquake in that city occur in 18J3.9, while the rental of the synagogal premises there is documented in Add.3358 and the emigration of Ashkenazi Jews to the land of Israel is reported in T-S 12.299.

On the competing claims to leadership by the Palestinian, Babylonian and Egyptian Jews, there is much material in the volumes by Mann and Gil just mentioned, as well as in H. Malter, *Saadia Gaon: His Life and Works* (Philadelphia, 1921), where the calendar controversy is discussed, in M. R. Cohen, *Jewish Self-Government in Medieval Egypt: The Origins of the Office of Head of the Jews, ca. 1065–1126* (Princeton, 1980) and in R. Brody, *The Geonim of Babylonia and the Shaping of Medieval Jewish Culture* (New Haven and London, 1998); see also, more generally, the helpful articles of M. Ben-Sasson, "Cairo Genizah Treasures and their Contribution to Jewish Historiography", *Bulletin of the Israeli Academic Center in Cairo* 21 (1997), pp. 3–12 and Jane S. Gerber, "My Heart is in the East" in *The Illustrated History of the Jewish People*, ed. Nicholas de Lange (Toronto, 1997), pp. 141–97. Much Genizah material is cited by E. Ashtor in his *The Jews of Moslem Spain* (3 vols., Philadelphia, 1973–84, based on the Hebrew edition of 1960–66) and the subject is well summarized by Jane S. Gerber, *The Jews of Spain* (New York, 1992). The best source for the medieval history of Maghrebi Jewry is H. Z. Hirschberg, *History of the Jews in North Africa* (2 vols.; Leiden, 1974–80, based on the Hebrew edition of Jerusalem, 1965).

Immigration and pilgrimage to the Holy Land during the classical Genizah period is again dealt with by Gil in his *History of Palestine* (Cambridge, 1992), pp. 609–31. There are numerous accounts of the general phenomenon during the late medieval and early modern periods; see, for example, on the Jewish side H. M. Adler, *The Itinerary of Benjamin of Tudela* (London, 1907) and on the Christian side H. F. M. Prescott, *Jerusalem Journey: Pilgrimage to the Holy Land in the Fifteenth Century* (London, 1954) and *Once to Sinai: The Further Pilgrimage of Friar Felix Fabri* (London, 1957). For details of a journey, see T-S Misc. 22.277 and special prayers are included in T-S Ar.53.2. The rediscovery of Kefar Marus through the Genizah documentation is reported in *Genizah Fragments* 8 (October, 1984), p. 4 and the relevant fragments are T-S K21.69, T-S Ar.49.164 and T-S AS 74.25 and 227. Details of Moses de Castro's letter and of other Jewish connections between Egypt and Palestine are given by Abraham

David in *Genizah Fragments* 15 (April,1988), p. 2, on the basis of Or.1080 J193 and T-S 13J24.21. For references to Joseph Karo, see *Genizah Fragments* 8 (October, 1984), p. 2 and the original Genizah manuscripts T-S Misc.10.80 and 13J24.28, while the Ari's business ventures are documented in T-S 12.589 which was published by E. J. Worman, "Un Document concernant Isaac Louria", *Revue des Etudes Juives* 57 (1909), pp. 281–82.

S. Schechter began the process of exploiting the Genizah source for writing about Sa'adya with his *Saadyana: Geniza Fragments of Writings of R. Saadya Gaon and Others* (Cambridge, 1903) and was followed by H. Malter with his extensive work *Saadia Gaon: His Life and Works* (Philadelphia, 1921), from which the quotation is here cited (p. 10). On the grammatical side, Solomon Skoss was among the earliest to examine the fragments of Sa'adya's work and published *Saadia Gaon: The Earliest Hebrew Grammarian* (Philadelphia, 1955). Among the most important reconstructions of his works that make significant use of Genizah material are the Hebrew editions of I. Davidson, S. Assaf and B. I. Joel, *Siddur R. Saadja Gaon* (Jerusalem, 1941, 2nd edition, Jerusalem, 1963); M. Zucker's *Rav Saadya Gaon's Translation of the Torah* (New York, 1959) and *Saadya's Commentary on Genesis* (New York, 1984) and Y. Ratzaby's publication of additional fragments of Sa'adya's commentaries, as in *Sinai* 109 (1992), pp. 97–117, 193–211 and *Sinai* 111 (1993), pp. 1–26; and N. Allony's *Ha-'egron* (Jerusalem, 1969). Currently in the press is an edition of his systematic chronicling of Jewish legal procedure *Sefer Ha-Sheṭarot* (*Book of Testimonies and Decrees*) by M. Ben-Sasson and R. Brody. The 1995 conference of the Society for Judaeo-Arabic Studies held in Strasbourg was devoted to "Saadiah Gaon: Pioneer of Judaeo-Arabic" and the proceedings are now being prepared for publication by P. B. Fenton. The autograph of Hai Gaon is to be found in T-S 12.829 and is discussed by Moshe Gil in *Genizah Fragments* 21 (April, 1991), p. 2, with a plate, based on his edition in *The Kingdom of Ishmael* (detailed among the Hebrew publications listed below), vol. 2, no. 38, pp. 114–18.

J. Yahalom has compiled a most informative and readable account of the life and work of Judah Ha-Levi, as reflected in Genizah sources, in his article "Judah Halevi and Mediaeval Hebrew Poetry", to be published in the forthcoming volume *Fragments Found and Fathomed*, ed. S. C. Reif (Cambridge, 2000) and summarizing a number of his earlier Hebrew articles. Among the most important sources in English, in addition to Yahalom, are the treatments of S. D. Goitein in his *A Mediterranean Society*, vol. 5 (Berkeley –Los Angeles–London, 1988), pp. 448–50, 464–65 and his article "The Biography of Rabbi Juda Ha-Levi in the Light of the Cairo Geniza Documents", *Proceedings of the American Academy for Jewish Research* 28 (1959), pp. 41–56. The fragment about Ha-Levi's voyage to Palestine is T-S AS 146.6, published by Goitein in the Hebrew article in *Tarbiz* 46 mentioned below.

Details of the Maimonides autographs are to be found in S. D. Sassoon's list in the introduction to *Maimonidis Commentarius in Mischnam*, ed. R. Edelmann

(Hafniae, 1956), with facsimiles in plates XX–LXI, with addenda provided by S. Hopkins, "A New Autograph Fragment of Maimonides' *Hilkhot Ha-Yerushalmi*", *Journal of Semitic Studies* 38 (1983), pp. 273–96, which deals with Genizah fragments T-S Ar.34.169 and T-S F17.7a. The appeal to Maimonides to accept the writer's son as a medical student is in T-S 16.291 and has been edited and translated by Joel Kraemer in his "Six Unpublished Maimonides Letters from the Cairo Genizah", *Maimonidean Studies* 2 (1991), pp. 73–80 while the text on sexual potency is to be found in T-S Ar.44.79, as described by H. D. Isaacs and Colin Baker, *Medical and Para-Medical Manuscripts in the Cambridge Genizah Collections* (Cambridge, 1994), p. 47. For some examples of letters and decisions by Maimonides, see Kraemer's article just mentioned and also his "Maimonides' Letters Yield their Secrets" *Genizah Fragments* 16 (1988), pp. 3–4 and "Two Letters of Maimonides from the Cairo Geniza", *Maimonidean Studies* 1 (1990), pp. 87–98; see also S. D. Goitein, *A Mediterranean Society*, vol. 2 (Berkeley–Los Angeles–London, 1971), pp. 159–61. The famous fragment concerning Isaac al-Dar'i is T-S 12.192, one of the two letters edited by Kraemer in 1990. Details of the biography of Maimonides supplied by Genizah material are provided by S. D. Goitein, *Letters of Medieval Jewish Traders* (Princeton, 1973), pp. 207–12 and "Moses Maimonides, Man of Action: A Revision of the Master's Biography in Light of the Geniza Documents", in *Hommage à Georges Vajda*, eds. G. Nahon and C. Touati (Louvain, 1980), pp. 155–67; P. B. Fenton, "A Meeting with Maimonides", *Bulletin of the School of Oriental and African Studies* 45 (1982), pp. 1–4, with two plates; and M. Ben-Sasson, "Maimonides in Egypt: The First Stage", *Maimonidean Studies* 2 (1991), pp. 3–30. The four fragments concerning his ransom, appointment, brother David and friendly meeting are T-S 16.9, T-S J2.78, Or.1081 J1 and T-S 8J14.18. For a general bibliography of publications on Maimonides in the European languages, see D. R. Lachterman, "Maimonidean Studies 1950–86", *Maimonidean Studies* 1 (1990), pp. 197–216.

Those who read Hebrew should also consult: M. Ben-Sasson, "Geniza Evidence on the Events of 1019–1020 in Damascus and Cairo" in *Mas'at Moshe: Studies in Jewish and Islamic Culture Presented to Moshe Gil*, eds. E. Fleischer, M. A. Friedman and J. A. Kraemer (Jerusalem, 1998), pp. 103–23. S. Stroumsa, "On Jewish Intellectual Converts to Islam in the Early Middle Ages", *Pe'amim* 42 (1990), pp. 61–75; M. A. Friedman, *Jewish Polygyny in the Middle Ages: New Documents from the Cairo Geniza* (Tel Aviv, 1986), especially pp. 332–39, concerning converts, the subject of T-S G2.66 and T-S 12.232; M. Gil, *The Tustaris: Family and Sect* (Tel Aviv, 1981); Y. Erder, "The Negation of the Exile in the Messianic Doctrine of the Karaite Mourners of Zion" and H. Ben-Shammai, "A Unique Lamentation on Jerusalem by the Karaite Author Yeshu'a ben Judah" in the Gil *Festschrift* just noted, pp. 56–81 and 93–102; S. D. Goitein, *Palestinian Jewry in Early Islamic and Crusader Times in the Light of the Geniza Documents* (Jerusalem, 1980); S. Assaf, *Texts and Studies* (Jerusalem, 1946); J. Prawer (ed.), *The History of Jerusalem: The Early Islamic Period*

638–1099 (Jerusalem, 1987); J. Prawer and H. Ben-Shammai (eds.), *The History of Jerusalem: Crusaders and Ayyubids (1099–1250)* (Jerusalem, 1991); J. Braslavi, *Studies in our Country: its Past and Remains* (Tel Aviv, 1954); A. David, "Jews in Crusader Acre in Light of a New Geniza Source" in *Mas'at Moshe* (see beginning of this paragraph above), pp. 158–63; Moshe Gil, *In the Kingdom of Ishmael* (4 vols., Tel Aviv and Jerusalem, 1997); A. Grossman, *The Babylonian Exilarchate in the Geonic Period* (Jerusalem, 1984); E. Bareket, *The Jewish Leadership in Fustat in the First Half of the Eleventh Century* (Tel Aviv, 1995) and *The Jews of Egypt 1007–1055* (Jerusalem, 1995), as well as her supplementary articles "The Jewish Leadership in Fustat in the First Half of the Eleventh Century", *Michael* 14 (1997), pp. 77–88 and "The Affair of Abraham b. Samuel ha-Sepharadi" in *Mas'at Moshe* (see beginning of this paragraph above), pp. 124–36; S. Sela, "The Headship of the Jews in the Fāṭimid Empire in Karaite Hands" in *Mas'at Moshe* (see beginning of paragraph above), pp. 158–63; H. Z. Hirschberg, *A History of the Jews of North Africa from Antiquity to our Time* (2 vols.; Jerusalem, 1965); M. Ben-Sasson, *The Jews of Sicily 825–1068: Documents and Sources* (Jerusalem, 1991) and *The Emergence of the Local Jewish Community in the Muslim World: Qayrawan 800–1057* (2nd edition; Jerusalem, 1997); E. Ashtor, *Toledot Ha-Yehudim Be-Miṣrayim Uve-Suryah taḥat Shilṭon Ha-Mamelukim* (3 vols., Jerusalem, 1944–70); E. Reiner, "Pilgrims and Pilgrimage to Eretz Yisrael 1099–1517" (doctoral dissertation, Hebrew University of Jerusalem, 1988); Zvi Ilan and Emmanuel Damati, *Meroth: The Ancient Jewish Village* (Tel Aviv, 1987); M. E. Artom and A. David, *From Italy to Jerusalem: The Letters of Rabbi Obadiah of Bertinoro from the Land of Israel* (Ramat Gan, 1997); A. David's article on T-S Misc. 22.277 in *Sefer Bar-Adon* (*Yisrael 'Am Va-'Areṣ* 7–8; Tel Aviv, 1994), pp. 223–30; S. D. Goitein, "Did Yehuda Halevi arrive in the Holy Land?", *Tarbiz* 46 (1977), pp. 245–50; E. Fleischer, "'The Essence of our Land and its Meaning': Towards a Portrait of Judah Halevi on the basis of Geniza Documents", *Pe'amim* 68 (1996), pp. 4–15. J. Blau's edition of *R. Moses b. Maimon: Responsa*, 4 vols. (Jerusalem, 1957–61 and 1986) is an essential reference tool and T-S 12.202 on the matter of the permitted marriage is edited there as no. 280, on p. 530. See also J. L. Kraemer, "Four Geniza Letters Concerning Maimonides" in *Mas'at Moshe* (see beginning of this paragraph above), pp. 381–400. For a general bibliography of publications on Maimonides in Hebrew, see Bitya Ben-Shammai, "Twenty-Five years of Maimonides Research: a Bibliography 1965–80", *Maimonidean Studies* 2 (1991), Hebrew section, pp. 17–42.

EIGHT

EVERYDAY
LIFE

"I promise my future wife that I shall walk the straight and narrow and avoid the company of rotten people..." [T-S 20.160]

"God knows, prices are so unpredictable these days..." [T-S 13J18.8]

"Trying to leave without paying your tax? You'd better come along with me, sir..." [T-S 13J16.10]

"The man is useless. I've been a frustrated woman for months now. Let's separate..." [T-S K25.205]

"Please don't spank my child for being late. His homework delayed him..." [Or.1081 J4]

"He doesn't understand his own sermons. He is an ignoramus, repeating things like a parrot..." [T-S 12.608]

It may not be polite but listening to snippets of other people's conversations can be a fascinating experience. Perhaps there is something of the voyeur in even the most bashful of us, making it impossible to resist the temptation to glance over a shoulder and see what someone else is reading or writing. Having glimpsed only a corner of the picture, our imaginations then complete the canvas, usually colourfully, sometimes wildly. Maybe we need to be reassured that other humans suffer the same experiences, emotions and reactions as we do. That is certainly true in the case of our attitudes to generations long since passed away. The diaries of Victorian and Edwardian women, the political and personal papers of imperial courts long since defunct, and the accounts given by soldiers and travellers of adventures enjoyed centuries ago have a remarkable power to stir excitement in the hearts of those who would deny that history is anything but dry and dull. Hollywood epics and historical novels cater to this fascination with what people once said and did, especially in private. The timelessness of Shakespearian tragedies on the one hand, as well as the popularity of classical pieces of art on the other, testify to the human need to identify with the thoughts and feelings of bygone ages. Most of us have at some time wished that we could have been present, preferably with a video-camera, at some famous events, or even ordinary incidents, in the history of at least one group of our ancestors.

Incredible as it may seem, the quotations at the head of this chapter are merely a tiny sample of the thousands of remarks recorded among the Jewish communities of the Arab world almost a thousand years ago. After William the Norman had conquered England, and while the primitive English were snatching territory from the boorish Scots and the feudal French, and fighting among themselves to see whether church, nobility or royalty would control their destinies, great Muslim empires held sway over much of the Mediterranean area and reached high levels of achievement in mathematics, medicine, poetry and religious thought. Egypt was at the centre of the Islamic political system of the day, and Cairo was its capital. There the Ben Ezra synagogue saw successive generations of refugees arrive from the Holy Land in flight from the Crusader aggressors, from North Africa to escape the cruel choice of the Qur'an or the sword, and from Spain out of the clutches of the bigoted Catholic inquisitors. Its unique Genizah archive is a rich source of information not only about major historical events and personalities, and the great variety of medieval Hebrew literature, but also about the daily life of the Jew in the Mediterranean area of the Middle Ages. It provides a remarkable insight into the Jewish past and the opportunity of thereby reaching a better understanding of Jewish identity in the present. Thanks to much recent work in conservation and research, a number of experts in the field, headed and inspired by the late Professor Shelomo Dov Goitein, have been able to reconstruct the everyday life of Mediterranean Jewry all those centuries ago. Primarily through their efforts, we can now enjoy some sample glimpses into the practical world of yesterday.

MARRIAGE ARRANGEMENTS

From at least as early as talmudic times, marrying into the aristocracy meant for the Jewish parent the opportunity of securing a son-in-law with an outstanding knowledge of Torah and Hebrew learning. In order

42 – Jewish marriage document describing a "mixed marriage" between a Karaite woman and a Rabbanite man (T-S 24.1) (Cambridge University Library)

to make such a *shiddukh*, or a match equally attractive from some other point of view, there were Cairene families who were willing to look as far afield as Lebanon (400 miles), Iraq (1,000 miles), Yemen (1,500 miles) or even Spain (1,500 miles). When such distances were involved (and even at shorter distances), the young couple obviously had little opportunity of making each other's acquaintance before the marriage. On some occasions, the prospective bride and groom were separated not only by geographical distance but also by religious allegiance. Before the rabbinic authorities put a stop to such practices in the time of Maimonides, marriages took place between the Rabbanite Jews, who looked to the Talmud as well as the Torah as their authority, and their Karaite counterparts, who followed only the letter of the biblical law. In those cases, each side agreed not to offend the religious susceptibilities of the other. In one such marriage, between the Karaite woman, Nesi'ah, daughter of Moses, and the leading Rabbanite, David, son of Daniel, the *ketubbah*, dated 1082, stipulates precisely what she will and will not do in religious matters. She will not violate her Karaite customs by sitting with him and enjoying the sabbath lights, nor will she eat that part of the animal's tail that is permitted by Rabbanite law. As far as the calendar is concerned, she refuses to profane any day declared to be a festival by her sect, but she does agree to observe his religious holidays too.

Within the Rabbanite community itself there were women who were able to insist on certain conditions, above and beyond what was regarded as standard, before they agreed to marry. For many, what was important to them in a community that countenanced polygyny, was the right to be the exclusive wife. Among the Palestinian Jewish women, but not among their Babylonian counterparts, it was an accepted practice to insist on the right to demand a divorce for no reason other than incompatibility, that is, in the event that the wife simply no longer cared for her husband. In such circumstances, however, she did agree to forfeit her alimony. Some women were concerned about protecting the inheritance rights of their children by an earlier marriage, while for others the matter of a fine funeral, or a beautifully illuminated marriage contract (*ketubbah*), clearly played on their minds. The conditions set by the bride, Fa'iza, the daughter of Solomon, in Fustat in 1047, identify her and her family as people who knew what they wanted from the bridegroom, Ṭuvia, son of Eli, and were obviously very much concerned that he might not be able to meet their standards. The central part of his declaration makes interesting reading:

> I shall behave towards her in the way that fine Jews behave towards their decent wives... I shall associate with good men and not corrupt ones. I shall not bring home licentious individuals, buffoons, frivolous men, and good-for-nothings. I shall not enter the home of anyone attracted to licentious behaviour, to corruption and to revolting activities. I shall not associate with them in eating, drinking or any other activity. I shall not purchase a slave-girl for myself, as long as this Fa'iza is my wife, unless she explicitly consents. I shall not leave Fustat, Egypt, to travel abroad, unless she specifically agrees.

Other, more unfortunate women, were delighted to have the opportunity to marry at all. In a case brought before the rabbinic court of David, son of Abraham and grandson of Maimonides, a woman agreed that her future husband should retain the right to have other wives. She felt obligated to him for having rescued her from her Arab captors by paying a ransom and was obviously aware that her bargaining position

43 – Bridegroom Ṭuvia ben Eli promises to behave and not to go "drinking with the boys" (T-S 20.160) (Cambridge University Library)

had been weakened by the fact that they had raped her, together with a number of other Jewish women, during captivity. There was an even sadder ending to another story which began with the husband giving his very attractive wife a conditional divorce to be activated if he failed to return from a trip abroad. After his lengthy absence, she took advantage of his offer and married a husband with more opportunity to stay at home. When the first husband heard of this, he returned home and, in the physical confrontation that followed, both men and the woman met their deaths.

WOMEN WITH CLAIMS

It should not be imagined that all women functioned only as housewives. Some provided medical services while others specialized in wholesale dealing, in the sale of flour, in the teaching of embroidery, in book sales, or in the making of perfumes. One of the most remarkable was Wuḥsha ("Desirée"), or Karima ("dear one"), daughter of Ammar, who was independently minded enough to make her own way in the commercial world, to fight for her financial rights in business deals, and to build up a large fortune as a banker. What is more, she divorced her husband after the birth of a daughter and then lived with a married man, contracting only the equivalent of a "civil marriage", and bearing him a son. The scandal led to her removal from the Iraqi synagogue on Yom Kippur but her gifts to charity appear to have regained for her at least the posthumous respect of the communal authorities. Some brides at the top of the social and economic scale brought into their marriages long lists of jewellery, clothing and linen up to the value of the average price of a house and a few even greeted their grooms with ten times that amount in goods, plus servants and real estate. At the other end of the scale, there were poor and orphaned brides who had to look to the community for assistance in setting up their homes.

Whatever financial backing they enjoyed, some marriages encountered problems that involved them in litigation, as is documented by many of the court records preserved in the Genizah. One woman complained to the authorities that in fifteen years of married life she had not only received neither gifts, jewellery nor clothes from her husband but that he distressed and beat her, and said that he would divorce her only if she renounced her rights to a settlement. Another unfortunate wife, in a bitter letter to her uncle, bewails the treatment she is receiving from her husband and her mother-in-law:

44 – Marriage document, including a stipulation that the bride may sue for divorce if she no longer cares for her husband (T-S 24.68) (Cambridge University Library)

> Soon my mother-in-law began to work against me, isolating me from everyone, and putting enmity against me into the heart of her son. The least that she did was to say to me "Go away, and become like your own notorious mother."

Husbands too sometimes had cause for complaint but they possessed a cruel and powerful weapon with which to terrorize their spouses. They could, and sometimes did, threaten to run off to some foreign part without divorcing their wives, thus leaving them in a perpetual state of marital limbo (*'agunah*), neither divorced nor living with a husband. One unhappy man made such a threat in the context of a demand to the head of his community for a judgement that would release him from some of the financial burden involved in making a settlement. He claimed that the marriage had been arranged against his will and that his wife's character and behaviour were so intolerable that three years with her had seemed to him like twenty. And now the final straw had been the arrival of his mother-in-law! Two other tragic cases involve the husband's failure to perform his sexual obligations to his wife. In one of these cases, the girl declares that she is still a virgin and that whenever her husband attempts to consummate the marriage he collapses in a convulsive fit, thereby terrifying and distressing her. Another records the plight of a wife who modestly describes herself as "a thirsty woman", denied any drink for nine months: "I am a thirsty woman; the man is useless. Let him separate; let's annul the marriage."

Other family troubles were, happily, of the more ordinary variety. A husband on a business trip to India writes to his wife about how much he yearns for her. He is particularly sad that he cannot provide her "rights on every sabbath and festival", a traditional time for sex. An itinerant cantor, away from home making a living by officiating at sabbath and wedding services, has obviously offended his wife in some way and tries to make it up to her by opening his letter to her in a warm and complimentary fashion. The quick change of emphasis from her to his son may not, however, have helped to patch things up:

> My greetings abound; may God's help soon be found, by the Jews all around. To my worthy and modest wife. I am aware of your admirable behaviour and there is no need for me to dwell on this here. In contrast to your own happy position, I am thoroughly miserable and miss you all, particularly the eyes of my beloved young son, whom I adore and cherish. In tears and anguish, I look for consolation at every corner, day and night, but I expect none, other than from God. I know that there is no need for me to lay down the law but do please think of your religious duties and conduct yourself in a way that brings you honour. Take every care of our dear, beloved child and spare no effort on his behalf. This will be a sure sign of your love. Do not worry at all about me. If only I could catch a swift cloud, I would return in record time. But, with God's help, I shall finish my business and come home quickly, with a pocket that is less than full but with a happy heart.

For her part, one wife was appalled by her husband's absence from home and the news that he might be contemplating a trip to Turkey. Writing on behalf of the whole family, both male and female, she lectured him in no uncertain terms about the damage that would be done to their reputation if he stayed away and how such behaviour would adversely affect the marriage prospects of their single daughter. A distinguished member of the community such as he should rejoin his family and if the reason for his reticence to return was related to tax problems, she suggested the name of an expert who could offer him sound advice in this connection. A distinguished merchant assured his wife that their enforced separation was making him just as depressed and lonely as she, while a wife dictated to her son a letter to the absent father of the household in which she brought him up to date with the latest domestic news:

> We have weaned the baby. Do not ask me what we suffer for him: trouble, crying, sleepless nights, so much so that the neighbours – God is my witness – are complaining. We incur great expenses for him: the doctor, medicaments, and two chickens every day.

ASPECTS OF EDUCATION

That particular Jewish mother might have preferred to be spending the money not on chicken soup but on the promotion of her children's

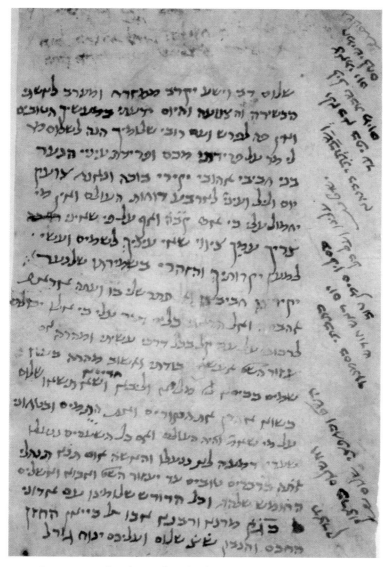

45 – Cantor regrets his absence from his family, particularly from his "darling little boy" (T-S 13J20.9) (Cambridge University Library)

Jewish education and communal involvement, matters that were traditionally regarded as of the utmost importance among her people. One lady of the house, clearly something of a matriarch, and a shrewd one at that, took the trouble of sending a Ḥanukkah gift to her

189

grandchild's private tutor. Two other female family members made efforts to involve themselves in synagogal matters. A mother and grandmother made a generous donation to the community on condition that their son/grandson would be invited to undertake the public reading of the Esther scroll on the feast of Purim and drew up a legal document to that effect, not only to protect their investment, as it were, but also to ensure that the arrangement could not be cancelled by the boy's father.

As far as boys were concerned, educational activity at home was soon complemented by attendance at school and the story there was apparently just as often one of naughtiness as of diligence. A scribbled note from a rather cross teacher informed the father of little Abu el-Ḥassan that his son had at first been most conscientious but that one of the class, egged on by the others, had soon put to a stop to this by breaking the newcomer's writing board. Few people in those days had qualms about the corporal punishment of children but even medieval fathers tried to rescue their sons from unnecessary floggings. Two little boys who came late to school brought a note explaining that the elder had been delayed by studying Arabic at home and the younger, who could not make his own way, had had to wait for his brother. The teacher is politely asked to refrain from spanking either for the tardiness of their arrival. One teacher had to admit that he had smacked his pupil excessively, and that if he had been a more robust child he might even have punished him more, but all to no avail. He appears to have been the child of elderly parents since the letter, reporting that the child is badly behaved, is addressed to his elder brother. In Goitein's translation, it reads:

> I have to inform you, my lord, that I have not been successful in educating this boy, Abu Mansur. Perhaps you can help me in this. Whenever I spank him, I do so excessively; but as soon as I begin, the schoolmistress rushes along and, after having smacked him four or five times, releases him. Had it not been for his illness, I would have killed him with beating, although as a poorly clothed newcomer, he is entitled to some consideration. He is impervious to argument and not at all quiet. As soon as he comes in, he starts fighting with his sister and cursing her incessantly, especially if I am not present. Perhaps you could threaten him with a little spanking and tell him to be reasonable, well-behaved and quiet. Whatever you decide, don't do anything which might anger your mother and father.

Education was admired and teachers were generally held in high regard. There was competition among them for pupils and this inevitably helped to keep the standard of teaching high. Some had entered the profession as immigrants into the community without other means and perhaps it

was they who suffered most from the late payment of fees There is certainly no lack of evidence for such tardy settlement of educational bills and Goitein's translation of one fragment exemplifies one such sad situation between the teacher and the communal treasurer regarding the fees of the orphans in his school:

> I now ask your excellency to kindly give an order to pay me their fees so that I should have something to spend for the holidays. I might perhaps like to taste a piece of meat, for I have not bought meat more than eight times from last Pentecost to this Pentecost. God knows that I would not have mentioned this to my lord, had I not known that my lord does not tolerate such a state of affairs.

Many of the adults also practised what they preached to their children by attending lectures and study courses at their synagogues. One letter speaks of candles burning on through the night to enable members of the Cairo community to study until dawn. It comes as no surprise to find many references to outstanding rabbis and to their advice being sought in matters of Jewish law and ritual by communities many hundreds of miles away. There is information about an Iraqi scholar travelling to Greece, as well as a French rabbi serving as a Jewish judge (*dayyan*) in Alexandria. It was not, however, usual for "western" rabbis to hold positions in the Egyptian communities since a kind of discrimination, reminiscent of the reverse situation in more modern times, was operated against them by the "orientals". They were sometimes ridiculed and even insulted for their lack of Arabic and their allegedly more primitive approach to the study of the Hebrew Bible and Jewish philosophy.

AWAY FROM HOME

Despite individual cases to the contrary, travel was the exception rather than the rule for scholars and for the many craftsmen and artisans –

represented in as many as 250 different trades – then living in the Egyptian Jewish community. Businessmen, on the other hand, had to travel the length and breadth of the Mediterranean, and to undertake voyages across the Indian Ocean, to make their livings. Such trips not only involved the painful separations already noted (sometimes even for a number of years); they also carried all the dangers associated with any form of travel in those turbulent times. A letter vividly describes a three-day Mediterranean storm followed by "the cracking of the ship like an egg in one's hands" and the rescue of a few survivors who were lucky enough to cling to some wooden debris. Other documents make it clear that even a relatively short voyage along the Palestinian coast from Egypt to Lebanon was not without its risks and could take over a week. The most dreaded outcome was capture by an enemy, or by pirates, who knew that Jewish communities everywhere would always be willing to pay generous ransoms to release any fellow Jews who were being held hostage. In fact, at one stage this cruel business became so profitable that the Jewish religious leaders had to cite talmudic law and forbid communities to pay more than the "going rate", for fear that giving in to blackmail would encourage the taking of additional hostages. It is not new for Jews to be forced to make harsh short-term decisions in order to protect themselves from worse developments in the long-term. Travel across land was usually by convoy in the traditional "caravan". Before setting out, Jews had to arrange either to pay extra if they wanted the whole entourage to stop for the sabbath, or to hire private guards to protect them while they raced to catch up with the others on Sunday.

There were some travellers who built new lives in and around the communities that they visited on business. Abraham Ben Yiju, who had family in Egypt, North Africa and Sicily, was a scholar, traveller and adventurer whose commercial activities in the twelfth century ranged from the Mediterranean Sea to the Indian Ocean. During his trips to the area of Tulunad, around the coastal city of Mangalore in southern India, he acquired an Indian slave who once got him into serious trouble in Aden. Having got drunk there on a shopping expedition, the slave burst into the office of the chief representative of the merchants and demanded money. Perhaps even more interestingly, Ben Yiju freed and converted a female Indian slave and took her into his household as wife or mistress. She bore the name Ashu and belonged to the matrilineal Nair caste on the Malabar coast. It seems that his dealings with her family involved him in a complicated financial tangle.

BUSINESS INTERESTS

Wide varieties of goods, ranging from bales of cloth, through animal hides and articles of clothing, to items of food and drink, were imported and exported by the Jewish merchants of Cairo (sometimes women as well as men). Their primary concern was not with particular commodities but with anything that could keep their capital working for them. As one entrepreneur put it, "Do not leave a single penny idle...buy when God gives you the chance and export on the first ship to set sail." The businessman's familiar plea that he has no ready cash was therefore already then a well-known one and one rich Tunisian, though well stocked with goods, could not find a few pounds (for a donation?) on the eve of the Jewish New Year. Others were perhaps a little more cautious and have left us evidence that they advised prospective buyers to take their time and choose their item well, since this was the way to make the best profit. There was after all the danger of price fluctuation. Merchants continually complain of this ("Prices are in God's hands; they follow no principle"), although such a tendency to grumble may be something of a professional characteristic, rather than a reflection of reality, since most of the documents indicate a reasonable degree of stability in prices. One Ashkenazi woman, writing in Yiddish to her son in Cairo in 1567 (and, by the way, complaining that she has not heard from him for ages!), tells him to bring her grandchildren to see her and claims about Jerusalem prices "Thank God, everything is cheap here."

In the middle of the eleventh century, the market price of a 100 lbs (about 45 kilos) of pepper could range, depending on circumstances, from 22 to 38 dinars (30 dinars was a moderate annual salary), with the average price settling around 34 dinars. One merchant, unable to obtain more than 32.5, held on to his partner's pepper until he got over 33, and managed to retain his own until there was a sudden leap in the price to over 36. Interestingly, he kept his partner informed of developments by letter, and suggested that they treat the whole load as a unit and share all the profit, as well as any loss. Such honesty and trust between partners was not untypical of business life since joint commercial ventures were sometimes a feature of relations between groups or families for a number of generations. There were even cases where Jews and Muslims who were partners arranged for profits made on the sabbath to be directed only to the latter. When David ben Solomon wished to move a huge amount of capital from Cairo to Qayrawan in 1267, he asked his friend Isaac ben Abraham to take the money as a loan from him in Egypt and to repay it to him later in the Tunisian city. Given that the amount involved was 600 pieces of silver, it is hardly surprising that this arrangement was made and notarized before a rabbinic court. There is certainly no shortage of documents relating to court cases in which claims are made for damages or the restoration of money or property.

Payment by cheque rather than by cash was also a procedure adopted in the Genizah period. You deposited your cash with a banker or broker and you made your payment by writing on a piece of paper the sum in Coptic numerals and words that the banker was to pay the specified bearer, together with the date, and a biblical verse intended to ward off any attempt at fraud! Other financial agreements were made and carried out without formal or legal endorsement and one merchant apologizes for requesting accounts from colleagues: "God forbid that I should request exact accounts from you or anyone else. I simply wanted to know how much I still owe and what you have shipped." The form in which accounts were recorded is also revealing. Complete and detailed account books have not survived but the Genizah has preserved entry combinations on waste book, journal and ledger sheets. From these it is clear that, in twelfth-century Egypt, one column was used for debits and another for credits, at least two centuries before this procedure was adopted in Italy and became generally standard. Apparently, then, merchants from Egypt and North Africa had a direct influence on the development of the double-entry method in Europe.

To ask for an overdue payment was even regarded as something of an impudence and "final demands" had consequently to be couched in the most delicate of terms. Abu Isḥaq Abraham ben Burayk's device with one of his debtors was to get a mutual friend to write and say that he – Abu Isḥaq – urgently wanted to travel to Spain but could not do so until he received settlement of that account. There were other occasions too when some action had to be taken that was unlikely to meet with one's correspondent's approval. A letter written from Alexandria to Qayrawan in 1052 reports that, in view of the unstable situation, the writer has just buried some cash in the earth. He knows that this will horrify his astute business associate, in this case his brother, who prefers to have his money working for him, but he claims that he would rather have criticism on this score than censure for losing the money. Obviously, not everyone maintained the highest standards of honesty. A case referred to Maimonides for a ruling dealt with the matter of a broker's son who had run off with Jewish and Muslim property. Either out of fear of the Jewish community and its possible sanctions, or out of loyalty and conscience vis-à-vis his co-religionists, he had secretly returned the goods belonging to the Jews.

TAXES ON RESOURCES

Where there is business, there is always a government ready to demand taxes and customs dues. It is hardly surprising, then, that the Genizah documents are not short of tales about the problems and harrassment faced by Jewish merchants some eight centuries ago. The police of the day apparently kept a particularly close watch on the boats sailing up and down the Nile and one unlucky dealer from Tunisia had no sooner boarded one of these than he found himself in the custody of five officers of the law. He obtained his freedom only after satisfying the authorities in the matter of some excise duty. Jews were doubly unfortunate since every non-Muslim was required by Islamic law to pay the government an annual poll tax of 2 dinars (as much as a low monthly wage), simply for existing, and as an indication of his inferior status. Jews from other countries were also obliged to pay up and there was even a special office to deal with those from Eretz Yisrael and its environs then resident in Egypt.

Poverty being what it then was, many Jews were terrified when the payment became due since they knew that they had to carry with them a receipt indicating that they had paid, or face a fine, a beating, imprisonment or, possibly, death in custody from starvation. Like later generations in Russia, some Jews tried to avoid the tax by going into hiding but then they could earn no wages and there are instances of wives and children perishing under such circumstances. A young man wrote to his mother of an incident one Sunday morning. As he set out on a journey, a policeman challenged him: "Do you intend to depart, still in possession of the government's unpaid poll tax? I shall not leave you until you accompany me to the police station." Among the greatest acts of Jewish charity was therefore the payment of this obnoxious tax for the poor, and the community sometimes had to arrange this. One letter written by Moses Maimonides himself introduces two friends of his to colleagues in another city and requests the community there to pay their poll taxes for them since they are on important business for him. Communal records also demonstrate how often payments were made to

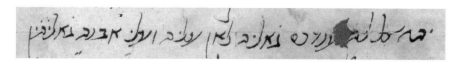

poor individuals, of both local and foreign backgrounds. Names and amounts are usually listed although anonymity is reserved for some in order to maintain their dignity. Letters requesting aid may be from individuals to individuals, or from communities to communities, such as from Palestinian Jews to their Egyptian co-religionists, and sometimes detailed explanations are given of the circumstances that have necessitated the appeal. In one case, a man who had known better times complains bitterly of the communal leader's lack of response to his appeal and stresses the gravity of his plight. He is most anxious to include wine and meat in his diet but is forced to restrict himself to bread and onions.

Another, and even more urgent drain on communal resources was the cost of ransoming captives. These sad victims had not only to be ransomed but also clothed, maintained and sent home. Meanwhile, the Muslim government insisted on receiving the poll tax and port duty on behalf of each of them. According to one historian's estimate, each captive cost the community more than the provision of bread for 150 needy folk over a period of two months. Nevertheless, no community ever thought twice about raising the necessary funds since there was no limit to the cruelties that could be visited on such hostages by their captors. In the matter of the provision of bread, mention may be made of a delightful letter in which a convert to Judaism thanks a noble Jewess for the bread she has charitably provided for him. Before becoming a Jew, he had enjoyed all manner of culinary delights, including delicious bread, but since coming to the Muslim countries he had had no success in locating any bread to compare with it, until he tasted hers. He then reciprocates by giving her one of his own recipes.

No doubt among those from whom funds were raised for the community were artisans who did financially well in economically good times. There were many trades practised by the Jews and the skills were passed on to the next generation by a system of apprenticeship. It appears that the formal arrangements for such vocational training were usually made orally but there are occasional Genizah items that shed light on specific cases. In one text we are informed that a silversmith had to serve an apprenticeship of two years while in another it would seem that a weaver could learn his trade in two months. It is possible that this particular young man already had some background in the trade since, as Goitein's translation informs us, the contract, from the year 1027, also stipulated a wage for him:

The aforenamed Bushr confirmed that he hired out his son Joseph to the aforementioned Barhūn for the duration of four months, beginning with the New Moon day of the month of Marcheshvan of the abovementioned year to the end of the month of Shevat against a payment of sixty dirhems per month, on condition that Joseph shall become proficient in the work on the loom. If Barhūn fails to advance Joseph in this craft so that he will become proficient like a regular craftsman, Barhūn must employ him for a period of another [four] months and pay him the wages of a craftsman.

IN THE SYNAGOGUE

Where there are Jews, there are synagogues, and rarely are such spiritual centres conducted along totally peaceful and harmonious lines. The synagogal affairs referred to in the manuscripts from medieval Egypt have a familiar ring to them. The Babylonian and Palestinian congregations in Fustat vied with each other for new members, the former boasting of the honours they gave to visitors and the fine cantors they engaged, while the latter parried with claims that they had more attractive Bibles and Torah scrolls (as well as beautiful carpets), that their services were shorter, and that young boys were permitted to take part in the services. At times, the tensions about who had the greater authority over the whole community grew so great that representations were made to the Muslim caliphate requesting a ruling. Palestine and Egypt had once been united in the matter of rabbinic authority but gradually the focus of power moved to those with connections to the Babylonian centres of talmudic expertise.

Apparently, such rivalries and other differences of opinion in the synagogue setting were not always of a friendly type and the sources indicate just how seriously people took such matters. A letter from Ramla in 1052 reports a "punch-up" on Yom Kippur between Jews from Tyre and others from Tiberias which had to be halted by the police. There are other reports of brawls, of disgust with lascivious behaviour, and of congregants being banned as persistent troublemakers. Such grave incidents were not as common as the more standard complaints. A devout young man is attracted to Messina in Italy as a place where he would make a good living. He decides against settling there because the morning service is already concluded by dawn, when it should be reaching only its climax, and there in no *minyan* at all for the afternoon service. Beadles are of course a favoured target for abuse. One is accused of conducting himself like a "boss" and not as a servant of the congregation. Another is upbraided for inducing his whole family of fifteen souls to take up full board and residence on the synagogue premises, and for even allowing them to play with pigeons (breeding and racing them?) on the roof.

Being called to the public reading of the Torah was a considerable honour and many complaints were filed with the authorities by those who disapproved of the selection procedures, or had not been given their full and accurate titles when being summoned to participate. Sometimes an official pre-empted a possible attack. One cantor informed Maimonides that he could not meet a request of his since he had to attend a poor man's circumcision ceremony, lest it be said that he favoured only the rich with his company. At other times, it was the official who did the complaining. Another cantor asked Maimonides for permission to abandon the recitation of some liturgical poems introduced in a small Egyptian village where he officiated. Although he received a response that was sympathetic to his disapproval of the novel poetry, he was advised, for the sake of communal harmony, to continue to recite it. A direct descendant of the same outstanding sage took a community to task for the preacher they engaged. He was an ignoramus who repeated, like a parrot, speeches on the mysteries of religion that he did not himself understand.

With regard to broader culture and its various aspects, it is hardly surprising to find that these reflect the achievements and interests of the Islamic world of the day. There are illuminations, diagrams and pictorial representations, generally of course without human faces, that are in use for illustrative and educational purposes. Verses and comments on verses may attract such artistic attention and there is one remarkable example, from among the later Genizah material, that is attached to the Arabic story of the lioness and her cub. Favourite targets for illustration were the beginnings of biblical books, Passover *haggadot*, marriage documents, and children's alphabet primers. There is also a coloured block-print, probably dating from the late fourteenth century, that contains the verse (Deuteronomy 28:6) "blessed are you in your coming in, and blessed are you in your going out" for use in a synagogue, in a classroom or perhaps in a *sukkah* on the festival of Tabernacles. The musical notes recorded by the proselyte, Obadiah Ha-Ger, have become one of the Genizah's most famous items and their Jewish religious authenticity is still the subject of controversy. Science and medicine are also the subject of many fragments.

MEDICINE AND MAGIC

Illness and its treatment were of major concern to the public and to the doctors who consequently represented one of the most important professions. Their training was based on the famous text-books of the ancient Greek masters, translated into Arabic, and updated to take account of the latest findings of leading experts. Jews co-operated widely

وأخذ علي باعلى الأنفس شتن الى الاسد

الغنى ... وجعلت ذلك له ما خبرها ا ستمح من ...

كليله ودمنا واقرأ ان دمنا ملا الصحنا ال

اقبات حتى دخلت على السفرانه مكببا بحزنا

فلما عاينت ذلك عرفت انه ليزد ذلك الاط

قتلا شازربه الاسد وامله

46 – The story of the lioness and the lion cub from the medieval Arabic tales *Kalīla Wa-Dimna*
(T-S Ar.51.60) (Cambridge University Library)

199

47 – Block-print predating the invention of conventional printing by a century
(Or.1080 J50) (Cambridge University Library)

with their Muslim colleagues and were even granted special certificates to enable them to practise on members of both communities. Some specialists were distinguished enough to work at the royal court or with other public figures and could command large fees, but most of them made their living from less grand clients. Doctors argued that fees were high because they had heavy responsibilities. It was not unknown for some of them to have to defend themselves against charges of negligence brought by disgruntled patients. They pointed out that while others were enjoying holidays and social gatherings, they were often required to be on call for medical emergencies. Their day-to-day activities kept them very busy and were remarkably varied. They might be called upon to provide certificates of ill-health for those applying for financial assistance from the community. Sometimes they were summoned to court to give specialist evidence. Many of them also tried to write medical guides on subjects of which they had acquired particular knowledge and there were those who were occupied with teaching the next generation of doctors.

It was of course the direct treatment of disease that took up most of their time. Many patients, suffering from a great variety of complaints, some physical and some mental, came to their offices and they had to

200

diagnose the problem, often by an examination of the patient's urine, and suggest the necessary treatment. Part of their training involved an understanding of how to make drugs and how to use them. They therefore functioned not only as medical practitioners but also as pharmacists, using many different kinds of plants, each with its own special effect. The most common complaints related to the eyes and they were fortunately able, even at that period, to perform operations to remove growths and obstructions. Headaches also troubled many folk and, in those cases, in addition to drugs, they were able to offer such external treatment as cold compresses. Large numbers in the community were troubled by sexually related matters. Men came to see doctors about impotence and fertility and were anxious to locate the best aphrodisiacs. Women asked about period pains and loss of blood, and about pregnancy and abortion. The medical experts did their best but there were often tragic aspects to these problems about which they could do little. They advised sensible diets, careful hygiene and the avoidance of excess in any human activity as the best ways of avoiding illness, particularly in connection with the digestive system, but not all patients took their advice. A fair proportion of them preferred to spend their money on astrologers, magicians and diviners who gave them amulets to wear and formulas to recite. The trained professionals resented such people as "quacks" but did acknowledge that there was a limit to what they themselves could do. Some admitted to their patients that true healing was in the hands of heaven.

There is no doubt that such "alternative medicine" also played a central role in the lives of many of the community in Genizah times. The origins of their mystical ideas and magical practices have to be sought in the Near East of many centuries earlier. There are parallels in ancient Mesopotamia although the immediate background appears to have been Palestinian, rather than Babylonian. When faced by a health problem, a romantic entanglement, or a personal disaster, many individuals sought solace and guidance in the use of herbal remedies, the wearing of amulets, the recitation of incantations, and the interpretation of dreams. Although biblical and rabbinic literature was used and cited, and references were made to divine power, there were also many more folkloristic aspects to these activities. Combinations of letters and numbers played a part and there were special roles for angels and other heavenly bodies. Much was made of the authority of such ancient figures as Noah and Shem on the one hand, and of the possibility of foretelling the future on the other. Some fragments relate to an individual circumstance while others provide general guidance for all manner of

201

problems. The language used may be Hebrew, Arabic or Aramaic but is primitive and popular rather than polished and literary. By way of examples, Judah ben Simḥah calls on the Lord, the Holy Name, the angel Meṭaṭron and the Prophet Elijah to guard him from "evil spirits, from every enemy and adversary, and from fear, trembling, terror, shaking, anguish, and from pain, discomfort, headache, faintheartedness and pains of the heart" while Abu al-'Iz ben Baqa', the shopkeeper, adjures all the holy letters "to gather the feet of every man and woman, and every merchant into the shop" so that they will "buy from him of their own free will"!

And so the everyday documents continue. A teacher asks for a salary advance to buy medicine for his sick child; a protest is made at the lease of a house to a Muslim because it faces the women's entrance to the synagogue; experiences are undergone which, in the words of a contemporary, "two camel-loads of paper would be unable to describe." Crusaders, slaves, postal services, leisure activities and a host of other fascinating topics – there is no dark recess of mundane, medieval life in the Mediterranean area that is not illuminated by the Genizah fragments and through the work done to decipher them by historians such as the late Shelomo Dov Goitein and his successors.

Guide to reading

Except where otherwise indicated, much of the information on which this chapter is based is provided in S. D. Goitein's classic set of volumes *A Mediterranean Society* (= *Med. Soc.*, 5 volumes, published respectively in 1967, 1973, 1978, 1983 and 1988, plus a sixth index volume, prepared by Paula Sanders, published in 1993, all of them in Berkeley, Los Angeles and London). Since only a small number of the secondary sources here cited are in Hebrew, they have not been separately noted as in other chapters. A first draft of this chapter, prepared with the assistance of Paul Fenton, who was then a colleague in the Genizah Research Unit at Cambridge University Library, appeared in the colour supplement of the *Jewish Chronicle* in London on 26 September, 1980, pp. 40–47. The topic of marriage is discussed in *Med. Soc.* 1, pp. 48–49 and in *Med. Soc.* 3, pp. 47–159, especially pp. 55–61, and some important fragments are T-S 18J4.5, T-S 20.6, T-S 13J25.20 and T-S 12.175. The "mixed" Karaite-Rabbanite marriage, T-S 24.1, was already dealt with by Schechter in *Jewish Quarterly Review* 13 (1901), pp. 218–21 and is noted by Goitein in *Med. Soc.* 3, p. 158. Two comprehensive studies of marriage documents, customs and lawsuits are M. A. Friedman's *Jewish Marriage in Palestine: A Cairo Geniza Study* (2 volumes; Tel Aviv and New York, 1980), especially vol. 1, pp. 312–46 and

379–450, and vol. 2, pp. 1–88, and his *Jewish Polygyny in the Middle Ages: New Documents from the Cairo Geniza* (Hebrew; Jerusalem, 1986). The right to a divorce is recorded in T-S 12.128, T-S 12.548, T-S 12.659 and T-S 24.30, while T-S 12.548 also alludes to some unusual conditions and T-S K10 contains a number of illuminated marriage documents.

The conditions extracted from Ṭuvia, son of Eli, recorded in T-S 20.160, are fully discussed and translated by Friedman in his article "Pre-Nuptial Agreements: A Geniza Study", *Diné Israel* 6 (1975), pp. cxi–cxiv, and noted by Goitein in *Med. Soc.* 3, p. 157. Friedman also deals with the court record relating to the rape victim, T-S 8K13.11, in *Jewish Polygyny*, pp. 95–106, and details of the *crime passionnel*, reported in T-S 8.111, are in *Med. Soc.* 3, pp. 80–81. Goitein summarizes the broad activities of women in *Med. Soc.* 3, pp. 312–59 and interesting examples of the professions they pursued are to be found in T-S 24.76, T-S 16.22, T-S 12.493, T-S 20.175 and T-S NS 320.7. The story of the notorious Wuḥsha is told by Goitein in "A Jewish Business Woman of the Eleventh Century", *Seventy-Fifth Anniversary Volume of the Jewish Quarterly Review*, eds. A. A. Neuman and Solomon Zeitlin (Philadelphia, 1967), pp. 225–47 and in *Med. Soc.* 3, pp. 346–52, the details derived from Add. 3420d, T-S 8J5.5, T-S Ar.4.5, T-S 10J7.10, T-S Misc.8.102 and T-S AS 145.3. Dowries are discussed in *Med. Soc.* 3, pp. 123–31 and the numerous relevant fragments are cited there by Goitein in notes 57–64 on p. 454; special attention is due to the remarkably affluent bride in T-S J1.29.

The wife/husband relationship receives Goitein's attention in *Med. Soc.* 3, pp. 160–223, with the two bitter complaints to be found in T-S 8J22.27 and 10J9.13 noted by him on pp. 186 and 175–76. Fragments that shed light on cases of wives being abandoned include T-S 12.179, T-S 18J2.10 and Or.1080 J7, as discussed in *Med. Soc.* 1, p. 58, and the dissatisfied husband, whose appeal is recorded in T-S 8J14.2, occurs in *Med. Soc.* 3, p. 204. The details of female sexual frustration are derived from T-S 10J4.11 and T-S K25.205 and are noted in *Med. Soc.* 3, p. 169, while the topic of the sad and lonely male occurs in T-S 10J16.14, Jewish Theological Seminary ENA 2739.16, and Westminster College Arabic II.51; see *Med. Soc.* 1, p. 68. The letter of the itinerant cantor, T-S 13J20.9 (here freshly translated), was published by J. Mann, *The Jews in Egypt and in Palestine under the Fatimid Caliphs* (reprinted edition with preface and reader's guide by S. D. Goitein; two volumes in one; New York, 1970), vol. 2, pp. 307–8 and mentioned by Goitein in *Med. Soc.* 3, p. 220. F. Kobler included a translation of the angry wife's letter (T-S 13J21.10) in his *Letters of Jews Throughout the Ages* (London, 1953), vol. 1, pp. 233–34, based on Mann's text in *The Jews in Egypt*, vol. 1, p. 242, but this is supplemented by the comments of Joel Kraemer, "Spanish Ladies from the Cairo Geniza", *Mediterranean Historical Review* 6 (1991), pp. 247–48. The merchant's loneliness occurs in the letter in T-S 16.278 (*Med. Soc.* 3, p. 222) while the fragment about chicken soup (David Kaufmann Collection X; *Med. Soc.* 3, p. 194) is not unique in mentioning this culinary delight, as noted in *Genizah Fragments* 35 (April, 1998), p. 1.

One of the most important studies of educational material in the Genizah is Goitein's article "Side Lights on Jewish Education from the Cairo Geniza", *Gratz College Anniversary Volume* (=*GCAV*), eds. I. D. Passow and S. T. Lachs (Philadelphia, 1971), pp. 83–110. The Purim reference (T-S NS J2) is cited there on pp. 92–93, together with the story of poor Abu el-Ḥassan's broken board (T-S Ar.53.65), and the Ḥanukkah gift (T-S 12.425) is reported in *Med. Soc.* 2, p. 188. The case in which the boys were apparently spared a beating (Or.1081 J4) is noted in *Med. Soc.* 2, p. 182 while the report about the failure of excessive physical punishment to make any impact, in the text of T-S 8J28.7, is translated by Goitein in *GCAV*, p. 91 and the complaint about non-payment of fees (British Library, Or.5542.23) is translated by him on pp. 96–97 of that article. For the mention of nocturnal study and adult education, see Jewish Theological Seminary ENA 191.2559 and *Med. Soc.* 2, pp. 192–95. The information about the travelling scholars is discussed in *Med. Soc.* 1, pp. 51–54 and 65–67 and the relevant manuscript sources from the Genizah are T-S 16.301, T-S 18J3.15, T-S 13J27.11 and ENA 2744. The number of trades known from the classical Genizah period is estimated at 250 by M. Ben-Sasson, "Cairo Genizah Treasures and their Contribution to Jewish Historiography", *Bulletin of the Israeli Academic Center in Cairo* 21 (1997), p. 9, and the most vivid description of a shipwreck occurs in T-S 12.114, David Kaufmann Collection XI and T-S 16.54; see *Med. Soc.* 1, p. 321. The whole subject is dealt with by Goitein in *Med. Soc.* 1, pp. 273–352 and among the most important fragments are: T-S13J36.6, T-S 8J19.27, T-S NS J3, T-S 10J17.18, T-S 10J18.1, T-S 13J20.25, T-S 8J28.12, T-S 24.78 and T-S 20.113.

An equally long list of fragments attests to the personal and professional activities of Abraham Ben Yiju. Goitein provided some detail when he included a missive from that colourful personality in his *Letters of Medieval Jewish Traders* (Princeton, 1973), pp. 201–6, but a more unusual treatment was the reconstruction of his life published by the Indian novelist, Amitav Ghosh. In his *In an Antique Land* (Harmondsworth, 1992), Ghosh, though not a professional scholar and therefore to be judged as a chronicler and not a semiticist, succeeds in building an intriguing picture of Ben Yiju that sometimes relates to Egypt today and at others to the medieval caliphate. He explains how a visit to Cambridge University Library and contact with Genizah scholars excited his interest in Jewish traders in India and provides a list of the relevant fragments on pp. 394–95. Goitein's unpublished Genizah corpus that he tentatively called the *India Book* will be an important source for the history of such trade when Mordechai Friedman completes the process of editing it and it duly appears in print. For a survey of the range of medieval Jewish trade in the Mediterranean as known from the Genizah source, see *Med. Soc.* 1, pp. 75–147 and 148–272. Notes advising a broad choice of commercial activities and concerning the lack of ready cash are in T-S 8J41.2, T-S 20.180, David Kaufmann Collection XXVIII and Dropsie College (now Center for Judaic Studies at the University of Pennsylvania) 389; see *Med. Soc.* 1, p. 200. Price fluctuation is mentioned in

T-S 13J18.8 (see *Med. Soc.* 1, p. 219) and the Yiddish letter from 1567 (T-S Misc.36.L.1) was published in the original by S. Assaf in *Zion* 7 (1941–42), pp. 68–71 and in English translation by F. Kobler in his *Letters of Jews Through the Ages from Biblical Times to the Middle of the Eighteenth Century* (London, 1952), vol. 2, pp. 364–67.

On the price of pepper, see Goitein's discussion in *Med. Soc.* 1, pp. 220–22, with the specific instance mentioned in the Bodleian Genizah fragment, Heb.a.3, f.13. Relations between business partners is covered in *Med. Soc.* 1, pp. 164–83 and it is P. B. Fenton who draws attention to the matter of sabbath profits in "Interfaith Relations as Reflected in the Genizah Documents", *Bulletin of the Israeli Academic Center in Cairo* 21 (1997), p. 26. The movement of capital from Cairo to Qayrawan is reflected in the notarized document T-S 12.515, published by J. Mann, *Texts and Studies in Jewish History and Literature* (2 vols., Cincinnati and Philadelphia, 1931–35), vol. 1, pp. 360–61. Remnants of medieval cheques are located in T-S Ar.30.184 and noted in *Med. Soc.* 1, p. 241 and embarrassment about requesting accounts underlies comments in T-S 12.335 and Bodleian Genizah fragment, Heb.c.28 (*Med. Soc.* 1, pp. 204–5). The relevance of the Genizah to the history of accounting has been demonstrated by M. Scorgie in his comments on T-S NS 321.7a and similar fragments in *Genizah Fragments* 29 (April, 1995), p. 2, based on his two 1994 articles in *Accounting Business and Financial History* and in *Accounting Historians' Journal*. For delicate requests for the payment of debts, see T-S 8J14.9 and T-S 13J29.1 (*Med. Soc.* 1, p. 258), and on the matter of the burial of cash, see T-S 13J26.9 (*Med. Soc.* 1, p. 265). Details of the property theft and its return to the Jewish owners occur in T-S Misc.8.90 and are cited by Goitein in *Med. Soc.* 2, p. 297.

Aspects of tax problems and related incidents are provided by Goitein in *Med. Soc.* 1, pp. 64 and 300, and *Med. Soc.* 2, pp. 95–96 and 380–94. The reference to the five policemen occurs in T-S 10J9.21; the account of the Sunday morning arrest is in T-S 13J16.10; and the letter by Maimonides is T-S 12.192. Other relevant fragments are T-S 20.174, T-S 13J36.2, T-S 10J17.20, Or.1080 J87 and T-S 12.289. The general theme of charity is closely studied by M. Gil in his *Documents of the Jewish Pious Foundations from the Cairo Geniza* (Leiden, 1976) and Mark Cohen is currently preparing a volume on communal payments for charitable purposes that are recorded in the Genizah texts. The letter of complaint is in T-S 8.24. The ransoming of captives is touched upon by Mann, *Texts and Studies in Jewish History and Literature* (2 vols., Cincinnati and Philadelphia, 1931–35), vol. 2, pp. 344–45 and by Goitein in *Med. Soc.* 1, pp. 329–30, *Med. Soc.* 2, pp. 137–38, and *Med. Soc.* 5, pp. 373–76 and 462–64. The primary Genizah sources are T-S 13J34.3, T-S 10J24.9, T-S 12.238 and T-S 16.9. The gift of bread is mentioned in the letter in T-S 12.244 and a paragraph is devoted to it in *Med. Soc.* 2, p. 129. One of the subjects covered in Goitein's article "Parents and Children: A Geniza Study on the Medieval Jewish Family", *Gratz College Annual of Jewish Studies* 4 (1975), pp. 47–68 is apprenticeship and the fragment here cited is from the Jewish

Theological Seminary ENA NS 2.II.41a, translated and discussed by Goitein on. pp. 47–50.

The particular tensions between Babylonian and Palestinian communities, such as those reflected in T-S 13J26.24, T-S 18J4.12, Alliance Israelite Universelle VII.A.17 and Dropsie College (now Center for Judaic Studies at the University of Pennsylvania) 354, are treated in *Med. Soc.* 2, p. 52; Goitein, *Palestinian Jewry in Early Islamic and Crusader Times in the Light of the Geniza Documents* (Jerusalem, 1980), pp. 52–69; M. Gil, *A History of Palestine 634–1099* (Cambridge, 1992), paras. 762–72, pp. 527–39; S. C. Reif, *Judaism and Hebrew Prayer* (Cambridge, 1993), pp. 154–64 and 181–91. Reports of synagogal brawls, as summarized by Goitein in *Med. Soc.* 2, p. 168, are found in T-S 13J16.21, T-S Ar.38.131 and Jewish Theological Seminary ENA 2736.20. For the story of the devout young man, see ENA 151.2557 (*Med. Soc.* 1, p. 98), and for the religiously questionable interests of the beadle, see T-S 18J4.12, discussed in the broader context of the activities of such officials in *Med. Soc.* 2, pp. 82–91. Information about the allocation of synagogal honours is given in *Med. Soc.* 2, p. 162, based on T-S NS J279 and T-S 8J41.11. The fragments dealing with the correspondence conducted with Maimonides and his family are Or.1080 J33, T-S 8J21.12 and T-S 12.608, as noted in *Med. Soc.* 2, pp. 89, 160 and 219.

The richest source for illustrated material in the Cambridge Genizah Collection are the binders T-S K5 and K10, many of which have already been researched by Professor Bezalel Narkiss and his team of Jewish art historians in Jerusalem and published in the *Journal of Jewish Art*. The lioness may be viewed in T-S Ar.51.60; the block-print in Or.1080 J50 (see *Genizah Fragments* 5 (April, 1983), p. 1, and 6 (October, 1983), p. 4); and the musical notes of Obadiah in T-S K5.41. The medical data is derived from *Medical and Para-Medical Manuscripts in the Cambridge Genizah Collections* by H. D. Isaacs, assisted by Colin Baker (Cambridge, 1994), which covers 1,616 Genizah fragments. The general information is owed to their introduction, pp. vii–xvii, and the details of particular diseases and treatments may be traced back to the relevant fragments by way of the excellent indexes. See also P. B. Fenton's brief but helpful summary "The Importance of the Cairo Genizah for the History of Medicine", *Medical History* 24 (1980), pp. 347–48. A delightful admission that healing is in God's hands is to be found in T-S AS 152.34, entry no. 1078 on p. 80 of the Isaacs volume, reproduced there in plates 16–17. Some magical content occurs in the para-medical items described by Isaacs but more specific coverage is included in J. Naveh and S. Shaked, *Amulets and Magic Bowls: Aramaic Incantations of Late Antiquity* (Jerusalem and Leiden, 1985) and *Magic Spells and Formulae: Aramaic Incantations of Late Antiquity* (Jerusalem, 1993); L. Schiffman and M. Swartz, *Hebrew and Aramaic Incantation Texts from the Cairo Genizah: Selected Texts from the Taylor-Schechter Box K1* (Sheffield, 1992); and P. Schäfer and S. Shaked, *Magische Texte aus der Kairoer Geniza*, two volumes so far published (Tübingen, 1994 and 1997). The theological background is provided in *Envisioning Magic: A Princeton Seminar and Symposium*, eds. P. Schäfer and H. G. Kippenberg (Leiden, New York and Köln, 1997), especially in the articles "Magic and Religion in Ancient Judaism" by Schäfer, pp. 19–43; "Jewish Magic in the Greek Magical Papyri" by H. D. Betz, pp. 45–63; and "On Judaism, Jewish Mysticism and Magic" by Moshe Idel, pp. 195–214. The two quotations given here are from T-S K1.94 and T-S K1.100, described by Schiffman and Swartz, with plates, on pp. 99–109. The three cases with which the chapter is concluded are from T-S 13J21.3, T-S 13J13.6 and T-S 13J16.7, noted by Goitein in *Med. Soc.* 2, p. 188, *Med. Soc.* 2, p. 293 and *Med. Soc.* 3, p. 177.

NINE

BOOKISH AND LETTERED

Though there is little remaining justification for it, the mention of the words "medieval" and "oriental" still convey to many people the opposite of modern, western civilization. What is envisaged is an age of intellectual darkness, an area characterized by the primitive, even by the heretical and the pagan. The theological and cultural reasons for such ideas are to be sought in the developments that took place in Europe as a result of the Renaissance and the Protestant Reformation of five hundred years ago and are still built into much of its culture. Whatever their background, these notions are gradually being revealed as historical delusions and an awareness has been growing that there is more to the achievements and culture of various Asian communities a thousand years ago than is dreamt of in some popular western philosophy. As far as Jewish intellectual history is concerned, a glance at the western centres at around the time of the Crusades, and an assessment of their level of development, will prepare the way for a description and evaluation of what the Genizah sources tell us about their eastern equivalents.

LITERACY AND LITERATURE

There were substantial Jewish communities in the Byzantine Empire, Italy and the Rhineland and by the tenth century the first two of these had already enjoyed a long, if chequered, history. They had produced liturgical poets, rabbinic scholars and Hebrew chroniclers of their own, probably as a result of their close relationship with the educational institutions of the Holy Land. For its part, the Franco-German centre was set to carry forward these Jewish cultural traditions but was still in its infancy. Foundations were being laid for cultural expansion when the communities of Christian countries became more organized and comfortable. There were undoubtedly internal developments in the early medieval Christian communities of the northern Mediterranean and of western Europe that led to an expansion of literacy. Whatever motivated that expansion, their relevance to the later history of European Jewish literacy was limited. The influences of the western Christian world on Jewish religious culture were not negligible but the western and eastern Jewish communities were certainly in contact both personally and by correspondence, and ideas forged in the one must have been imported into the other. In that case, the trend towards a wider and more intensive degree of Jewish literacy may well have originated at an earlier period, further south and east. With the extensive documentary evidence from the Genizah, we are now able to test whether that theory is borne out by the facts.

It was once common for those with an interest in the events of yesteryear to raise questions or provide answers about who reigned when, which battles took place where, and how a certain idea or invention came on to the scene. Today, it is more fashionable to concentrate on the quality of life enjoyed by different folk at various times and to ask how literate they were, which languages they used and why, and who had the benefit of education. Those newly confronted with early medieval Jewish manuscripts and their importance are often therefore interested in knowing more about the history of Jewish literacy, languages and learning, and researchers are now in a position to slake their thirst for such knowledge.

If literacy means composing literature, spreading a written tradition among parts of the population, and authorizing texts that shape the lives and ideals of the community, it must be acknowledged that Jewish literacy made considerable progress during the geonic (pre-medieval) period. Standard texts of the leading religious works were edited, rational methods of interpreting literature were introduced, and written guidance was provided for both ritual and theology. Given the literary nature of the Jewish religious tradition, it is clear that such developments affected a substantial proportion of the Jewish population rather than an élitist minority.

The text of the Pentateuch stood at the centre of the tradition and confronted the ordinary Jew in synagogue, home and school. It was not the rabbi who functioned as the intermediary between the people and its God but sacred scripture and its interpretation. According to rabbinic Judaism, communion with the divine could be experienced through the learning process, so that education developed a function akin to worship. Not a specially ordained priest but any Jew educated enough in the sources to be called rabbi, "my teacher", could lead his co-religionists through the intricacies of the traditions, the knowledge and the practice.

Hebrew was an essential element of Jewish life and even the rare Jew who had for some reason remained illiterate could not help but be caught up in its appearance, recitation and sound.

FROM SCROLL TO CODEX

What is equally important is that it was a change in how such culture was transmitted that led to these achievements. The contents of scrolls were copied on to bound volumes (codices), to which later generations added their own notes. Such codices began as no more than a few folded leaves but eventually evolved into substantial volumes with many folios. By being committed to a written form in these codices, oral traditions acquired a new degree of authority. The centralization and organization of the Jewish community under Islam made possible the wide distribution and acceptance of such texts. When the caliphate disintegrated and smaller independent Jewish communities emerged, they already had a corpus of written sources to which they looked for instruction and inspiration. The fact that leading scholars chose to summarize the religious traditions in such published forms indicates that there existed a large enough body of literate Jews to make the whole exercise worthwhile.

Turning to the history of the Jewish book, one finds an almost total absence of Hebrew manuscripts between the second and the ninth centuries and it is unlikely that this is merely an historical accident. Rather, the dominant tendency during these centuries was the oral one and the trend was reversed only with the expansion of the use of the codex, for the reasons just described. Texts other than Hebrew Bible scrolls then began to make a wide appearance. Although the number of complete Hebrew codices that have survived from the ninth and tenth centuries is still only in single figures and their content predominantly biblical, the evidence of the Genizah leaves little room for doubt that many of its fragments originally belonged to codices of various types of literature originating in the oriental communities of those centuries. The Hebrew codex apparently made its appearance in the eighth century, perhaps under the influence of Islam, which had borrowed the medium from the Christian and Classical worlds. Within three centuries, it became the standard medium for textual transmission.

When the eighth-century post-talmudic tractate, *Massekhet Soferim*, dealt with the transcription and recitation of sacred texts, it was primarily concerned with the writing of a biblical scroll. The position totally changed within two or three centuries by which time there were

48 – A ruling board for the scribe or his trainee (T-S K11.54)
(Cambridge University Library)

already standard practices for Jewish scribes copying all kinds of literature on to codices. With similar developments taking place among the Muslims, the Jews were gradually replacing papyrus with vellum as the primary material for the transcription of texts and would soon begin to adopt paper. Quires were composed, catchwords included, sections numerated, lines justified, margins set, and the ruling-board (*maṣṭara*) was employed to facilitate the planning of the lines. Studies of Genizah fragments are gradually revealing how this whole process developed from a primitive to a fairly sophisticated level. As the process reached its zenith, pride was taken in producing particularly beautiful codices of the Hebrew Bible. The codex's versatility, capacity, and ease of reference meant that it was widely adopted for the circulation of the literature that had been created and expanded in the previous few centuries.

Where there are sets of volumes, there is inevitably a need to store them together and one would expect to encounter the earliest history of the Jewish library among oriental Jews. It has indeed recently been demonstrated that in the Jewish communities of North Africa in the ninth and tenth centuries texts were being widely copied and circulated and that extensive libraries, covering various languages, were being amassed and sold. Such libraries included not only the classical Jewish

49 – An inscription prepared for a bookcase speaks out in favour of knowledge (T-S Ar.5.1) (Cambridge University Library)

212

sources but also the newest commentaries on the one hand and more general learning on the other. They were actively built up by individuals, sometimes businessmen rather than specialized scholars, and by communities, through gifts, appeals and purchases, and they were made available for academic use by students and for ritual use by congregants.

50 – A Latin note (inverted, bottom right) has been added (by a Crusader?) concerning the authorship of a commentary on Isaiah (T-S 12.722) (Cambridge University Library)

213

By creating, copying and disseminating the contents of these libraries, the Maghrebi Jews of means introduced a wide variety of literary works to other communities and thereby exercised a powerful influence on the levels of Jewish cultural achievement. The impressive contents of the Cairo Genizah are in no small degree due to the arrival there of many Jewish refugees from Tunisia and to the transfer of the bibliographical riches of the North African communities to the Egyptian centre. Book-lists are also a common feature of the Genizah discoveries and demonstrate the existence of reference literature for educational activities by the community. Bibles, prayer books, talmudic texts and commentaries, Jewish legal and theological tracts, as well as scientific, medical and philosophical works, are among the items that are regularly listed, sometimes in the context of a public sale. It is remarkable that a bibiophile, who was having a book-case made, prepared a delightful text in praise of such an item of furniture and its educational importance, with the apparent intention of having it engraved on the front. Equally remarkable is the fact that when the Egyptian Jewish community raised funds in the twelfth century for the ransom of Jews who had been captured by Crusaders in the Holy Land, they also made arrangements to pay the conquerors for the safe return of Jewish books. In one case, a Latin note describing the contents of a commentary on Isaiah has survived, testifying to an interest on the part of at least one Crusader in the intellectual aspect of his booty or its resale commercial value.

A VARIED USE OF SEMITICS

While literacy may be defined as an acquaintance with literature, it may mean, and indeed more often today does mean, the ability to read and write a language or more than one language. If we are to understand the Jewish situation in this connection during the Genizah period, we should abandon an exclusive concern with the history of literature and attempt a consideration of the more mundane aspects of Jewish life more than a thousand years ago, particularly the matter of the languages used. Much of what has earlier been said about books, transmission and authority applies to Hebrew volumes but, as in earlier generations, Jewish society was effectively trilingual. Hebrew, Aramaic and Arabic were used in a variety of contexts by different people for sundry reasons, with each of these languages exercising an influence on the others. Hebrew obviously continued to be the language of the formal cycles of biblical readings, was adopted for masoretic notes on the biblical text, and was retained as the language of the *midrashim*, or rabbinic commentaries on the Hebrew

Bible. It was also used for the statutory prayers and for the composition of liturgical poetry, although in the latter case it must be stressed that it took on all manner of novel linguistic elements in order to allow the poets full rein for their lyrical originality. It remained the "holy tongue" and left a particularly strong linguistic legacy with the communities that were closely influenced by the Palestinian centre, which had laid so much stress on the Hebrew Bible and studies of its linguistic structure. There was, however, constant tension about whether the biblical or the rabbinic variety of Hebrew was the authoritative form for post-biblical works, as well as persistent competition from its two sister languages.

The language that had once been a vernacular in Roman Judea, Aramaic, was restricted to a more scholarly role, being used for the Talmud, both Babylonian and Palestinian, and for commentaries on it and codes extracted from it. It became the language most closely associated with the theory and practice of Jewish religious law. It was also employed for the *targumim* (the Aramaic biblical renderings that had once served to inform and edify Aramaic-speaking Jews but had since developed a literary life of their own) and for some parts of the liturgy. Some of the earliest prayers survived in Aramaic because they had been composed in what had been a popular language while some of the latest liturgical material was written in Aramaic because that gave it a high level of intellectual sophistication. In many ways the use of Aramaic among the Jews of that period resembles that of Latin among medieval Christian scholastics, its function having evolved from a vernacular used by the majority into an almost esoteric medium for the intellectually initiated. Given the specialized and limited employment of the language, the manuscripts and printed texts of Aramaic Jewish literature gradually became corrupted on the one hand and the subject of misguided "correction" on the other. Thanks to the early texts now available from the Genizah, it has proved possible to distinguish the Palestinian and Babylonian forms of the language and to reconstruct their pointing, grammar, and vocabulary. Since such forms ultimately go back to the talmudic period, a linguistic link has been reforged between the early medieval and the late Classical period, thus permitting a better understanding of the development of Jewish literature and culture in a period that was, to a considerable extent, previously obscure.

Arabic was of course the dominant language of the huge Islamic empire of the Genizah period and it is hardly surprising that it had also become the vernacular of Jews and Christians living there. What is interesting is that although the Jews used it widely, they preferred to read and write the language in Hebrew and not in Arabic script. This

51 – A trilingual version in Hebrew, Aramaic and Judaeo-Arabic of the Joseph story
(T-S B1.25) (Cambridge University Library)

Arabic, currently entitled Judaeo-Arabic, preserves more vernacular forms and later dialectical features than classical Muslim Arabic, and is also characterized by the occurrence of many Hebrew, as well as some Aramaic words and phrases. Arabic proper, if it may be described as such, was used only rarely by a minority of Jews while Judaeo-Arabic was so widespread that, according to one estimate, it is represented in almost half of the texts recovered from the Genizah. As Norman

216

Stillman has succinctly put it, "Judaeo-Arabic holds a place of special significance. It has had the longest recorded history... It has had the widest geographical diffusion... It was the medium of expression for one of the foremost periods of Jewish cultural and intellectual creativity." It was Judaeo-Arabic that was chosen for biblical commentary and translation; for studies of rabbinic literature and Jewish religious law; and to provide grammatical, liturgical and philosophical guidance. Folklore and belles-lettres are well represented and there are important works in the fields of science and medicine. Among the more mundane items are letters, accounts, lists and legal documents. As in so many areas covered by the Genizah, many of the texts are the oldest or even the only extant versions of particular works and their discovery has therefore led to the rewriting of Jewish literary history. In their transcriptions of the pentateuchal text, the Arabic-speaking Jews of the early Middle Ages, arch-linguistic conservatives that they were, did not always opt for one language or another but sometimes composed trilingual versions in which the Hebrew, the Aramaic and the Judaeo-Arabic of each verse appeared side-by-side.

But the situation was never quite so clear-cut. Mundane letters were also written in Hebrew, poems were composed in Aramaic, rubrics for the Hebrew prayers were couched in Judaeo-Arabic and Hebrew vowel-points were attached to Judaeo-Arabic texts. Sometimes the same work was composed in both Hebrew and Judaeo-Arabic. The Karaites, in fact, took to writing Hebrew texts in Arabic script with Hebrew vowel-points and also composed a highly Arabicized Hebrew that would appear to have been comprehensible to nobody but themselves. Some generations of Karaites preferred Arabic while others reverted to Hebrew. This variety in the choice of the language written in particular contexts demonstrates that there was more at stake than the simple matter of comprehensibility. The choice may have amounted to a polemical statement, a way of demonstrating one's adherence to a particular tradition or one's departure from it, or an expression of literary, social or educational innovation.

EXOTIC JEWISH LANGUAGES

As is well known, Jewish use of languages other than Hebrew by way of Hebrew script and characteristic, Jewish vocabulary, was not restricted to the Arabic-speaking world. Elsewhere too, the Jews were anxious to have their linguistic cake and to eat it. While assimilating culturally by adopting the local language, they maintained their Jewish identity by

52 – Yiddish letter from a Jerusalem woman to her son in Cairo, 1567
(T-S Misc.36 L1) (Cambridge University Library)

218

hebraizing various aspects of its form. What is perhaps less widely appreciated is the degree to which such Jewish languages, defined by socio-linguists as "ethnolects", are represented among the Genizah manuscripts. In addition to Judaeo-Arabic, although in much more limited number, the Genizah researcher encounters texts in Judaeo-Greek, Judaeo-Spanish, Judaeo-German (Yiddish) and Judaeo-Persian. Although we are here more interested in the significance of such texts for the history of Jewish literacy and culture, it should not be forgotten that they provide essential evidence for those researching the earliest histories of the non-Semitic languages on which they are based.

Given that the Jews of so many centuries in such a large number of countries were under the influence of Islamic culture and Arabic language, it is easily forgotten that an equivalent Greek influence once existed among numerous Jewish communities. Not only did it flourish in the Classical and Byzantine worlds, when it was endemic to talmudic and midrashic literature; it also left its mark in the medieval period within the Islamic empire and at its edges, in such places as Egypt, Asia Minor and the Greek Archipelago. It is therefore not surprising to find Genizah fragments written in Judaeo-Greek that testify to a fairly broad use of such language, as a vernacular and in literature, among some Jews, particularly, no doubt, those who had come from areas of Byzantine influence. As with other such Jewish languages, one encounters a considerable knowledge and input of Hebrew. The number of items is not vast, and one has to make allowance for the fact that what has survived may have done so by accident and may not be representative. Nevertheless, the contents of a recently published set of Greek Jewish texts from the Genizah are sufficiently varied to permit the assumption that what is being uncovered here is a mere remnant of a linguistic phenomenon that was once extensive and significant.

The interpretation of the Hebrew Bible was clearly of importance to those who used Judaeo-Greek. Various parts of Scripture are dealt with, sometimes by way of the translation of difficult words, sometimes via running translations or commentaries. The approach may be grammatical, theological or midrashic and there are sometimes links with earlier Greek translations of the Bible or with known medieval Jewish commentaries. The Mishnah also apparently attracted similar attention and the Passover Haggadah makes a number of appearances, its Hebrew text interspersed with Judaeo-Greek guides to the ritual procedure. As so often with Genizah material, the mundane is not absent from the Judaeo-Greek picture. A marriage settlement drawn up in 1022 in

Mastaura (Lydia, Asia Minor) between Namer, son of Elkanah, and Evdokia, daughter of Caleb, provides intriguing details of money, clothing, jewellery and household items. There is also a business letter that deals with the sale of hides, some of them sent with a Christian priest, and – ubiquitous items among Genizah texts – a letter from a husband to his wife complaining about the miseries he is undergoing during his travels, and another from a mother to her son cajoling him to come and fetch her from Alexandria to Fustat.

In any discussion of intellectual and linguistic influences on Judaism, major attention has to be given to the Jewish presence in Spain, particularly during the five centuries before the expulsion in 1492. During the early part of that period, when Spain was under Muslim control, there developed a rich cultural heritage in Arabic that made a major impact on Jewish life and literature. Leading Jews such as Moses

ben Maimon and Judah Ha-Levi brought that outstanding tradition from al-Andalus, as they called it, to North Africa and Egypt, and it is powerfully represented in the Cairo Genizah. Although that Jewish culture, from the "golden age of Spanish Jewry", bequeathed much that is still practised and enjoyed in modern Judaism, it remained part of the Muslim-Jewish symbiosis characteristic of Arab lands. After the reconquest of Spain by the Christians, a new expression of Spanish Jewish civilization got under way, this time expressed in Judaeo-Spanish. This culture is no less deserving of description as "golden", and it did not disappear when the Iberian peninsula was emptied of its Jews. Those who had once lived there carried its banner high to many Jewish communities around the world and, despite what they had suffered, remained closely attached to their hispanic identity.

Such a Sefaradi identity was maintained with great pride and confidence and those who inherited it never forgot the high levels of social, economic and political success that they had once enjoyed in the Spanish homeland. They did everything they could to impose it wherever they settled and the evidence of their activity in Egypt and the surrounding area is clearly to be found among the Cairo Genizah fragments written in Judaeo-Spanish and dating mainly from the fifteenth to the seventeenth century. The range of the literature represented among these manuscript remnants is wider than that of the Judaeo-Greek items emanating from the same source, and more akin to those written in Judaeo-Arabic, although the numbers are far fewer. Some texts provide translations and commentaries on biblical, rabbinic and liturgical texts. There are intriguing collections of ballads, songs and proverbs. The scientific, medical and folkloristic fields are well represented and some fragments relate to astrology and the calendar. Above all, there are personal letters written by and about Sefaradi Jews on their Mediterranean wanderings. Money is lent; charity is sought; travel instructions are given; and family matters are discussed. Another superb example of Jewish maternal pressure occurs in a sixteenth-century letter (translated by Eleazar Gutwirth) from doña Gamila, widow of Rabbi Yom Ṭov Shalom, to her son, Abraham:

> Know as it pleases you that Esther married. May you marry your sons with greater advantage. May they never be orphans…and more tears flowed from my eyes than from a fountain, for I found myself with no other support than the Lord, blessed be he, and your brother-in-law, who did come. And you do not send me even two lines with him. Even if he did not call on you, you could have sent him two lines [for us] with those who come and go. You could have done so, not for me but for your sister who, saying "Oh, to receive two lines from my brother!" is tearing out her heart and does nothing but cry from your lack of affection.

If such Jewish motherly emotions are recorded in Judaeo-Arabic and in Judaeo-Spanish, it is hardly surprising that they are also to be found in Judaeo-German form, that is, in Yiddish. What is perhaps surprising is that such a language is also to be found in the Genizah but when one recalls that there was a substantial Ashkenazi community in Jerusalem in the sixteenth century, the occurrence is more easily explained. Members of that community sometimes made their way to Egypt to seek their fortune, or at least a basic livelihood, and it was natural for them to correspond with their families in Yiddish. We are fortunate in having a number of such letters written in 1567 by Rachel Zussmann to her son Moshe, who was working in Cairo as a religious scribe. Interestingly, this literary lady begins her letters in Hebrew and after a few lines of formal greeting switches to *mamaloshen*. There is also a fifteenth-century fragment of a Yiddish translation of the mishnaic tractate *Avot*, which may also have found its way to Egypt through the land of Israel or in the belongings of a visiting Ashkenazi trader. One of the most important documents for the early history of Yiddish, a codex containing the repertoire of a troubadour in the form of rhymed fables

especially about such topics as Moses, the Garden of Eden, Abraham and Joseph, as well as the item of German mythology known as *Dukus Horant*, is also located in the Cambridge Genizah Collection and may have made its way to Cairo in a similar fashion. On the other hand, it is not absolutely clear that it was actually acquired by the University Library together with the other Genizah items and it is just possible that its provenance is to be sought elsewhere. Be that as it may, the presence of even some Yiddish pieces is further evidence of the broad literacy documented in the Genizah.

As far as Judaeo-Persian is concerned, there is no full list of Genizah items in this language but from the preliminary findings it is clear that there were Jews who were using that dialect for mundane and literary texts a thousand years ago. Various literary compositions and documents have surfaced, including two Karaite commentaries on Daniel and fragments of grammatical writings. Perhaps it was the Karaite Jews of Egypt and Palestine who brought the language with them when they emigrated there from the east and continued to use it as a means of retaining a distinct religious and linguistic identity.

LANGUAGE AND IDEOLOGY

However interesting and informative such exotic Jewish languages, their use in the oriental Jewish communities of the pre-modern period can in no way be compared to that of the three dominant languages earlier discussed, namely, Hebrew, Aramaic and Arabic. The use of Judaeo-Arabic as an alternative Jewish language may have something to do with the tendency to treat new literature as deserving only of the vernacular, while venerating older literature by continuing to use the ancient tongues in which it had long been transmitted. It may also be related to the level of education available to those making most use of a particular genre. Alternatively, there may have existed in the Jewish mind of the period a distinction between the literary, aesthetic and solemn significance of Hebrew and the communicative value of Arabic as a widespread vernacular. Whatever the reasons, this trilingual circumstance was a major factor in the blossoming of philological study among the Jews. Familiar as they were with the forms occurring in three Semitic languages, they were able to construct theories about the general form of these languages and how they related to one another and to use the characteristics of one to explain the anomalies of another.

It was not without good reason that the Arabs referred to the Jews (as to the Christians) as *ahl al-kitāb*, "the people of the book". The literary output and the linguistic competence just described presupposes an almost obsessive concern with the written word. While that concern had its origins in the biblical period, it had to a large extent been transferred to the area of oral transmission in talmudic and immediately post-talmudic times insofar as the rabbinic traditions were concerned. Only with the passion of the rabbinic authorities to establish their whole ideology and practice as central and definitive did it return to its original form, or even to an extension of that form. The Rabbanites were anxious to refute the accusation made by such theological opponents as the Karaites that their oral traditions were a travesty of the original, sacred

53 – Hebrew alphabet primer for Jewish children (T-S K5.13)
(Cambridge University Library)

223

scripture, prone to error and alterations. They therefore embraced the written medium once again and utilized it to publicize an ever-expanding variety of works that adopted the latest ideas to defend and promote their own theological position. The ninth-century head of the Sura academy, Naṭronai ben Hilai, expressed his dissatisfaction that other disciplines were being neglected in order to concentrate on Talmud ("hence they have concentrated on the Talmud alone and neglected Bible and Mishnah"). The more catholic outlook that lay behind that complaint was fast becoming the norm by the end of the geonic period. This regeneration of broader interests, as in the golden age of Spanish Jewry, combined with an enthusiastic adoption of the codex to produce a wealth of new, scholarly texts. The question that remains to be answered is to what extent it may be assumed that the wider availability of such texts was paralleled by a broadly based knowledge of them on the part of what may be referred to as the Jewish masses.

GENIZAH AND BROADER EDUCATION

What may be said about the extent of Jewish literacy some eight centuries ago? The evidence from the Genizah convincingly demonstrates that written material of a great variety of content existed in the Jewish community in and around Cairo from the tenth to the thirteenth century. In the region of at least 210,000 manuscript fragments, yielding a total of at least three times that number of individual leaves, the majority of them dating from those centuries, have survived the ravages of time and the elements, to excite the interest of the modern researcher. One may therefore confidently assume that the original hoard deposited in the Ben Ezra synagogue was greatly in excess of that number and itself represented only a proportion of what was actually produced in the communities in and around Cairo. Also relevant to the discussion is the fact that Cairo was not renowned for being the most scholarly or literate of the Jewish societies of the period. Indeed, much of this material emanated from circles that were not primarily concerned with scholarship, religion or science. Its particular value lies in the fact that it represents what has been referred to as "counter-history" rather than the views of the leadership, and as such it provides ample testimony to the whole gamut of education from the elementary to the advanced, and from children's alphabetical exercises to adults' guest lectures. What is more, while explicit dates are not usually given, it is possible that hundreds of the fragments predate the tenth century, therefore bearing direct witness to the heart of the geonic age, while the customs reflected in the collection as a whole appear to be relevant to a much wider geographical area than Cairo and its environs. If an attempt is now made to summarize what is known about such customs, this should provide some sense of the wider literacy of that time and place and demonstrate that the dissemination of texts had a major impact on large sections of the Jewish people.

It was degrading for a Jew to be unable to participate fully in those aspects of the synagogal service that involved simple recitation of Hebrew and a mark of some distinction to be knowledgeable enough to undertake the rarer and more difficult readings on behalf of the congregation. The basic aim of elementary education was therefore to set him on the road towards these achievements. Most of the male community achieved at least the simplest level of reading and writing Hebrew, while the fewer more educated members became familiar with more difficult, biblical and rabbinic texts. One father was conscious of the fact that an opportunity to demonstrate his prowess in public was a necessary incentive for his son. He therefore instructed his son's teacher to prepare him for the recitation in the synagogue of passages from the Prophets and the Esther Scroll (as is clear from Goitein's translation):

I have requested you several times to teach my little one every week the portion from the Prophets belonging to the weekly lection. Likewise, it is customary for teachers to let the boys read the sections of the Bible appropriate to each season, such as the Book of Esther for Purim, and the Song of Songs for Passover, as well as other texts recited during the holidays. For if I do not ascend the platform with him, having him read in the synagogue, he will not learn at all. So please, teach him the portions from the Prophets and the Scroll of Esther.

The drive for literacy in Hebrew also provided Jews with the opportunity of writing Judaeo-Arabic, that is, recording their own vernacular in a script more familiar to them than Arabic. Not that Arabic itself was ruled out. Some Jews were taught the required calligraphy and such a competence could qualify them for those administrative, religious, medical and commercial professions for which it was required. Generally, however, such competence was required only by those in contact with the Muslim world. Interestingly, even when preparing a text for ultimate transmission outside the Jewish community, the writer would prepare a draft in Judaeo-Arabic. Once this was deemed satisfactory, the relevant Arabic text could be drawn up, perhaps by a professional, and forwarded as necessary. Knowledge of Arabic was

54 – Jottings by a young Jewish child in the 11th century (T-S K5.19)
(Cambridge University Library)

regarded as a practical necessity for some professionals and not a required element in the programme of instruction aimed at Jewish literacy.

BOYS AND GIRLS

If numeracy may be included under the general heading of literacy, it should be noted that references are also found to arithmetic, although less frequently than to Hebrew and Arabic. One mother had a contract drawn up according to which her son would be taught Arabic script and arithmetic at an agreed fee of two dinars. His language lessons were intended to train him to write a well-composed Arabic letter without spelling mistakes, while his education in arithmetic aimed at mastery in the abacus, decimals, and accounts. Classes in various subjects took place in the synagogue, in the communal study-centre, at the teacher's residence or in the pupil's home, and were conducted by a professional teacher. The fees were paid by the parents, or if the parents lacked the means or the children were orphans, the community met the cost. Reinforcement of these lessons, or education in wider religious practice,

226

was the task of the father in the synagogue and of either or both parents in the domestic setting. Being largely phonetic, Hebrew could be taught analytically letter by letter, although there is evidence of at least one pedagogical innovator who preferred the global method. That teacher, in a small provincial town in Egypt in the twelfth century, incurred the wrath of a rabbinic judge in Cairo who gave strict instructions for him to revert to the more traditional methods. Scrap paper was used for practice and, copies of books being an expensive item, one text was often used for the whole class. Pupils therefore had to acquire the ability to read the text from whatever angle at which they might be seated in relation to the script. Alphabet primers were among the few items of Hebrew literature that attracted illumination, presumably with the intention of exciting the interest of the budding scholars, and individual wooden boards were also in use.

Girls did not automatically receive such an education but occasionally there were parents who made such arrangements for them, usually for biblical studies. Some succeeded so well that they became professional teachers themselves, while others developed skills as calligraphers. In one sad little manuscript, a father bewails the loss of just such a daughter, mournfully remembering her intellect, her knowledge of the Torah and her piety, and poignantly recalling the lessons he used to give her. The fact that there are a number of letters in which wives are directly addressed by their husbands, as against others in which a male colleague is requested to pass on written information by word of mouth to the writer's spouse, appears to demonstrate that women were not universally illiterate. Since there are specific letters and documents written in female hands, it is clear that some women were acquainted not only with reading but also with writing. It should, however, be acknowledged that even these occurrences are in the legal, communal and personal spheres, rather than in the literary.

One mother was so anxious that her daughter should receive a sound education that she made a death-bed request in a letter written in her own hand to her sister. She asked her to take on the responsibility for ensuring this, although she was aware that this would strain the family resources. The text is at once moving and instructive, well worth citing, at least in part (in Goitein's translation):

This is to inform you, my lady, dear sister – may God accept me as a ransom for you – that I have become seriously ill with little hope of recovery, and I have dreams indicating that my end is near. My lady, my most urgent request of you, if God, the exalted, indeed decrees my death, is that you take care of my little daughter and make efforts to give her an education, although I know well that I am asking you for something unreasonable, as there is not enough money – by my father – for support, let alone for formal instruction. However, she has a model in our saintly mother ... my lady, only God knows how I wrote these lines!

Those boys who advanced to higher levels of learning developed a more educated hand and the range of styles recorded among the Genizah texts begins at the primitive and advances to the most expert. Some young men spent many years at talmudic centres of learning both at home and abroad, maintained by communal and individual subscriptions. Adults who were engaged in making a living nevertheless devoted time, sometimes daily, to studying traditional Jewish literature, biblical and rabbinic, with friends, or attending courses given by local scholars or lectures delivered by specially invited authorities. The learning process often took place late in the evening, or during the night, and Maimonides makes a point of stressing how important it is to use the dark hours profitably in this way. Communities ensured that there was accommodation available for such devoted study, usually on the synagogal premises, and there is evidence that points to the availability of reference literature. Even if Cairo was better known among the communities of the Jewish world for its economic activity than for its academic prowess, there are still clear indications in the Genizah of a fairly high level of literacy. Scholarly notes, invitations to lectures, details of refresher courses – all point to an intense degree of educational activity, while the remainder of the evidence confirms that it was not an élitist or an exclusivist preoccupation.

By the middle of the classical Genizah period, then, literacy for the Jews of the communities living under Islam constituted a fairly complex and sophisticated level of education for a broad section of the community in a variety of Jewish and non-Jewish subjects. By this time, too, their Jewish brethren in Christian Europe were following their lead and had established a sound base for a later flowering of Hebrew and Jewish letters in that centre that was to have important cultural consequences for the modern western world. The paradox is that while these centres to the north flourished, so their counterparts to the south, under harsher Muslim régimes than those of the Genizah period, began to decline, and a process got underway that was to stand the geography of Jewish educational achievement on its head.

Guide to reading

For overviews of general developments in the Jewish Middle Ages, see S. W. Baron, *A Social and Religious History of the Jews*, especially vols. 6–7 (New York, London and Philadelphia, 1958); *The World History of the Jewish People. Medieval Period. Dark Ages*, edited by Cecil Roth (Tel Aviv, 1966); S. D. Goitein, *A Mediterranean Society: The Jewish Communities of the Arab World as Portrayed in the Documents of the Cairo Geniza* (= *Med. Soc.*, 5 volumes, plus a sixth index volume, prepared by P. Sanders; Berkeley, Los Angeles and London, 1967–93); *A History of the Jewish People*, ed. H. H. Ben-Sasson (E. T., London, 1976); *The Jewish World: Revelation, Prophecy and History*, ed. E. Kedourie (London, 1979); T. and M. Metzger's *Jewish Life in the Middle Ages* (London and New York, 1985); and the relevant essays in *The Illustrated History of the Jewish People*, ed. Nicholas de Lange (Toronto, 1997). M. Waxman, *A History of Jewish Literature*, vols. 1–2 (second edition; New York, 1960) provides the literary background while *Communication in the Jewish Diaspora: The Pre-Modern World*, ed. Sophia Menache (Leiden, New York and Köln, 1996) deals with medieval Jewish literary contact. Although it is in many ways dated, there is still much of interest and importance in Israel Abrahams, *Jewish Life in the Middle Ages* (Philadelphia, 1896). The situation in Christian Europe may be compared by consulting the various essays in *The Uses of Literacy in Early Mediaeval Europe*, ed. R. McKitterick (Cambridge, 1990).

Information about the Jewish adoption and use of the codex may be found in. S. Lieberman, *Hellenism in Jewish Palestine: Studies in the Literary Transmission, Beliefs and Manners of Palestine in the I Century B. C. E. – 4 Century C. E.* (2nd edition, New York, 1962), pp. 203–9; E. G. Turner, *The Typology of the Early Codex* (Philadelphia, 1977); C. M. Roberts and T. C. Skeat, *The Birth of the Codex* (2nd edition, London, 1983); R. H. Rouse and M. A. Rouse, "Codicology, Western European" in *Dictionary of the Middle Ages*, vol. 3 (New York, 1983), pp. 475–78; M. Beit-Arié, "How Hebrew Manuscripts are Made" in *A Sign and a Witness: 2,000 years of Hebrew Books and Illustrated Manuscripts*, ed. L. S. Gold (New York and Oxford, 1988), pp. 35–46; I. M. Resnick, "The Codex in Early Jewish and Christian Communities", *Journal of Religious History* 17 (1992), pp. 1–17; S. C. Reif, "Codicological Aspects of Jewish Liturgical History", *Bulletin of the John Rylands University Library of Manchester* 75 (1993), pp. 117–31, and "The Genizah and Jewish Liturgy: Past Achievements and a Current Project", scheduled to be published in the proceedings of a conference on 'Avodah and 'Ibada arranged by Seth Ward at the University of Denver in March, 1998.

Papyrus is still used for some of the older Genizah material (e.g. T-S 6H9–21) and there are also examples of cloth being used for the recording of texts (e.g. T-S 16.31). See C. Sirat, *Les papyrus en caractères hébraïques trouvés en Egypte* (Paris, 1985) and in her brief note on T-S 6H9–21 in *Genizah Fragments* 5 (April, 1983), pp. 3–4. The pentateuchal codex was known to the oriental Jews as *mashaf torah*, as in e.g. T-S 12.791, or *mashaf de-'orayta*, as in e.g. T-S A41.41. For details of books, scribes and orality, see *The Hebrew Book: An Historical Survey*, eds. R. Posner and I. Ta-Shma (Jerusalem, 1975); M. Beit-Arié, *Hebrew Codicology* (Paris, 1976; 2nd edition, Jerusalem, 1981); S. D. Goitein, *A Mediterranean Society*, vol. 2 (Berkeley, Los Angeles and London, 1971), pp. 228–40; S. C. Reif, "Aspects of Mediaeval Jewish Literacy" in *The Uses of Literacy in Early Mediaeval Europe*, ed. R. McKitterick (Cambridge, 1990), pp. 134–55; B. Gerhardsson, *Memory and Manuscript* (Uppsala, 1961; republished with a new preface by the author and a foreword by J. Neusner, together with *Tradition and Transmission in Early Christianity*, Grand Rapids and Livonia, Michigan, 1998); M. J. Carruthers, *The Book of Memory: A Study in Medieval Culture* (Cambridge, 1990); and W. A. Graham, *Beyond the Written Word: Oral Aspects of Scripture in the History of Religion* (Cambridge, 1987; paperback edition, 1993). On book-lists, see Goitein, *Med. Soc.* 2, pp. 206 and 248, *Med. Soc.* 5, pp. 3–4 and 425, and on the ransom of books (the Latin note is in T-S 12.722), see *Med. Soc.* 5, pp. 85, 376 and 529. Goitein discusses the proposed engraving in his "Books Migrant and Stationary: A Geniza Study" in *Occident and Orient: A Tribute to the Memory of Alexander Scheiber*, ed. R. Dan (Budapest and Leiden, 1988), pp. 179–98, citing T-S Ar.5.1 and T-S NS J271. The sale of the library of Rabbi Abraham Ḥasid is documented in T-S 20.44; see E. J. Worman, "Two Book Lists from the Cambridge Genizah Fragments", *Jewish Quarterly Review* 20 (1908), pp. 450–63.

The development of Hebrew over the centuries and its varying form in different contexts is touched upon by W. Chomsky, *Hebrew the Eternal Language* (Philadelphia, 1964); E. Y. Kutscher, *A History of the Hebrew Language* (ed. R. Kutscher, Jerusalem, 1982); and A. Sáenz-Badillos, *A History of the Hebrew Language* (E. T., Cambridge, 1993). A useful summary of the various Aramaic dialects has been written by K. Beyer, *The Aramaic Language: Its Distribution and Sub-Divisions* (E. T., Göttingen, 1986) and important work has also been done by M. Sokoloff, as in the conference papers he edited in *Arameans, Aramaic and the Aramaic Literary Tradition* (Ramat Gan, 1983), and in *A Dictionary of Palestinian Jewish Aramaic of the Byzantine Period* (Ramat Gan, 1990). Basic work on Judaeo-Arabic as an independent Jewish language has been done by Joshua Blau, the world's expert in the field, in his *The Emergence and Linguistic Background of Judaeo-Arabic* (Oxford, 1965); *A Study of the Origins of Middle Arabic* (Jerusalem, 1981); and *Studies in Middle Arabic and its Judaeo-Arabic Variety* (Jerusalem, 1988). Colin Baker has produced a useful summary of the relevant Genizah genres in his "Judaeo-Arabic Material in the Cambridge Genizah Collections", *Bulletin of the School of Oriental and African Studies* 58 (1995), pp. 445–54, and Meira Polliack has provided important guidance to Judaeo-Arabic literary types in her published lecture "Genres in Judaeo-Arabic Literature" (Halmos lecture series, Tel Aviv University, 1998). See also the essays on a variety of Judaeo-Arabic topics in *Genizah Research after Nintey Years: The Case of Judaeo-Arabic*, eds. J. Blau and S. C. Reif (Cambridge, 1992). The quotation from Stillman is from *The Language and Culture of the Jews of Sefrou, Morocco: An Ethnolinguistic Study* (Manchester, 1988), pp. 3–4.

For some very helpful remarks and bibliography about "ethnolects", see "Adaptations of Hebrew Script", in two parts by Benjamin Hary and H. I. Aronson, in *The World's Writing Systems*, eds. P. T. Daniels and W. Bright (New York and Oxford, 1996), pp. 727–42. The unusual occurrence of particular Jewish languages in unexpected contexts is noted and documented in S. C. Reif, "Aspects of Mediaeval Jewish Literacy" in R. McKitterick's volume earlier mentioned, pp. 148–49, and Khan has dealt with the Arabic transcriptions of the Hebrew Bible in his *Karaite Bible Manuscripts from the Cairo Genizah* (Cambridge, 1990). The Judaeo-Greek texts have recently been edited by Nicholas de Lange in his *Greek Jewish Texts from the Cairo Genizah* (Tübingen, 1996), which includes the marriage settlement (T-S 16.374), the business letter (T-S 16.289), and the two other pieces of correspondence (T-S 8J19.33 and Or.1080 J1) mentioned here; for some of the historical background, see S. B. Bowman, *The Jews of Byzantium* (Alabama, 1985). The standard works on medieval Jewish Spain are E. Ashtor's *The Jews of Moslem Spain* (3 vols., Philadelphia, 1973–84, based on the Hebrew edition of 1960–66) and Y. Baer's *The Jews in Christian Spain* (2 volumes, arising out of the earlier German work of 1929 and 1936 and based on the second Hebrew edition of 1959) and a brief guide to the Judaeo-Spanish Genizah items is E. Gutwirth and S. C. Reif, *Ten Centuries of Hispano-Jewish Culture* (Cambridge, 1992), where doña Gamila's letter (T-S NS 298.11) is translated on p. 26, with a plate at the end of the booklet. In the matter of Yiddish items in the Genizah, Simon Hopkins provides information about new discoveries and those that preceded them in his article "A Fragment of *Pirqe Avot* in Old Yiddish", *Proceedings of the World Congress of Jewish Studies 1981* 8/3 (Jerusalem, 1982), pp. 153–57. The Genizah fragments here referred to are T-S Misc.36.L.1, T-S E3.114 and T-S 10K22. S. Shaked is the leading authority in the field of Judaeo-Persian and has summarized the situation and published some texts in his "Two Judaeo-Iranian Contributions: Fragments of Two Karaite Commentaries on Daniel in Judaeo-Persian" in *Irano-Judaica: Studies Relating to Jewish Contacts with Persian Culture throughout the Ages*, ed. S. Shaked (Jerusalem, 1982), pp. 304–22.

Part of the relationship between the different Jewish languages is discussed by R. Drory, "Words Beautifully Put: Hebrew versus Arabic in Tenth-Century Jewish Literature", *Genizah Research*, eds. Blau and Reif (cited in the previous paragraph but one), pp. 53–66, with extensive bibliography, and other aspects of the topic are dealt with in G. Khan, *Karaite Bible Manuscripts from the Cairo Genizah* (Cambridge, 1990). A general sense of the cultural message of Karaism may be derived from such volumes as *Karaite Anthology: Excerpts from the Early Literature*, ed. L. Nemoy (New Haven and London, 1952); Z. Ankori, *Karaites in Byzantium: The Formative Years 970–1100* (New York and Jerusalem, 1959); *Karaite Studies*, ed. P. Birnbaum (New York, 1971); and *Studies in Judaica, Karaitica and Islamica presented to L. Nemoy*, ed. S. R. Brunswick (Ramat Gan,

1982). The quote from Natronai appears in S. W. Baron, *A Social and Religious History of the Jews*, vol. 6 (New York, London and Philadelphia, 1958), pp. 235–36. On the general value, historical signficance and dating of the Genizah material in this context, see Goitein, *Med. Soc.* 2, p. 173; Beit-Arié, *Hebrew Codicology* (third paragraph of this guide to reading), pp. 9–19; and S. A Hopkins, "The Oldest Dated Document in the Geniza?" in *Studies in Judaism and Islam Presented to S. D. Goitein*, eds. S. Morag, I. Ben-Ami and N. A. Stillman (Jerusalem, 1981), pp. 83–98.

Genizah material relating to education, in addition to being dealt with by Goitein in the Hebrew volume cited in the first paragraph dealing with Hebrew publications below, is covered by that same outstanding researcher in *Med. Soc.* 2, pp. 173–83 and 185–90 and in his "Side Lights on Jewish Education from the Cairo Geniza", *Gratz College Anniversary Volume* (=*GCAV*), eds. I. D. Passow and S. T. Lachs (Philadelphia, 1971), pp. 83–110. The limited use of Arabic by Jews is explained by Geoffrey Khan in "The Arabic Fragments in the Cambridge Genizah Collections", *Manuscripts of the Middle East* 1 (1986), pp. 54–60 and "Arabic Documents in the Cairo Genizah", *Bulletin of the Israeli Academic Center in Cairo* 21 (1997), pp. 23–25. The fragments relating to the preparations for synagogal reading, to the study of Arabic and arithmetic, and to the global method are T-S Ar.30.36, T-S NS J401 and T-S 13J23.20, which are edited, translated and discussed by Goitein in *GCAV*, pp. 89, 93–94, 97–99, 102, 106–7 and 109–10. The references to teachers' fees are to be found in the same volume, pp. 94–97 and 107–8, citing T-S 13J6.27, T-S NS 321.28 and T-S 10J18.15. On girls and women, see *Med. Soc.* 2, pp. 183–85 and for women's letters see the forthcoming volume by Joel Kraemer, *Women's Letters from the Genizah*. The loss of the little girl is recorded in Jewish Theological Seminary, ENA 2935.17 and dealt with by Goitein in *GCAV*, p. 87, while the woman's death-bed request occurs in Genizah Misc. 6* in the same library and receives the attention of Goitein in *GCAV*, pp. 85–87 and 100–1. The advice of Maimonides is to be found in his code, *Mishneh Torah, Talmud Torah*, 3.13, as translated by M. Hyamson, *The Book of Knowledge* (Jerusalem, 1965), p. 60a. See also J. Mann, "Listes des Livres provenant de la Gueniza", *Revue des Etudes Juives* 72 (1921), pp. 163–83 and *Texts and Studies in Jewish History and Literature* (2 vols., Cincinnati and Philadelphia, 1931–35), pp. 643–84.

The remainder of this list provides some additional material for the Hebrew reader. On medieval history, see M. D. Herr, "On the Meaning of the Term 'Middle Ages' in Jewish History" in *Culture and Society in Medieval Jewry. Studies Dedicated to the Memory of H. H. Ben-Sasson*, eds. M. Ben-Sasson, R. Bonfil and J. R. Hacker (Jerusalem, 1989), pp. 83–97. A. Grossman, *The Early Sages of Ashkenaz: Their Lives, Leadership and Works* (Jerusalem, 1981) and *The Early Sages of France: Their Lives, Leadership and Works* (Jerusalem, 1996). M. Ben-Sasson and A. Grossman, *Ha-Qehillah Ha-Yehudit Biymey Ha-Beynayim* (Jerusalem, 1988). On education, see S. Assaf, *Meqorot Le-Toledot Ha-Ḥinukh Be-Yisrael* (4 vols.; Tel Aviv, 1925–43); Nathan Morris, *A History of*

Jewish Education (3 vols.; Jerusalem, 1960, 1964 and 1977); S. D. Goitein, *Jewish Education in Muslim Countries Based on Records from the Cairo Geniza* (Jerusalem, 1962); and J. Safran, *Studies in the History of Jewish Education* (Jerusalem, 1983).

On the codex, see M. Haran, "The Codex, the *Pinax* and the Wooden Slats", *Tarbiz* 57 (1988), pp. 151–64, with an additional note in *Tarbiz* 58 (1989), pp. 523–24; S. Z. Havlin, "From Scroll to Codex", *Alei Sefer* 16 (1990), pp. 151–52 and 160–61; M. Bar-Ilan, "Ha-Ma'avar Mi-Megillah Le-Qodeqs", *Sinai* 107 (1991), pp. 242–54; S. C. Reif, "Liturgical Texts from the Genizah; How their Physical State Relates to their Content" in *From Qumran to Cairo* (Hebrew), ed. J. Tabory (in the press). For information about libraries in the Genizah period, I am indebted to M. Ben-Sasson for providing a copy of his unpublished Hebrew paper "*Sifriyot Ha-Magreb Bi-Genizat Qahir*". That the practice of writing on only one side was also used for rabbinic texts is documented by an early Genizah manuscript, T-S AS 74.324, published by M. Bregman, "An Early Fragment of Avot de-Rabbi Natan from a Scroll", *Tarbiz* 52 (1983), pp. 201–22. The reference to *Soferim* is to *Massekhet Soferim* 3:6 and see also *Sefer Halakhot Gedolot*, ed. E. Hildesheimer, 3 volumes (Jerusalem, 1971, 1980, 1988), vol. 1, p. 404. Details of the Latin note by the Crusader are given by B. Kedar in *Jerusalem in the Middle Ages: Selected Papers* (Jerusalem, 1979), pp. 107–11.

Concerning the various "Jewish" languages, see the Haifa periodical *Jewish Languages*; A. Bendavid, *Leshon Ha-Miqra U-leshon Hakhamim* (Tel Aviv, 1967); S. Federbush, *Ha-Lashon Ha'Ivrit Be-Yisrael Uva-'Amim* (Jerusalem, 1967); J. Blau, *A Grammar of Mediaeval Judaeo-Arabic* (Jerusalem, 1961); Geoffrey Khan, "A Geniza Fragment of a Judeo-Arabic Lament" in *Mas'at Moshe: Studies in Jewish and Islamic Culture Presented to Moshe Gil*, eds. E. Fleischer, M. A. Friedman and J. L. Kraemer (Jerusalem, 1998), pp. 184–97. J. Hacker deals with the Sefaradi emigrés' dominance of the communities where they settled in his article "Patterns of the Intellectual Activity of Ottoman Jewry in the 16th and 17th Centuries", *Tarbiz* 53 (1984), pp. 569–603, which appeared in English in *Jewish Thought in the Seventeenth Century*, eds. I. Twersky and B. Septimus (Cambridge, Mass., and London, 1987), pp. 95–135. In the Yiddish field, see Simon Hopkins, "A Geniza Fragment of Pirqe Avot in Old Yiddish", *Tarbiz* 52 (1983), pp. 459–67, with plate, on T-S E3.114.

The relationship between the different Jewish languages is discussed by R. Drory, *The Emergence of Hebrew-Arabic Literary Contacts at the Beginning of the Tenth Century* (Tel Aviv, 1986) and by David Téné in his article on comparative linguistics and linguistic knowledge (no English title) in *Hebrew Language Studies presented to Professor Zeev Ben-Hayyim*, eds. M. Bar-Asher, A. Dotan, G. B. Sarfati and D. Téné (Jerusalem, 1983), pp. 237–87. Hebrew sources concerning the history of Jewish education have already been cited above in the first paragraph of this Hebrew list.

TEN

A CENTURY
REACHED

Minor personal activity may ultimately have major historical impact and this is nowhere truer than in the case of Solomon Schechter's trip to Cairo in the winter of 1896–97. Inspired, as he clearly was, by the discovery of a Hebrew text of Ben Sira, he set out to locate the source of the numerous fragments of medieval Jewish literature then surfacing in a variety of institutions in the western world, but he could have had no more than an inkling as to what he would discover. Given his broad rabbinic knowledge, his sparkling imagination and his enthusiasm for manuscript research, there was every prospect that he would achieve a greater degree of success than his predecessors and contemporaries in obtaining access to the literary and documentary treasures that had been amassed in the Genizah of the Ben Ezra synagogue of Fustat (Old Cairo) and in exploiting its contents. Even he, however, aware as he certainly was of the inability of one generation to conclude the work on these discoveries, could not have foreseen that a hundred years after his expedition to the Egyptian capital the whole world of Jewish scholarship would still be buzzing with excitement at the novel nature of so much of the material that his efforts had brought to light. Indeed, it may confidently be asserted that there is hardly an area of research in hebraica and judaica from the rise of Islam until the Ottoman hegemony that has not been monumentally affected by the study of the worn, fragmentary and often barely legible leaves emanating from the Cairo Genizah.

Between 1996 and 1998, the centenary of Schechter's retrieval of such a thrilling cache of texts was marked around the world in a number of ways. A major conference took place in December, 1996 under the auspices of the Jewish National and University Library, the Hebrew University and Tel Aviv University, and plans were made for the publication of many of the lectures. The First International Ben Sira Conference was held in the Netherlands and its lectures soon appeared in print. From June to October, 1997, the Israel Museum in Jerusalem mounted a major exhibition, including some fifty Cambridge Genizah fragments and a few from the Jewish National and University Library, that created great excitement and was viewed by over 70,000 visitors. Cambridge University Library and the Jewish Museum in New York arranged similar presentations of Genizah manuscripts in the latter half of 1997 and early in 1998, and both the Israel Academy and Cambridge University arranged suitable lecture series, with a view to publication. The World Congress of Jewish Studies, with the co-operation of the Ben-Zvi Institute and the Society for Judaeo-Arabic Studies, devoted part of its Jerusalem 1997 conference to the Genizah theme; and plans got underway for exciting developments on the Internet through the joint efforts of Cambridge University Library and Princeton University. There were also numerous television and radio programmes, newspaper and magazine articles, and individual essays in scholarly periodicals. It seemed suddenly to become apparent to those who had not previously appreciated that fact that the Genizah material is no less significant than the Dead Sea Scrolls for the history of Jewish life and thought and for tracing the interaction of various religious groups within the mono-theistic tradition.

It is therefore most appropriate to put on record here some information, much of it fresh, about scholars, events and policies that will illuminate the Genizah story at Cambridge from the time of Schechter's discovery until the centenary of the gift that was officially made by him and Taylor in October, 1898. Obviously the data relating to such developments over the century is too extensive to be presented in anything but a limited fashion and will have to be treated more comprehensively elsewhere. There is, for instance, much to be written at a later date about Schechter's views on Genizah research and on his fellow scholars, and about the varying attitudes to the Genizah Collection on the part of Cambridge dons and librarians. What can in the meantime be done in this context is to offer an overview of the major developments in five periods, namely, 1890–1909, 1909–1934, 1934–1955, 1955–1973 and 1973–98.

AN EXCITING LAUNCH

The first period to be discussed may conveniently be defined as covering the years 1890, when Schechter took up his post at Cambridge, to 1909, when Ernest Worman, who had taken over responsibility for the Genizah Collection soon after Schechter's departure, died a premature death. Without in any way undermining the key role of Schechter and his fellow Cambridge dons in arranging for the bulk of the contents of the Cairo Genizah to be brought to Cambridge University Library and for serious work to be undertaken on the conservation and identification of the fragments, today's historian must also recognize the pioneering efforts of Elkan Nathan Adler of London and Solomon Aaron Wertheimer of Jerusalem in earlier years. These two scholars obtained a substantial number of fragments before Schechter's visit, the former content to remove one sackful and to leave the remainder, and the latter forced by impecunious circumstances to sell his literary treasures as soon as he had completed examining and copying them. In Adler's own words, Neubauer rated him soundly "for not carrying the whole lot away" and Schechter admired his continence "but was not foolish enough to follow" his example. Adler's collection was of course sold to the Jewish Theological Seminary in 1922, when he was suffering the results of unwise financial investments, and Wertheimer's items made their way to various libraries at the end of the last century. In addition, it should not be forgotten that the Reverend Greville Chester, an Anglican clergyman, Egyptologist and author, obtained various items in the early 1890s and presented them to Oxford and Cambridge, that Neubauer was one of the first scholars to predict the importance of potential discoveries

55 – Contents of a Genizah crate before conservation and sorting
(Cambridge University Library)

in the *genizot* of the Near East, and that Cyrus Adler purchased a batch of Genizah manuscripts in Egypt in 1891.

The collection that Schechter brought from Cairo, though by far the largest, was not the only set of Genizah fragments to find its way to Cambridge University Library. In addition to those sold by Wertheimer and presented by Greville Chester to the Library before Schechter's visit to Cairo, substantial Genizah material was also obtained from W. S. Raffalovich in 1897–98; from Reginald Henriques in 1898; from Mrs Agnes Lewis in 1926; from the Israel Abrahams Collection in 1961; and from the Sassoon Collection, via the British Ministry of Education, in 1981. Although, for convenience, reference is here generally made to the Cambridge Genizah Collection, it is actually more accurate to speak of the Cambridge Genizah Collections.

After his triumphant return from Cairo in the spring of 1897, Schechter settled down to five years of devoted labours on the manuscript fragments that he had convinced the Chief Rabbi of Cairo, Aaron Raphael Ben Shim'on, to present to the University of Cambridge on behalf of the Cairo Jewish community. Although the famous photograph portrays a lonely figure, dedicatedly pursuing his close

study of the contents of many boxes, Schechter was fortunate in being able to enjoy the support of Francis Jenkinson, who was Cambridge University Librarian from 1889 until 1923. Jenkinson assisted with the sorting and transcription, when he was knowledgeable enough to do so, and carefully arranged all aspects of the fragments' conservation. Schechter also benefited from the enthusiastic assistance of a number of Cambridge hebraists. The Master of St. John's College, Charles Taylor, who had guided and financed his trip to Cairo, and was the co-donor of the Taylor-Schechter Collection to the University of Cambridge, jointly edited the Ben Sira fragments with him. He also set to work on the Greek palimpsests, overwritten with later Hebrew texts, with Francis Burkitt, soon to become University Lecturer in Palaeography and later Norrisian Professor of Divinity, and the result was the publication of two volumes that have remained standard reference texts through the decades. Two other Christian scholars, the redoubtable Mrs Agnes Lewis and Mrs Margaret Gibson, applied themselves to the study of the Syriac items and produced an edition of thirty-four of these.

The work of four other scholars, who were introduced in an earlier chapter, also complemented early efforts to describe the Genizah material. Herman Leonard Pass prepared an excellent summary of the biblical contents of the Taylor-Schechter Collection and began work on the miscellany of apocryphal, pseudepigraphical and other literary pieces in Hebrew, Aramaic and Judaeo-Arabic that are contained in T-S A45. In 1901–2, Hartwig Hirschfeld examined the Arabic and Judaeo-Arabic parts of the Collection and produced a preliminary survey of their contents. He also separated 255 "especially important" items and sorted the remainder into a number of cardboard boxes. Ernest James Worman was the first to publish many of the Genizah's historically significant pieces, thus laying foundations for the later work of Solomon Skoss, Jacob Mann, D. H. Baneth and S. D. Goitein, while Paul Kahle, then a young and promising semiticist, was a pioneer in the process of identifying and classifying the unusual biblical items to be found in the newly arrived material.

PILOTLESS PROGRESS

Following Schechter's departure in 1902, and the deaths of Taylor in 1908 and Worman in 1909, Israel Abrahams and Herbert Loewe, whose interest in the Genizah was by no means central to their overall scholarly activities, were successively appointed as Schechter's heirs in the lecturership in talmudic and rabbinic literature. It is therefore hardly surprising that the period from 1909 until 1934, when the Library moved to its present site westwards over the river Cam, pales in comparison with its earlier equivalent. The staffing and financial problems caused by the First World War and the subsequent economic depression meant that little of the Library's resources could be channeled into what the majority of the University's senior membership no doubt saw as a somewhat recondite preoccupation. Unlike the situation at the British Museum and the Bodleian Library, where more specialized posts had been created, the position at Cambridge University Library was that one orientalist, E. J. Thomas, appointed in 1909, was expected to oversee all literatures in an area ranging from Casablanca to Yokohama, although his own special interest was in Buddhism. The description of special collections could not therefore be added to the responsibilities of Library staff but had to be undertaken by experts from among faculty members at Cambridge or elsewhere.

As far as Hebrew manuscript research was concerned, the emphasis moved from the Genizah material to the preparation of a long-overdue catalogue of the thousand Hebrew manuscript items, most of them codices, that had been acquired by the University Library over a period of some four centuries but had been only partially described. Building on the earlier foundations laid by S. M. Schiller-Szinessy, Schechter himself and Stanley Cook, Herbert Loewe, despite having to expend much energy in commuting between Cambridge and Oxford in order to make an insecure living teaching rabbinics, completed a handlist in 1927. As far as the Genizah was concerned, only those few fragments that had been acquired between 1890 and 1896 were deemed numerically less daunting than the other collections and included in the work. The boxes A-K, bound volumes, and pieces mounted on glass had been sorted according to subject, given classmarks and, in some cases, briefly described by Worman but there were still boxes of Arabic and miscellaneous material that had not been accorded similar treatment. Andrew Baldrey, originally employed as a bindery assistant in 1884 at a weekly wage of twenty-five shillings, had become what would in current terminology be described as the Library's conservation specialist for the Genizah Collection by the time that Schechter left Cambridge. He continued to look after the physical needs of the fragments and by the time of his retirement in 1926 he knew more than any other member of staff about these precious pieces of judaica, without being able to read a single word in any of them. The Library had indeed recognized his expertise by increasing his annual salary from £110 to £300 in 1920.

When Schechter required photographs of Cambridge Genizah material to be sent to New York, it was Baldrey who undertook the task and he no doubt acted in a similar capacity for the other individual scholars who, during the period under discussion, carried the torch of Genizah learning into the dark recesses of medieval Jewish scholarship. The strong connection between rabbinic scholarship and Christ's College, established in the third quarter of the nineteenth century,

continued through Norman McLean, University Lecturer in Aramaic and then Master of the College, and Israel Abrahams, and was well represented at this time by one of its fellows, W. A. L. Elmslie, who used a number of Genizah fragments for his edition of *The Mishna on Idolatry: 'Aboda Zara* (Cambridge, 1911). Other distinguished scholars such as Moses Gaster, C. D. Ginsburg and E. N. Adler, made pilgrimages to Cambridge to study or view items of interest, to be welcomed by the friendly and helpful Jenkinson, while the American Jewish philanthropist, James Loeb, who established the famous Classical Library series, also put in an appearance.

Undoubtedly of the greatest significance during the second and third decades of this century was the research done by Jacob Mann. Mann had come to London from his native Galicia in his youth and had studied at Jews' College and the University of London from 1908 until 1915. By 1916 he had already analysed a list of historical fragments, which he requested Jenkinson's permission to publish, and a stream of papers and volumes were to establish him as an outstanding pioneer in the use of the Genizah material for writing whole new chapters of medieval Jewish history in the Near East. It seems likely that the early inspiration for Mann's scholarly interests and the attention he paid to the Genizah was none other than the Principal of Jews' College, Adolph Büchler, himself no mean historian. Büchler and his uncle, Adolf Neubauer, had been among the first scholars to tackle the fragments in Oxford between 1891 and 1893. Another major research figure at that time was the German scholar, Paul Kahle, who had taken an interest in the biblical, masoretic and targumic fragments from as early as 1899 in Cambridge and was

240

preparing seminal publications that were to prove indispensable for decades. In New York, at the Jewish Theological Seminary of America, a team of scholars had worked with Schechter and continued his researches after his death, particularly by means of some fragments borrowed from the Cambridge Collection. The team included Louis Ginzberg, Israel Davidson, Alexander Marx and Israel Friedlaender and resulted in the publication of a number of works. There is, however, more to the tale of the Loan Collection (now called T-S Misc.35–36) than is revealed by such a brief bibliographical summary and it certainly merits recounting in the present context.

When Schechter left Cambridge in 1902, he was careful not to leave behind him all the literary treasures of the Genizah for other researchers to inherit. In addition to taking with him Cairo fragments that he regarded as his private property, he made careful arrangements to borrow from the Taylor-Schechter Collection those items that he had found particularly interesting and that he planned to publish. So it was that some 251 pieces, 41 of them conserved in glass and the others unbound, followed him to New York within a few months. The idea was that Schechter and the distinguished group of scholars that he would soon succeed in attracting to the Seminary would decipher and edit the texts within a short time and restore them to Cambridge. Taylor assured the Vice-Chancellor that the process would take no more than two or three years to complete but by 1910, two years after his death, only three fragments had made their way back to England. Schechter's death in 1915 induced more than a mild attack of panic at the University Library but the head of the institution, Francis Jenkinson, was still personally attached enough to the memory of Schechter to agree to the further extension requested by the Seminary's librarian, Alexander Marx. For eight more years, the Seminary pleaded the extenuating circumstances created by the First World War, a lack of research time, and problems relating to the publications programme.

When Jenkinson died in 1923 and the University Librarianship was taken over by A. F. Scholfield, the relaxed attitudes of the nineteenth century gave way to a more authoritarian approach and a concern for efficient management. Scholfield, an Old Etonian, had been Keeper of the Archives for the Government of India and Librarian of Trinity College, and had no great liking for loose ends. He soon began a correspondence aimed at ensuring the swift return of the fragments from the Seminary, devoting a number of letters to close enquiries about the precise progress being made in New York and the exact date when the project might be concluded. He even enlisted the services of Israel

Abrahams, who was on a visit to New York in 1924, to put pressure on the Seminary, with the result that its President, Cyrus Adler, agreed to effect the immediate return of the fragments. Four finally limped home in November of that year. Cambridge seems finally to have lost its patience when the Seminary requested that any material returned should be withheld from other scholars for some time longer and its angry response brought the return, in March 1925, of all the remaining items – minus 5! Scholfield angrily declared this to be a lesson to the Library not to lend manuscripts and he had passed on to the great heavenly library before these missing items were finally found in 1968 among Schechter's transcriptions of their texts and returned to Cambridge.

The University Librarian, in a manner that was less than pleasant, also put pressure on Loewe to complete his handlist, and soon called for reports on the current state of the Genizah Collection. When these were duly delivered, it turned out that little progress had been made in a quarter of a century. The Arabic and miscellaneous Hebrew boxes were not properly classified or numbered and there were still crates whose value was· seriously questioned. Baldrey described twenty-six wooden cases as "containing Bible 2nd selection, arranged according to books, and rubbish which has been examined several times by various scholars." Another library assistant, one B. C. Nightingale, whose alternative view had apparently been sought by Scholfield, was less respectful of these fragments, later to become the New Series and Additional Series, and less loyal than Baldrey to what he misguidedly saw as the outdated views of the first Genizah generation. The boxes contained "nothing of any interest or value. The late Librarian [Jenkinson] would not allow anything to be destroyed which is the only reason why they were not burned years ago." Had these fragments been left to the mercies of such unimaginative and short-sighted curators, today's Genizah scholarship would have been far less extensive than it has happily turned out to be. Imagine, if you can, Genizah research without the last letter written by David, the brother of Maimonides, before he was drowned in the Indian Ocean; without the exchange of poems between Dunash ibn Labraṭ and his wife; without the evidence of Judah Ha-Levi's 'aliyah to the Holy Land; and without the earliest Hebrew block-print. Fortunately, Scholfield, whose love of order was greater than his impatience with orientalia, decided that caution was the best part of valour and either before the move to the new library building, or soon afterwards, made proper order among the fragments of the Old Series and, though removing the "crates of rubbish" from prime library space, kept them under his protection.

MANY CLIMB ABOARD

In the old building the Genizah Collection had been kept in the Cairo Room and brought by "boys" (i. e., assistants) from there to Room Theta, where it could be consulted by interested scholars. From 1934 onwards it was stored directly under the splendid Anderson Room, which then served as the area for the consultation of manuscripts. Once again, no member of the Library staff was specifically appointed to look after the fragments but, during the twenty-year period leading up to the beginning of what may justifiably be called "the Goitein era", research in the Genizah field benefited from the devoted efforts of two librarians who were obliged to cover a wide area of oriental material. Both arrived at the Library as youngsters, employed to fetch and carry; both were sent to study for degrees in the University and served in the armed forces during the Second World War; and both became widely acknowledged experts in the Library's oriental collections.

James Pearson was engaged as a "boy" from 1928 until 1932 before taking a degree in oriental languages and returning to the Library in 1938 as Under-Librarian in the Oriental Section. Twelve years later he moved on to direct the Library of the School of Oriental and African Studies in the University of London, where he was elected Professor of Oriental Bibliography in 1972. Don Crane served as an assistant in the Oriental Section from 1937, three years after he arrived in the Library, and retired as Under-Librarian and the senior orientalist in 1980. In addition to their work on orientalia in general and on the Hebrew codices in particular, these two devoted librarians kept the Genizah Collection in good order, began to compile lists of published references to the Cambridge fragments, and attended to the needs of visiting and corresponding scholars. When the eight-hundredth anniversary of the birth of Maimonides occurred in 1935, it was Herbert Loewe who suggested an exhibition and no doubt chose the items to display. Neither Pearson nor Crane appear to have been involved in that initiative, but from 1937 onwards they took on a variety of such oriental responsibilities and fulfilled them in efficient fashion. E. J. Thomas, their mentor, retired in 1940 and left the oriental department in their capable charge.

While many of the scholarly seeds had been sown in the 1920s, the 1930s saw a blossoming of Genizah research in the fields of Hebrew poetry, geonic responsa and documents relating to the history of Palestinian Jewry. The study of the many thousands of poems, a large proportion of them and their authors hitherto unknown, was inspired and led by the Research Institute for Hebrew Poetry, founded in Berlin in 1929 by Salman Schocken and transferred to Jerusalem in 1934. By means of visits to Cambridge and the acquisition of many photographs of Genizah manuscripts, a whole group of scholars, led by Hayyim Brody and including A. M. Habermann, Jefim Schirmann and Menahem Zulay, scoured vast numbers of texts for poetic compositions, identified wherever possible their authors, and produced critical editions of the works found.

In those days, Genizah research was still the exception rather than the rule among scholars of Judaic studies and it was very much left to a few individuals to obtain access to the sources and prepare books and articles, as and when they were able. In the field of rabbinic literature, B. M. Lewin ploughed a lonely furrow but succeeded in preparing the ground more than adequately for the many studies of post-talmudic developments that were to emerge at a later date. His monumental thesaurus of geonic literature remains a basic reference tool and he shed new light on halakhic relations between Babylon and Eretz Yisrael in the pre-Crusader period. Simcha Assaf, on the other hand, did not draw the line at exploiting the Hebrew and Aramaic Genizah texts for retrieving halakhic material and locating historical documentation for Palestinian Jewish life in the geonic period. He also turned his attention to the Arabic items and enlisted the support of his colleague at the Hebrew University, D. H. Baneth, in the edition of such texts and their translation into Hebrew. The joint endeavours of these two scholars, added to the achievements of Mann, undoubtedly provided much of the raw material for the subsequent rewriting of medieval Jewish history in the Orient.

As earlier indicated, Paul Kahle was among the first non-Jews to engage in Genizah research, especially in the fields of Hebrew vocalization, Masorah and Targum. By 1928 he had already headed an institute for oriental studies at the University of Bonn for five years, had important publications to his name, and enjoyed a reputation for devoted and intensive research. For the benefit of his students and colleagues, he not only arranged for copies of important manuscript material to be sent to Bonn but also succeeded in borrowing the precious manuscripts themselves from Russia, the United States, Netherlands and France, as well as from Oxford and Cambridge. Between 1928 and 1932 he persuaded Cambridge to lend him a number of priceless Genizah fragments, sometimes for many months, and it was only the rise to power of Hitler in 1933 that brought this arrangement to an abrupt end. The University Library obviously had visions of its material attracting the unwelcome attention of the book-burning Nazis and swiftly effected its return to England via diplomatic channels. Remarkably, Kahle obtained the loan of a Latin manuscript from Cambridge in 1934 and was still sufficiently engrossed in his Semitic researches to request more Genizah fragments in 1938. Needless to say, on this occasion his approach met with a negative response. Indeed in that same year, instead of scholarly texts making their way from Oxford and Cambridge to Germany, Germany's leading expert in biblical texts from the Genizah fled in the opposite direction and Kahle spent the rest of his career in England. It was there that he produced his excellent volume *The Cairo Geniza,* for so long an indispensable guide to the subject.

Inevitably, the Second World War years found both the European centres of Hebrew manuscript resources and the scholars who generally exploited them engaged in more pressing matters and it was not until the founding of the State of Israel in 1948 that the prospects for the organized examination of the Cambridge Genizah Collection again became a reality. By that time, the Hebrew University had been in existence for twenty-three years and its well-established Institute of Jewish Studies and School of Oriental Studies were strongly influencing scientific research in the Genizah field. The disturbances in British Mandatory Palestine and the subsequent Israeli War of Independence stalled scholarly progress but by 1950 matters were sufficiently stable to permit the establishment in Jerusalem of an Institute for the Photography of Hebrew Manuscripts. The Institute, first directed by Nehemiah Allony, originally belonged to the Ministry of Education and Culture but was attached to the Jewish National and University Library in 1963. That initiative was characteristic of the Jewish State's commitment to encouraging the conservation, copying and description of all major collections of hebraica around the world and was a factor in the creation of a renewed interest in the Cambridge Genizah Collection. No doubt the excitement about the Qumran discoveries also played a part.

Internally at Cambridge University Library, it was again the appointment of an assistant, this time a woman, to a junior post that was ultimately destined to create an environment in which that renewed interest could be encouraged and promoted. Susan Skilliter was still a teenager, barely out of school, when she began to work at the Library in 1949 but she applied herself well to her tasks. She soon earned both increases in salary and the Library's assistance in registering her as a student of oriental languages at Cambridge. She successfully completed her degree in 1954, after three years' absence from the Library at Newnham College. She returned in the summer of 1954 as Assistant

56 – Professor Shalom Spiegel of the Jewish Theological Seminary in New York with a crate of
fragments at Cambridge University Library, *c*.1960 (Cambridge University Library)

Under-Librarian to join Don Crane and take charge of the Oriental
Section (Pearson having left in 1950), precisely when Shelomo Dov
Goitein, then of the Hebrew University of Jerusalem, was spending four
months examining the Genizah collections of Cambridge, Oxford,
London and Manchester. In that year Goitein began to assist the Library
with the organization and description of some of the neglected material
and built a good working relationship with the University Librarian, H.
R. Creswick (who had succeeded Scholfield in 1949), and with Miss
Skilliter. Because of this, and the fact that he had already worked on the
material purchased from Raffalovich and classmarked Or.1080 and
Or.1081, he was asked to comment on the value, or otherwise, of a vast
amount of Genizah material, then kept in crates under the roof, with the
word "rubbish" written on the side of the largest. Goitein was
astonished at the size of that crate and at the extent and nature of this
neglected archive. He stressed that these fragments were equally
important as those already contained in the respected and frequently
consulted Old Series, and thus was born the New Series.

FULL SPEED AHEAD

Goitein generously spread the word about the expanded Collection, Creswick encouraged (more gently than Scholfield) scholars and scholarship, while Skilliter and Crane did their best to cope good-naturedly with the greatly increased number of researchers interested in consulting the fresh material, and in looking again at the established parts of the Collection. Given the extent of their numbers, it is not possible to detail all their research activities and the discoveries they each made between 1955 and 1972. It will have to suffice in the present context to mention briefly the achievements of a few. Goitein and a whole school of young scholars, beginning with Norman Golb, most of whom had had the benefit of his training and advice, rewrote the history of Jews in Arab lands in the Middle Ages. Alexander Scheiber and Shalom Spiegel illuminated the dark corners of medieval Hebrew literature, while Naphtali Wieder brought to light the earliest versions of the Jewish prayer-book and Jacob Teicher, then Lecturer in Rabbinics at Cambridge, did similar groundwork for the first printed hebraica. Missing links in the history of talmudic study were located by Shraga Abramson and similar lacunae in Hebrew grammar and lexicography were made good by Nehemiah Allony and in Bible commentary by Moshe Zucker. Schirmann and other students of liturgical poetry continued the work they had earlier commenced, and Shelomo Morag and Alejandro Díez-Macho updated and expanded Kahle's pioneering efforts in masoretic studies.

But the process of creating the New Series (containing some 42,000 items) was not all sweetness and light. Since no librarian was exclusively responsible for the Genizah Collection or qualified enough to identify and classify its contents, it was left to visiting scholars to remove items from crates and suggest how and where they might be placed. This was not always done in the most professional manner and differences of opinion led even to the changing of classmarks. Erwin Rosenthal, who was Reader in Oriental Studies at Cambridge and Fellow of Pembroke College, was fond of (privately) reporting that Moshe Zucker's exploits with some of the crates were such that the Library had to be persuaded to allow him further access. A project to microfilm the whole Collection got under way in 1956 and brought the texts of the fragments within the reach of any interested scholar with access to a microfilm reader but the application of modern techniques of conservation had not yet been undertaken. Evidence of this may still be found in the fact that many of the microfilms processed at that time record fragments in an unconserved, and sometimes barely legible state. The Library's annual reports for the years 1955 to 1961 testify to the excitement of Goitein's discoveries and to the assistance received with the New Series from such visiting scholars as Schirmann, Spiegel and Allony, as well as to a growing frustration on the part of the orientalist librarians, and a final snapping of their patience:

> The great collection of fragments from the Genizah of Old Cairo, known as the Taylor-Schechter Collection, attracts more and wider attention year by year, and orders for microfilms and other photographs become more and more numerous. This causes a great deal more handling of the fragments by the Library staff and the photographer than is desirable on account of their fragility and the Syndicate have therefore ordered that a complete negative microfilm copy of the Collection shall be made for Library use...
>
> This collection of fragmentary Hebrew and Arabic manuscripts and printed remains from the genizah of Old Cairo came to the Library some sixty years ago. The fragments then selected for cleaning, mounting and addition to the Library's shelves numbered approximately 50,000 items. The remainder were left in thirty crates in a Library store. A recent cursory examination of the crates brought to light documents important for the work of Mr. S. D. Goitein, Director of the School of Oriental Studies in the Hebrew University of Jerusalem; these were original letters relating to the spice trade between India, South Arabia and East Africa in the eleventh and twelfth centuries. – from the *Annual Report for 1955–56*
>
> Thanks to the efforts of Professor Schirmann, Professor Spiegel, Dr Allony and other visiting Hebrew scholars from Jerusalem or America, the number of boxes in the New Series of the Taylor-Schechter collection has risen to 307... This energetic activity of a few devoted visitors during the summer vacation, although undoubtedly of the utmost value, interrupts the normal working procedure of Miss Skilliter and Mr Crane. – from the *Annual Report for 1959–60*
>
> Relief in the number of visitors to be served has, however, been more than offset in the Anderson Room by the great increase in the number of items to be fetched from the Taylor-Schechter Geniza [*sic*] collection. World-wide interest in this collection has developed since the war. There is rarely a day in the year when someone is not working on Geniza fragments. Very often there are several visitors simultaneously. More visitors have come because of the recent discovery of the importance of that part of the collection which was put aside as of little interest when the collection first came to the Library. This part of the collection is still in

much the same primitive state as it was when it arrived in large crates from Cairo some sixty years ago. There are times when the inadequacy of the Anderson Room as a place for research on such material is exasperating both to the staff and to the public. – from the *Annual Report for 1960–61*

The only hebraist in the Faculty of Oriental Studies with a genuine concern for the Genizah Collection to be placed at the centre of oriental scholarship and a close personal interest in researching its contents was Dr Jacob Leib Teicher and he often made the point to his Faculty colleagues that the time had come for the appointment of a scholar to

57 – Professor S. D. Goitein at Cambridge University Library
in the 1960s with Professor Alexander Scheiber of
Hungary and Professor Norman Golb of the USA
(Cambridge University Library)

249

take specific responsibility for the Genizah Collection in the University Library. The Regius Professor of Hebrew at the time, David Winton Thomas, was, like almost all his predecessors, primarily interested in biblical or "Old Testament" Hebrew, rather than in the wider area of three thousand years of Hebrew language and literature. Nevertheless, at Teicher's urging and with the Professor's full co-operation, an approach was made to the Syndics of the Library by the Faculty Board of Oriental Studies and a joint committee was set up to consider the creation of a Genizah post in the Library. Among the members were Creswick, Teicher and Thomas. Its recommendations of 21 December, 1960 (expressed in a memorandum submitted to the Council of the Senate in February, 1961) were that funds be sought for the appointment of a "mature scholar" as an Under-Librarian who would arrange for the sorting, identification and cataloguing of the Collection; and would record all published work relating to it. He would also arrange for visiting scholars to contribute their areas of expertise to the cataloguing programme; and would initiate and manage a plan that would "bring credit to the University and to its Library and...would be a signal service to Hebrew scholarship." It was envisaged that adequate accommodation would be required and would have to be made a part of the Library's extension plans.

When, for various reasons, these recommendations could not be implemented by the University, the joint committee met again in January, 1964 and suggested a more modest project as the first stage of its long-term plan. A more junior scholar would be appointed as Assistant Under-Librarian and would work under the supervision of an Honorary Curator, the appointment would be for a period of five years, and outside funding would be sought for a substantial part of the cost. When that funding was made available by the British Academy in 1965, Dr Henry Knopf, already employed to deal with the Hebrew printed books in the Library, was appointed as the first full-time librarian with responsibility for the Cambridge Genizah material and, as well as dealing with queries and visitors, began to catalogue the biblical fragments. The office was put on a more permanent basis by the Faculty's agreement to suppress an Aramaic lectureship and in 1970 Knopf was appointed to the retirement age, on condition that he teach some Rabbinics for the Faculty, by way of compensation for their loss of a post. During Knopf's term of office, which he resigned in 1972 to take up a library post at Bar-Ilan University in Israel, a number of important developments took place. A start was made on the cataloguing of the biblical fragments, additional boxes were appended to the New Series, the microfilming project made good progress, material was added to the

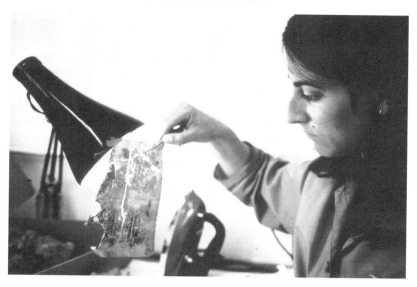

58 – Conservation of Genizah fragments at Cambridge University Library in the 1970s (Cambridge University Library)

59 – Research on Genizah fragments by Rabbi Dr E. J. Wiesenberg at Cambridge University Library in the 1970s (Cambridge University Library)

Library's record of its published Genizah items, and the steady stream of researchers working on the Collection continued unabated. Even more importantly, a project was commenced to conserve, in accordance with the latest techniques, the New Series, and was initially funded by a grant made available by Yeshiva University in New York. But the lack of funding for any additional staff to meet the needs of the Collection meant that progress was inevitably limited and it was estimated that the conservation of the New Series and the description of the biblical fragments were, if continued at that pace, likely to take about fifty years.

A RECENT LOG

Eric Ceadel, who had been appointed to the University Librarianship in 1967, and the Regius Professor of Hebrew, John Emerton, who had taken up his post in 1968, were consequently enthusiastic about the plans that I drew up and submitted to them soon after my appointment to be responsible for the Collection in 1973. With their co-operation, and that of Ceadel's successors, Fred Ratcliffe from 1980 and Peter Fox from 1994, and the encouragement of both the Faculty of Oriental Studies and the Library Syndicate, a fully comprehensive programme of work on the Collection was undertaken in the context of a newly created Genizah Research Unit. That programme has ensured that the developments recorded in Cambridge during the past twenty-five years are in no way unworthy of all the earlier achievements. With the assistance of external funding, extra staff were employed and the microfilming and conservation of all 140,000 fragments, expected to take another fifty years, was completed in 1981. The embarrassment of the remaining thirty-two crates of unclassified material was removed when they were sorted in 1974 and 1975 into the Additional Series under a variety of subject headings. A busy team of researchers catalogued about 45,000 fragments, and some 50,000 published references to Cambridge Genizah items were located and published, with the help of a special computer program. Cambridge University Press joined forces with Cambridge University Library to publish ten volumes in the newly established *Genizah Series*. Fourteen visiting scholars were encouraged to play an active role in the description of the Collection and co-operative projects were undertaken with the Israel Academy, Jewish National and University Library, Hebrew University and Jewish Theological Seminary of America. The future of Genizah research was not neglected and a team of young researchers was a regular feature of the Unit. After periods in the Unit, ten of them found important posts in oriental faculties and libraries in various countries. Appeals were made to funding bodies, philanthropists and interested individuals and over £1m was raised from outside sources in support of the Unit's projects. A serious attempt was made, through a regular newsletter *Genizah Fragments* and various other publications, and through the media, to bring the results of Genizah research to a wider public and it became almost commonplace for important exhibitions of hebraica around the world to include Cambridge Genizah items. Information about these items and manuscript images began to be accessible on the Internet.

60 – His Royal Highness, Prince Philip, Chancellor of the University of Cambridge, discusses some Genizah fragments with the Director of the Research Unit, Professor Stefan Reif, 1986 (Cambridge University Library)

The progress made at Cambridge contributed to an explosion of Genizah research throughout the field of Jewish studies so that it is no longer possible even to attempt to list the hundreds of scholars outside Cambridge University Library whose research is heavily dependent on the material that Schechter brought from Cairo. Ezra Fleischer and Joseph Yahalom in liturgy and poetry; Israel Yeivin, Ilan Eldar, E. J. Revell and Geoffrey Khan in Masorah; Jacob Sussmann, Menahem Kahana and Robert Brody in Talmud; Joshua Blau, Haggai Ben-Shammai and Simon Hopkins in Judaeo-Arabic; Malachi Beit-Arié and Colette Sirat in palaeography; Moshe Gil, Menahem Ben-Sasson and Mark R. Cohen in medieval Jewish history; Mordechai Friedman on Palestinian marriage documents and Joel Kraemer on women's correspondence; Shaul Shaked and Peter Schäfer on material relating to magic; Michael Klein on Targum and Paul Fenton on Jewish mysticism; Abraham David on sixteenth-century Palestinian Jewry and Eleazar Gutwirth on Judaeo-Spanish – these scholars have been among the most active and industrious, but the list could be greatly multiplied. A hundred years after Schechter's remarkable scholarly prescience, Louis Ginzberg's tribute, paid in 1916 in his preface to the German original of his *An Unknown Jewish Sect*, is truer than ever: "So long as there are Jewish houses of learning the name of Solomon Schechter will be mentioned in them, and even though he may no longer be among us, yet he is with us."

Guide to reading

That Schechter was already aware of the importance of his discoveries after a short time is clear from the articles published by him in *The Times* of 3 August, 1897, and *Jewish Chronicle* of 1 April, 1898, and reproduced as "A Hoard of Hebrew Manuscripts" in the second volume of his *Studies in Judaism* (Philadelphia, 1908), pp. 1–30. L. Ginzberg also saw their great significance as he notes on p. viii of the English foreword to his *Genizah Studies in Memory of Doctor Solomon Schechter I: Midrash and Haggadah* (New York, 1928). The papers of the Ben Sira conference have appeared in *The Book of Ben Sira in Modern Research*, ed. P. C. Beentjes (Berlin and New York, 1997) while those of the December 1996 meeting will appear in *Te'uda* 15, edited by M. A. Friedman, and those of the World Congress of 1997 in its volumes of proceedings. Guides to the Jerusalem and Cambridge Genizah centenary exhibitions have appeared, respectively, as *The Cairo Genizah: A Mosaic of Life*, ed. Daisy Raccah-Djivre (Jerusalem, 1997) and *History in Fragments: A Genizah Centenary Exhibition*, eds. Shulie and Stefan Reif (Cambridge, 1998) and the Israel Museum also produced in this connection *The Genizah News*, ed. Ioram Melcer (Jerusalem, 1997). The fiftieth anniversary of the Dead Sea Scrolls and the centenary of the Genizah were jointly marked by a conference arranged in February 1998 at the Hebrew University by Michael Stone and Esther Chazon for the Orion Institute on the subject of the Damascus Document and the papers are scheduled for publication in 1999.

Some details concerning Worman, Adler, Wertheimer and Chester appear in *Ernest James Worman 1871–1909* (Cambridge, 1910), containing contributions by R. B. Johnson, G. J. Gray, H. T. Francis and F. J. H. Jenkinson, I. Abrahams and C. Joseph; E. Levine, "Elkan Nathan Adler: In Memoriam", *Jewish Historical Society of England Miscellanies 5* (1948), pp. 117–27 and *Encyclopaedia Judaica* 2, cols. 275–76; *Encyclopaedia Judaica* 16, col. 459 and the booklet *Ktav Yad Ve-Sefer Institute* (Jerusalem, 1990); and J. Foster, *Alumni Oxonienses* I (Oxford, 1888), p. 244; *Crockford's Clerical Directory for 1892* (London, 1892), p. 244; and the *Balliol College Register, 1833–1933*, ed. I. Elliott (Oxford, 1934), p. 5. Adler's comments come from his article "The Hebrew Treasures of England", *Transactions of the Jewish Historical Society of England* 8 (1918), p. 16, and there is further information on his Genizah collection in Neil Danzig's important volume *A Catalogue of Fragments of Halakhah and Midrash from the Cairo Genizah in the Elkan Nathan Adler Collection of the Library of the Jewish Theological Seminary of America* (New York and Jerusalem, 1997). Details of the various Genizah collections at Cambridge University Library are provided in S. C. Reif, *Hebrew Manuscripts at Cambridge University Library: a Description and Introduction* (Cambridge, 1997), p. 32. Genizah research in America, beginning with Cyrus Adler in 1891, is neatly summarized in Menahem Schmelzer's pamphlet *One Hundred Years of Genizah Discovery and Research: The American Share* (National Foundation for Jewish Culture Lecture Series, no. 2, New York, 1998). Victor (Lebedev) Bochman's article "Hidden Treasures: 100 Years since the Discovery of the Cairo Genizah", *Ariel* 106 (1998), pp. 7–14 has useful information concerning the Arabic and Karaite material but suffers from a number of inaccuracies.

The productive relationship between Schechter and Jenkinson is fully discussed in S. C. Reif, "Jenkinson and Schechter at Cambridge. An Expanded and Updated Assessment," *Transactions of the Jewish Historical Society of England* 32 (1993), pp. 279–316 and appreciations of Taylor appear in *Eagle* 30 (1908–9), pp. 64–85 and 197–204; *Dictionary of National Biography. Supplement 1901–11* (London, 1912), pp. 480–82; and *Who Was Who 1897–1915* (London, 1986, sixth edition), p. 513, and of Burkitt in *Proceedings of the British Academy* 22 (1936), pp. 445–84 and *Dictionary of National Biography. Supplement 1931–40* (London, 1949), pp. 124–25. The volumes produced were S. Schechter and C. Taylor, *The Wisdom of Ben Sira...from Hebrew MSS in the Cairo Genizah Collection* (Cambridge, 1899); *Facsimiles of the Fragments hitherto recovered of the Book of Ecclesiasticus in Hebrew* (London, 1901); F. C. Burkitt (with preface by C. Taylor), *Fragments of the Books of Kings according to the Translation of Aquila* (Cambridge, 1897); and C. Taylor, *Hebrew-Greek Genizah Palimpsests from the Taylor-Schechter Collection* (Cambridge, 1900).

There is a delightful description of the lives of Mrs Lewis and Mrs Gibson in A. Whigham Price, *The Ladies of Castlebrae* (Gloucester, 1985), and their study was entitled *Palestinian Syriac Texts from Palimpsest Fragments in the Taylor-Schechter Collection* (London, 1900). For information on Pass and Hirschfeld, see J. A. Venn, *Alumni Cantabrigienses II/V* (Cambridge, 1953), p. 42; and *Jews' College Jubilee Volume*, ed. I. Harris (London, 1906), pp. cxii–cxvi. Details of the work done by Pass were prepared for the Library Syndicate and presented to them at their meeting of 24 October, 1900 (minute 10), and appear in the *Cambridge University Reporter*, no. 1360 (12 June, 1901), pp. 1088 and 1107–8. T-S A45 was subsequently described by S. A. Hopkins, *A Miscellany of Literary Pieces from the Cambridge Genizah Collections* (Cambridge, 1978). Hirschfeld's report was published in *Cambridge University Reporter*, no. 1463 (23 June, 1903), pp. 1068–69; see also S. C. Reif, "Introductory Remarks. Semitic Scholarship at Cambridge," in *Genizah Research after Ninety Years: The Case of Judaeo-Arabic*, eds. J. Blau and S. C. Reif (Cambridge, 1992), pp. 1–4. On Worman, see *Ernest James Worman 1871–1909* (Cambridge, 1910) and *Cambridge University Reporter*, no. 1711 (23 June, 1908), p. 1243. Data on Schechter's two successors at Cambridge is to be found in H. M. J. Loewe, *Israel Abrahams. A Biographical Sketch* (Cambridge, 1944), *The Times*, 12 October, 1940, p. 6; *Jewish Chronicle*, 18 October, 1940, p. 5; *Encyclopaedia Judaica* 11, col. 447; and *Who Was Who III, 1929–40* (London, 1967; second edition), p. 822. Further information on Thomas and orientalia is in F. H. Stubbings, *Emmanuel College Magazine* 40 (1957–58) pp. 106–8; *Cambridge University Reporter* no. 1705 (2 June 1908), p. 1030; (16 June, 1909), p. 1178; and no. 1809 (17 June, 1910), p. 1247.

The story of the various attempts made over the years to describe the Hebrew manuscripts at Cambridge University Library is told in S. C. Reif, *Hebrew Manuscripts at Cambridge University Library: a Description and Introduction* (Cambridge, 1997), pp. 1–35, in which volume there also appears (pp. 37–44) the preface that H. M. J. Loewe wrote for his unpublished "Handlist of Hebrew and Samaritan Manuscripts in the Library of the University of Cambridge", (MS Or.1770–72 in Cambridge University Library). The information about Baldrey has been extracted from the Library's confidential staff records for those years and from a letter from Schechter to Jenkinson, 27 October, 1910, Cambridge University Library MS Add.6463.7061. The connection between Christ's College Cambridge and rabbinic scholarship in the late nineteenth century has been traced by S. C. Reif, "William Robertson Smith in Relation to Hebraists and Jews at Christ's College Cambridge," in *William Robertson Smith. Essays in Reassessment*, ed. W. Johnstone (Sheffield, 1995), pp. 210–24. Elmslie is noted in the *Biographical Register of Christ's College*, ed. J. Peile, vol. II (Cambridge, 1913), p. 874, and details of the visitors to Cambridge are provided in Jenkinson's personal diary, 25 November, 1909 (Add.7432), p. 329; 20 December,

1910 (Add.7433), p. 354; 6 July, 1913 (Add.7436), p. 187; 28 August, 1913 (Add.7436), p. 240; and 6 September, 1917 (Add.7440), p. 249.

Accounts of the lives of Mann, Büchler and Kahle may be found in V. E. Reichert, "Jacob Mann 1888–1940", *American Jewish Year Book* 43 (1941), pp. 407–14; I. Epstein, "Adolph Büchler (1867–1939). The Man and the Scholar" in *Studies in Jewish History. The Adolph Büchler Memorial Volume*, eds. I. Brodie and J. Rabbinowitz (London, 1956), pp. xiii–xxx; and Matthew Black, "Paul Ernst Kahle 1875–1965", *Proceedings of the British Academy* 51 (1965), pp. 485–95. Jenkinson mentions Mann's work on the Genizah fragments in his desk diary, 8–9 June, 1916 (Add.8754), p. 47. An account of the early Genizah rivalry between Oxford and Cambridge is given in S. C. Reif, "The Discovery of the Cambridge Genizah Fragments of Ben Sira: Scholars and Texts", in *The Book of Ben Sira*, pp. 1–22, and the whole story of the Cambridge "Loan Collection" (i.e. T-S Misc.35–36) is recounted in S. C. Reif's Hebrew article, with the English title "The Cambridge Genizah Story: Some Unfamiliar Aspects", scheduled for publication in *Te'uda* 15 (both volumes noted in the first paragraph of this reading list). Obituaries and tributes to Scholfield appeared in *The Times*, 20 October, 1969, p. 10, and 23 October, p. 12; and in *Who Was Who VI 1961–70* (London, 1979; second edition), p. 1009. The report of Andrew Baldrey, presumably to Scholfield, was written on University Library notepaper and dated 3 September, 1927. It does not vary greatly from the report of twenty-one years earlier published in Cambridge University Reporter, no. 1609 (2 June, 1906), pp. 1008–12. Nightingale's note is signed "B. C. N." and dated 15 August, 1927 and Taylor-Schechter departmental records include a note of Genizah material headed "Copy of the labels on 25 wooden boxes and 1 cardboard box taken to the Arts School basements, 19 February". The four particularly exciting fragments here mentioned are Or.1081 J1, T-S NS 143.46, T-S AS 146.6, and Or.1080 J50.

J. D. Pearson described his early days in the Library and his first encounters with Genizah researchers in "Curiosities of Bygone Days", *Genizah Fragments* 28 (1994), p. 2. His final entry in *Who's Who* appeared in the 1997 edition, p. 1517 and a full obituary, by B. C. Bloomfield, was published in *The Independent*, 9 August, 1997, p. 16. There is an appreciation of Crane by Jill Butterworth in the *Cambridge University Staff Bulletin*, no. 657 (29 July, 1994), pp. 2–3 and other data is derived from the Library's staff records of the 1930s. See also S. C. Reif, *Published Material from the Cambridge Genizah Collections. A Bibliography 1896–1980* (Cambridge, 1988), introduction, p. vii, and *Hebrew Manuscripts at Cambridge University Library. A Description and Introduction* (Cambridge 1997), p. 34. The background to the Maimonides exhibition is documented in *Cambridge University Reporter*, no. 3049 (3 December, 1935), p. 362; and in the Library Syndicate minutes for 20 February, 1935, which make it clear that the initiative was that of Loewe.

The Genizah evidence in the field of Hebrew poetry was published in *Studies of the Research Institute for Hebrew Poetry* 1–7 (Hebrew; Berlin and Jerusalem,

1933–58); see also *Encyclopaedia Judaica* 8, col. 1407. Lewin's *Oṣar Ha-Ge'onim* was published in 13 volumes between 1928 and 1962 and details of his work are given in his *Festschrift, Sefer Ha-Yovel... B.M. Lewin*, ed. J. L. Fishman (Maimon) (Hebrew; Jerusalem, 1940), pp. 1–32. On the pioneering efforts of Assaf and Baneth, see *Sefer Assaf*, eds. M. D. Cassuto, J. Klausner and J. Guttmann (Hebrew; Jerusalem, 1953), pp. 7–32 of the Hebrew pagination; and S. D. Goitein, *A Mediterranean Society* 1 (Berkeley and Los Angeles, 1967), pp. 25–26. The contribution of Kahle is assessed in the obituary by Black mentioned in the sixth paragraph above and details of his relationship with the Genizah manuscripts at Cambridge University Library appear in S. C. Reif's forthcoming Hebrew article in *Te'uda* 15. On developments at the Hebrew University, see *The Hebrew University of Jerusalem 1925–1950*, ed. M. Spiegel (Jerusalem, 1950), pp. 42–66 and 88–97, and for a potted history of what became the Institute of Microfilmed Hebrew Manuscripts, see B. Richler, *Guide to Hebrew Manuscript Collections* (Jerusalem, 1994), pp. 83–84. *Newnham College Roll. Letter* (January, 1986), pp. 69–71, contains appreciations of Susan Skilliter by Ann Williams and Carmen Blacker and there is an obituary of University Librarian Creswick in *The Times*, 24 October, 1988, p. 16; see also *Who Was Who VIII* 1981–1990 (London, 1991), p. 171.

The story of how he came to be involved in Genizah research is told by S. D. Goitein in his "Involvement in Geniza Research," in *Religion in a Religious Age*, ed. S. D. Goitein (Cambridge, Mass., 1974) pp. 139–46, and the numerous articles and monographs produced by the scholars mentioned stand testimony to the major expansion of this field of Jewish studies in the post-War period; see *Encyclopaedia Judaica* 16, cols. 1333–42; N. Golb, "Geniza Studies in Jerusalem," in *Studies and Reports* (of the Ben-Zvi Institute), vol. 2 (Jerusalem, 1956), pp. 11–18; S. Shaked, *A Tentative Bibliography of Genizah Documents* (Paris, 1964); and S. C. Reif, *Published Material* (mentioned in the last paragraph but one). On Rosenthal, see S. C. Reif's biographical appreciation, and the subsequent bibliography of his work, in his *Festschrift*, edited by J. A. Emerton and S. C. Reif and entitled *Interpreting the Hebrew Bible* (Cambridge, 1982), pp. 1–26, as well as his brief article "Undreamed-of Treasures", *Genizah Fragments* 4 (October, 1982), p. 3. On Shalom Spiegel's work on liturgical poetry, see his *The Father of Piyyut: Texts and Studies toward a History of the Piyyut in Eretz Yisrael*, selected from his literary estate and edited by Menahem H. Schmelzer (Hebrew; New York and Jerusalem, 1996). The three Annual Reports from which the quotations have been drawn appeared in the *Cambridge University Reporter* of 29 May, 1957 (no. 4049, p. 1402); of 7 June, 1961 (no. 4254, p. 1810); and of 14 March, 1962 (no. 4290, p. 1162).

There is a tribute to Teicher in *The Times*, 21 November, 1981, p. 8, and details concerning the life and work of D. W. Thomas are given in *The Times*, 20 June, 1970, p. 12; 24 June, 1970, p. 12 and 30 June, 1970, p. 12; *Who Was Who VI 1961–70* (London, 1979; 2nd edition), p. 1111; and J. A. Emerton, "The Work of David Winton Thomas as a Hebrew Scholar", *Vetus Testamentum* 41 (1991), pp. 287–303. Copies of the two memoranda concerning the initiative for a Genizah appointment are in the Taylor-Schechter departmental records; the other members of the joint committee were Mr. James Kinnier Wilson, University Lecturer in Assyriology, and Professor E. C. Ratcliff, Regius Professor of Divinity; see also Cambridge University Reporter, no. 4290, p. 1160. The appointment to the revised Library post is recorded in *Cambridge University Reporter*, no. 4509 (11 May, 1966), pp. 1801–2; no. 4726 (7 October, 1970), pp. 92–93; and no. 4732 (18 November, 1970), p. 228, and details of the conservation project appear in S. C. Reif, "1898 Preserved in Letter and Spirit", *Cambridge Review*, no. 2266 (29 January, 1982), pp. 120–21. Information about Ceadel may be found in *The Times*, 23 November, 1979, p. VI; and *Who Was Who VI* (cited above), p. 137, and about Ratcliffe and Emerton in *Who's Who 1998*, pp. 612 and 1641. The progress of work on the Cambridge Genizah material has been monitored in the Library's annual reports, published in the *Cambridge University Reporter*; in the Unit's newsletter *Genizah Fragments*, beginning in April, 1981; and in *Encyclopaedia Judaica Year Book 1983/5* (Jerusalem, 1985), pp. 163–71. Details of the Genizah publications of the scholars listed appear in the *Index of Articles on Jewish Studies*, published in Jerusalem, beginning in 1969 and the Ginzberg quote is from *An Unknown Jewish Sect* (revised and updated translation of *Eine unbekannte jüdische Sekte*, New York, 1922; New York, 1976), p. xix.

The volumes that have to date appeared in the *Genizah Series* published for Cambridge University Library by Cambridge University Press, and edited by S. C. Reif, are as follows:

2. *Hebrew Bible Manuscripts in the Cambridge Genizah Collections*
   Volume 1 *Taylor-Schechter Old Series and other Genizah Collections in Cambridge University Library*, by M. C. Davis, incorporating material compiled by H. Knopf (1978)
   Volume 2 *Taylor-Schechter New Series, and Westminster College Cambridge Collection*, by M. C. Davis (1980)
3. *Miscellany of Literary Pieces from the Cambridge Genizah Collections*, by Simon Hopkins (1978)
4. *Vocalised Talmudic Manuscripts in the Cambridge Genizah Collections*
   Volume 1 *Taylor-Schechter Old Series*, by Shelomo Morag (1988)
5. *A Hand-list of Rabbinic Manuscripts in the Cambridge Genizah Collections*
   Volume 1 *Taylor-Schechter New Series*, by Robert Brody, incorporating material prepared by E. J. Wiesenberg (1998)
6. *Published Material from the Cambridge Genizah Collections: A Bibliography 1896–1980*, edited by Stefan C. Reif (1988)
7. *Palestinian Vocalised Piyyut Manuscripts in the Cambridge Genizah Collections*, by J. Yahalom (1997)
8. *Targumic Manuscripts in the Cambridge Genizah Collections*, by Michael L. Klein (1992)

9. *Karaite Bible Manuscripts from the Cairo Genizah*, by Geoffrey Khan (1990)
10. *Arabic Legal and Administrative Documents in the Cambridge Genizah Collections*, by Geoffrey Khan (1993)
11. *Medical and Para-Medical Manuscripts in the Cambridge Genizah Collections*, by Haskell D. Isaacs, with the assistance of Colin F. Baker (1994)

Additional volumes expected to appear in the near future are:

1. *An Introduction to the Cambridge Genizah Collections*, by Stefan C. Reif
2. *Hebrew Bible Manuscripts in the Cambridge Genizah Collections*
   Volume 3 *Taylor-Schechter Additional Series 1–31*, by M. C. Davis
   Volume 4 *Taylor-Schechter Additional Series 32–225*, by M. C. Davis
12. *Arabic and Judaeo-Arabic Manuscripts in the Cambridge Genizah Collections*, by Colin F. Baker and Meira Polliack
13. *Published Material from the Cambridge Genizah Collections: A Bibliography 1980–1995*, edited by Stefan C. Reif, Geoffrey Khan and Erica Hunter

INDEX

INDEX OF SUBJECTS AND SOURCES

INDEX OF MANUSCRIPTS CITED

INDEX OF NAMES, PLACES AND INSTITUTIONS